LO.05 28

D0789749

Inside British Society

Inside British Society

Continuity, Challenge and Change

Edited by

Gordon A. Causer
Lecturer in Sociology
University of Southampton

WHEATSHEAF BOOKS · SUSSEX

ST. MARTIN'S PRESS · NEW YORK

First published in Great Britain in 1987 by
WHEATSHEAF BOOKS LTD
A MEMBER OF THE HARVESTER PRESS PUBLISHING GROUP
Publisher: John Spiers
16 Ship Street, Brighton, Sussex
and in the USA by
ST. MARTIN'S PRESS, INC.
175 Fifth Avenue, New York, NY10010

British Library Cataloguing in Publication Data
Inside British society : continuity, challenge
   and change.
   1. Great Britain—Social conditions
   ——1945—
   I. Causer, Gordon A.
   941.085'8   HN385.5
ISBN 0-7450-0348-6
ISBN 0-7450-0398-2 Pbk

St. Martin's Press
ISBN 0-312-01151-2
Library of Congress Cataloging-in-Publication Number 87-42635
Printed in Great Britain by Billing & Sons Limited, Worcester.
Typeset in Times 11/12pt by Witwell Ltd, Liverpool

THE HARVESTER PRESS PUBLISHING GROUP
The Harvester Group comprises Harvester Press Ltd (chiefly
publishing literature, fiction, philosophy, psychology, and science and
trade books); Harvester Press Microform Publications Ltd (publishing
in microform previously unpublished archives, scarce printed sources,
and indexes to these collections) and Wheatsheaf Books Ltd (chiefly
publishing in economics, international politics, sociology, women's
studies and related social sciences).

Contents

List of Contributors vii
Preface and Acknowledgements xi

1. Introduction: Britain in the 1980s:
   Economic Restructuring and Political Change
   Gordon A. Causer 1

2. The Economy
   Gordon A. Causer 20

3. Management
   J. H. Smith 38

4. Trade Unions
   Jon Clark 58

5. Social Security and the Division of Welfare
   Roger Lawson 77

6. Housing
   A. M. Rees 98

7. The Family
   Graham Allan 120

8. The National Health Service
   Joan Higgins 141

9. The Police
   J. P. Martin 162

10. Education
    Eric Briggs   182

11. The State
    John A. Hall   200

Bibliography   223
Author Index   239
Subject Index   244

The Contributors

GRAHAM ALLAN (Lecturer in Sociology) received his Ph.D. from the University of Essex and previously taught at the University of Exeter. His main teaching and research interests are in informal social relationships and domestic life. His publications include *A Sociology of Friendship and Kinship* (Allen and Unwin, 1979) and *Family Life* (Basil Blackwell, 1985).

ERIC BRIGGS (Lecturer in Social Administration) studied sociology at the University of Essex and worked at the London School of Economics before moving to Southampton. He has researched and written on various aspects of the social security system, and is currently engaged in research on the consequences of social security fraud.

GORDON A. CAUSER (Lecturer in Sociology) was educated at the Universities of Reading and York. He has published papers on aspects of class structure and business organisation, and is currently engaged, together with colleagues from the New Technology Research Group, on a study of scientific and technical personnel in high technology firms.

JON CLARK (Senior Lecturer in Sociology) was a research fellow at the London School of Economics and the University of Paris before moving to Southampton, where he is currently chairman of the department. He has published extensively in the fields of labour law and technological change, and is co-author (with fellow members of the New Technology Research

Group) of *The Process of Technological Change* (Cambridge University Press, 1987).

JOHN A. HALL (Senior Lecturer in Sociology) was educated at Exeter College, Oxford, Pennsylvania State University and the London School of Economics. He has lectured widely in Europe and the United States and is at present on extended leave as Associate Professor of Sociology and Social Studies at Harvard University. He is the author of several books, including *Diagnoses of Our Time* (Heinemann, 1981), *Powers and Liberties* (Basil Blackwell, 1985) and *Raymond Aron* (Polity Press, 1987), and editor of collections on the state, the rise of the West and the neglected political theorists of the period 1848 to 1945.

JOAN HIGGINS (Senior Lecturer in Social Administration) taught at Portsmouth Polytechnic before moving to Southampton. Her main interests are in the fields of health policy and comparative social policy, and she is the author of a number of books and articles, including *The Poverty Business* (Basil Blackwell, 1978) and *States of Welfare* (Basil Blackwell, 1981). Her study of private health care, *The Business of Medicine*, will be published by Basil Blackwell during 1987.

ROGER LAWSON (Senior Lecturer in Social Administration) previously taught at the Universities of Cardiff and Glasgow and has been Visiting Professor at the University of Frankfurt and Research Fellow at the Institute for International Social Law in Munich. He has published extensively on social policies in Western Europe and is editor (with Vic George) of *Poverty and Inequality in Common Market Countries* (Routledge and Kegan Paul, 1980) and (with Robert Walker and Peter Townsend) of *Responses to Poverty: Lessons from Europe* (Heinemann, 1984).

J. P. MARTIN (Professor of Sociology and Social Administration) was a founder member of the Cambridge Institute of Criminology before moving to Southampton. He is the author of several books in the field of criminology, including *The Police: A Study in Manpower* (with Gail

Wilson—Heinemann, 1969) and *Licensed to Live* (with John Coker—Basil Blackwell, 1985). He was a member of the Jellicoe Committee on Boards of Visitors in Penal Institutions, and is currently a member of the Hampshire Probation Committee.

A. M. REES (Senior Lecturer in Social Administration) was previously at the University of Durham. His interests include nineteenth- and twentieth-century social history and the study of social security and housing policy. He is the author (with Eric Briggs) of *Supplementary Benefits and the Consumer* (LSE Occasional Paper in Social Administration, 1980) and of a completely revised fifth edition of *T. H. Marshall's Social Policy* (Hutchinson, 1985).

J. H. SMITH (Professor of Sociology) undertook research for the Acton Society Trust and taught at the London School of Economics before taking up the post of Professor of Sociology at Southampton in 1964. He has been a Rockefeller Fellow in the Social Sciences and a Fellow of the Center for Advanced Study in the Behavioral Sciences at Stanford, California. He has published widely on the sociological aspects of management, and is currently completing a long-term study of the pioneering work of Elton Mayo.

THE DEPARTMENT OF SOCIOLOGY AND SOCIAL ADMINISTRATION, UNIVERSITY OF SOUTHAMPTON

The Department of Sociology and Social Administration at the University of Southampton was established in its present form in 1966. Since then it has developed an extensive programme of teaching and research in the fields of sociology and social policy. In recent years members of the department have made important contributions to the sociological literature in a number of areas, including the historical development of social structures, the effects of technological change, comparative social policy, the sociology of family life and the study of mental illness. The department's concern with the practical application of sociological knowledge has been expressed in its development of specialist degree options in health care, health visiting and industrial relations, which it offers alongside a wide range of single and joint honours degrees in Sociology and Social Policy. The department's strong interest in the empirical study of British social structure and social policy is reflected in the present volume, which draws upon many years of research and teaching to present an analysis of the challenges faced by some of the central social institutions of British society in the 1980s and beyond.

Preface and Acknowledgements

A little over a year ago I broached with a number of my colleagues in the Department of Sociology and Social Administration at the University of Southampton the possibility of preparing a book which would address itself to the present state and condition of British society. While there exist a number of texts which provide an excellent introduction to the principal features of British social structure (e.g. Noble, 1981; Abrams and Brown, 1984) we felt that there was a need for a volume which addressed itself to those issues and areas which are the subject of popular and political debate beyond the confines of academic social science. In particular it was our view that many of the established institutions of British society were increasingly under challenge, whether from political leaders who cast doubt on their ability to meet what they perceived as the needs of the country, or from underlying economic and social trends which called into question their existing modes of operation. Our concern in this book is therefore to examine the nature of these challenges and the responses to them. We believe that such a discussion will be of value to those studying sociology and social policy, whether it be at A level, in undergraduate courses on British social structure and social policy, or on courses leading to the qualifications of various professional bodies.

Initial drafts of all chapters, with the exception of the Introduction, were discussed at a series of departmental seminars in the academic year 1985/86, and we have all benefited from the comments of our collaborators. No attempt has been made, however, to impose a spurious consensus upon contributors, and the reader will no doubt detect points of divergence and disagreement among us in our treatment of related issues. Nor have we attempted to achieve a comprehensive coverage of all aspects of British society. In particular, our focus upon the 'challenge to the institutions' has meant that a number of issues which have concerned British social scientists in recent years, such as changing patterns of urban development and the position of women, are treated only in a somewhat indirect fashion. We are also uncomfortably aware, our title notwithstanding, of a certain 'anglocentric' bias in what we have written, particularly in those areas, such as policing and education, where arrangements in Scotland differ from those in England and Wales. We hope that we may be able to address ourselves more directly to some of these issues in subsequent collaborative volumes.

As is always the case, we have incurred a number of debts in the writing of this book. In particular we should like to thank those of our colleagues and research students who, while not contributing to this book, have made valuable contributions in the seminars at which the papers were discussed. In addition Graham Allan wishes to thank Graham Crow for his comments on an earlier version of Chapter 7, while Jon Clark gratefully acknowledges the comments made on an earlier version of Chapter 4 by Steve Jary, Lord Wedderburn and David Winchester. Thanks are due to George Sayers Bain and Robert Price for permission to reproduce the tables on union membership and female participation in Chapter 4, and to Robert Price for providing updated information on union membership. Edward Elgar, managing director of Wheatsheaf Books during the preparation of this volume, encouraged us greatly by indicating his interest at an early stage of the planning process. And we owe a special debt to Julie Zillwood for cheerfully deciphering our first, second and third thoughts and producing the final typescript so efficiently. All contributors, of course, acknowledge their own ultimate responsibility for what they have written.

Gordon Causer
Southampton, September 1986

1 Introduction: Britain in the 1980s: Economic Restructuring and Political Change

Gordon A. Causer

INTRODUCTION

In 1973 the countries of the advanced capitalist world entered a period of slow growth, accelerating inflation and rising unemployment from which, despite periodic upturns and the eventual, if perhaps temporary, taming of inflation, they have still failed completely to recover. Within that international context Britain, as will be seen in the following chapter, has fared particularly badly. Today there is a tendency to look back to the period before the first 'oil shock' of 1973 as, if not a 'golden age', at least a period of prosperity and stability, compared with which Britain in the 1980s is seen as a society subject to increasing stresses and tensions and, in more extreme formulations, as a society in 'crisis' or 'decline'. The long-standing concern over the relatively poor performance of the British economy has been intensified by the rapid growth in unemployment and by its persistence at historically high levels despite the gradual recovery of the economy from the depths of the acute downturn of 1979–81. At the same time the problems of the economy appear to be increasingly paralleled in the wider social structure. The relative radicalism of Labour's 1974 electoral programme, followed by the Conservative Party's move to the Right under Margaret Thatcher, seemed to represent a break with the supposed political consensus of the post-war period (Krieger, 1986). The Conservative stance on public expenditure in particular could be interpreted as a response to the 'crisis of the welfare state', or the 'overload' of public demand on governments, analysed variously by writers of both Right and Left in the 1970s (Brittan, 1977; Gough, 1979). More generally, the apparent breakdown of consensus at national level seemed to mirror an underlying breakdown in the relatively stable pattern of political support in the electorate at large which had characterised the immediate post-war era. Through the 1970s political scientists analysed the gradual weakening of traditional political alignments, evidenced in a growing swing in party support from one election to the next and in periodic upsurges of support for third parties—the Liberals and, in Scotland and (to a lesser extent) Wales, the nationalist parties (Nairn, 1977; Sarlvik and Crew, 1983). While support for the latter has receded in the 1980s, the emergence of the Liberal/SDP Alliance as a grouping commanding one-quarter of the votes cast in the 1983 General Election appeared to signal an end to the established system of two-party politics.

Beyond the party political arena other signs of destabilisation have elicited increasing concern. Most dramatic has been the occurrence in 1981, and again in 1985, of serious outbreaks of rioting in inner city areas, bringing to mainland Britain scenes of violence hitherto confined largely to Northern Ireland. The sense of a generalised breakdown in law and order was reinforced by the violence and counter-violence associated with the miners' strike of 1984–85, and by a continuing increase in crime rates. The latter, while perhaps exaggerated by the popular press, has been real enough in its incidence and effects, particularly in inner city areas (Kinsey *et al.*, 1986).

By the mid-1980s, therefore, a combination of relative economic decline, rising unemployment, political fragmentation and public disorder combined to present an image of a society in some disarray, with which the image of an earlier, more stable social order could be contrasted. However, as Graham Allan (Chapter 7 this volume) points out, the notion of a breakdown in social integration is not novel, but recurs in almost every generation. Furthermore, it is the burden of a number of contributions to this volume that both the stability and consensus of the past and the degree of change in the present can be overstated. Roger Lawson, for example (Chapter 5) points out that the apparent consensus on welfare in the 1950s was much weaker than it perhaps appears in retro-spect. My own discussion of the economy (Chapter 2) reminds us that even before the oil shock of 1973 the state of the British economy had become a subject of almost chronic political concern. Nor was Britain entirely free of internal disorders in the decade or so after the Second World War, as the 'race riots' of 1958 in Nottingham and Notting Hill indicate. The present is characterised, as our title suggests, by continuities with the past as well as changes, and the balance between the two varies over time and from one sphere to another.

However, in giving due acknowledgement to continuities with the past, it is important not to lose the baby along with the bathwater. British society *is* undergoing substantial changes, and it is precisely the interaction of these changes with the continuities inherited from the past which gives rise to the challenges which are analysed in succeeding chapters. While these changes are clearly bound up with the recessions which have beset the world economy since 1973, they cannot be viewed simply as an effect or consequence of them. As Howard Newby had commented:

It is now generally recognised that the 1980s have witnessed, and will continue to witness, a major transformation of the economic and social structure of all the advanced capitalist societies. Moreover, this process is seen to be a fundamental *restructuring* of these societies and not—whatever the commonly-offered rhetoric on these matters—a simple recession. These are major changes, not temporary phenomena, and there will be no 'return to normal' should the general level of economic activity recover. (Newby, 1985, p. 1)

The purpose of the present chapter is to delineate some of the characteristics of this restructuring as it is taking place in Britain today as a background to the discussion of specific institutions in the chapters that follow.

ECONOMIC RESTRUCTURING

Economic restructuring is a continuing process in British society today, and any characterisation of it is necessarily somewhat tentative. None the less, four aspects of the process appear relatively clear—the sectoral shift in employment, the locational shift in employment, the rise in (largely female) part-time employment, and the restructuring of labour markets and employment conditions. These four elements are empirically interrelated but can be separated out analytically.

Sectoral shifts

As noted in Chapter 2 below, employment in manufacturing industry (as a proportion of the total labour force) reached its peak in the mid-1960s and has steadily declined thereafter—a process accentuated by the wave of business failures and labour 'shake-outs' in the period 1979–81 (Smith, K., 1984, Ch. 1). By the mid-1980s employment in manufacturing accounted for around one-quarter of employment in Britain, compared with over one-third twenty years earlier (Johnson, 1985, pp. 34–5). The important point, however, is that the decline has been absolute as well as proportionate (see Table 4.1, p.60) and has not been accompanied by a commensurate decline in manufacturing production. Between 1982 and 1986, as manufacturing output slowly recovered from the trough of 1979–81, manufacturing employment declined by a further 440,000. Therefore, as far as manufacturing is concerned, we encounter a situation of 'jobless growth', in which increased production is achieved without a corresponding increase in employment. Three factors appear to be responsible for this process:

(a) the decline of traditional, often labour-intensive, industries, and the consequent increased importance of modern industries which are more capital-intensive or which (as in the case of many high-technology products) increasingly locate their assembly activities in low-wage Third World countries;

(b) the pursuit by many employers, often under the exigencies of recessionary conditions and intensified competition, of a strategy of reducing their workforce, seeking greater flexibility in the use of labour, and so on;

(c) the introduction of labour-saving technologies. Although early projections of job loss as a consequence of the introduction of microelectronic technologies have proved exaggerated, and job losses due to the introduction of new technology have been greatly outweighed by direct job loses due to recession, recent research suggests that the rate of job loss from this source may be accelerating. In any event, the significance of introducing new technologies lies not only in the job losses they directly cause, but also in the loss of new jobs which might otherwise have been created (Northcott and Rogers, 1984; Northcott, 1986).

The concomitant of the decline in manufacturing employment has been a rise in the proportion of employment located in the service sector, which by the mid-1980s accounted for nearly two-thirds of employment, divided almost equally between public and private sectors. Within the broad category of services, however, there has been substantial variation. Thus the proportion of the labour force employed in distributive services has remained almost stable for most of the post-war period, while growth has occurred in services to producers (due in part to the contracting-out of services, such as cleaning, previously performed by 'in-house' employees) and in the 'social services' of public administration, defence, education and health (*Bank of England Quarterly Bulletin*, 1985). It is indeed in the public sector that the greatest absolute growth in employment has occurred during the post-war period. But while the growth in service sector employment to some extent compensates for the decline in jobs in manufacturing, the jobs created are often filled by women working part-time, rather than the predominantly male labour force displaced by the shrinkage of manufacturing employment.

Locational shifts in employment
It is now commonplace to identify the 'North/South' divide as a major fissure in British society, the relative prosperity of the South of England being contrasted with depressed economic and employment conditions in the rest of the country. This image, however, requires some qualification. To an extent it carries over into the last decade an imagery shaped by both the inter-war depression and the circumstances of post-war affluence. During the latter period above-average unemployment remained a problem primarily in those areas, such as the North-East of England and the industrial belt of Scotland,

characterised by the decline of such traditional industries as shipbuilding. What characterises the present situation, however, is the way in which unemployment has spread to encompass the areas where employment opportunities expanded during the post-war boom, such as the West Midlands (Spencer *et al.*, 1986). The 'North', in short, has moved further south. By early 1986 only the East Midlands, East Anglia, the South-East and the South-West had unemployment rates significantly below 15 per cent, and even within these 'prosperous' regions unemployment was high by post-war standards. Only the South-East region registered an unemployment rate below 10 per cent, and then only by the barest of margins (Morgan, 1986, p. 12). Furthermore, there is significant intra-regional variation, so that inner London, for example, was by mid-1985 exhibiting rates of unemployment similar to those of Scotland, Wales and the North-West (Buck *et al.*, 1986, p. 2). To understand these distributions we must examine the changing pattern of employment location in the post-war period. In a recent paper Philip Cooke (1986) has delineated three stages in the spatial development of the UK economy:

(a) The early industrialisation of such areas as Clydeside, North-East Lancashire and South Wales. These areas were badly affected by the inter-war depression and by the post-war decline of traditional industries. The latter trend was somewhat offset by a process of industrial diversification, often through the establishment of branch plants by companies whose headquarters lay elsewhere, which were often attracted by schemes of regional aid. The process of recession and international competition, however, has led to significant closures of such plants, leaving these areas substantially dependent on public sector and local/regional private sector service employment.

(b) A second 'wave' of industrialisation in the inter-war and post-war period, centred on such industries as motor vehicles, plane manufacture, domestic appliances and consumer electrical goods, and concentrated heavily in the West Midlands and outer London. The development of these industries led to substantial migration into these areas, but employment here too has been badly hit by the combination of recession and international competition.

(c) A third 'wave' (or perhaps, Cooke suggests, only a 'ripple') of development in the 'high-tech' industries of aerospace, pharmaceuticals, computers, telecommunications and consumer electronics. Employment in these fields is heavily concentrated in the outer metropolitan area and parts of the South-East, though with outlying 'islands' in Central Scotland and the eastern areas of South Wales (Cooke, 1986, p. 245).

It seems fairly clear that, in manufacturing at least, the 1960s and 1970s were characterised by a general trend to the 'decentralisation' of employment away from large urban centres. This reversal of the long-standing trend to centralisation played an important part in generating problems of high unemployment in the inner cities. The reasons for this decentralisation are debatable but among the relevant factors appear to be constraints upon expansion in existing locations, the differing capacity of localities to generate new enterprises, the effects of regional aid, and the desire of companies to decentralise their manufacturing activities to draw upon pools of relatively cheap and unorganised labour (Massey and Meegan, 1982; Fothergill and Gudgin, 1983; Massey, 1984). These trends in manufacturing are also significant for the development of service sector employment, in that concentration of administrative functions in certain areas encourages the associated development of 'business services' (market research, computer services, etc.), while the relative prosperity of an area shapes the extent of growth in the provision of services to private consumers.

Whether these trends continued in the 1980s is more problematic. In the depths of recession the branch plants created by the decentralising process of earlier decades may have been particularly vulnerable, and localities in a number of regions are becoming increasingly dependent for employment on locally based institutions (Townsend, A. R., 1983; Cooke, 1986). Thus the processes which helped to remove employment from the inner cities may now be resulting in declining opportunities in the areas to which employment was relocated. Furthermore, the depressed economic conditions and living standards of both inner city areas and 'declining' regions make them unpropitious sites for the development of successful entrepreneurial activities.

Male and female employment

Few trends in British society in recent years have been more striking than the growth in female part-time employment. Between 1974 and 1984 the number of full-time male and female employees declined by 11.47 per cent and 9.27 per cent respectively, while the number of women in part-time work increased by 21.86 per cent. Furthermore, these global figures mask the very rapid growth that has taken place in certain fields, for part-time female employment has declined in many areas of manufacturing while increasing rapidly in some parts of the service sector. Over the same period, for example, the number of part-time female employees in textiles fell by 54.47 per cent while the numbers employed in hotels and catering rose by 61.3 per cent.

Three factors seem to be involved in this trend. Firstly, the post-war period as a whole has undoubtedly seen a normative change in attitudes to married women working and a move away from the emphasis on the full-time housewife role in the inter-war and immediate post-war period. Secondly, the sectoral shifts of employment noted above have been associated with a decline in 'male' industries (as well as some—such as textiles—with a long tradition of female employment) and an increase in some forms of service employment where women have traditionally been concentrated, often in part-time work (Beechey, 1986, pp. 93-4). Thirdly, the relocation of employment noted in the previous section has often been associated with a desire on the part of employers to recruit labour which is cheaper, more readily available and (often) with fewer traditions of collective organisation. Female employees, especially those working part-time, appeared to meet these needs, and one correlate of the decentralisation of employment discussed earlier has been an increase in part-time female employment in those areas where it has traditionally been low (Winckler, 1985; Townsend, A. 1986).

This rise in the significance of part-time female employment has two consequences. On the one hand it reinforces the conception of women as secondary or supplementary wage-earners within the family, and as a labour force especially suited to certain types of occupation (light assembly, clerical work, and so on). Thus, despite women's increased participation in the labour force, their economic dependence within the family and the long-established pattern of occupational segregation are sustained, and even reinforced. As Martin and Roberts note, women's return to work on a part-time basis is frequently associated with downward mobility from their earlier occupational positions in full-time work (Martin and Roberts, 1984, p. 147). On the other hand, as several contributors to this volume indicate, the growth in female part-time employment, coupled with the general growth in unemployment, has led to an increasing economic differentiation *between* families and households. Largely because social security regulations offset wives' earnings against husbands' entitlements, the wives of men in work are around twice as likely to be in employment as the wives of the unemployed. Consequently a division is opening up between households with two (or more) wage-earners and those with none, who are consequently almost wholly dependent on state benefits (Pahl, 1984, pp. 313–14).

The restructuring of labour markets and employment conditions

The changing pattern of female employment just discussed can be seen as part of a wider restructuring of labour markets and employment conditions which, if not caused by the recession, has nevertheless been greatly facilitated by it. In the 1970s dual labour market theory, and the more elaborated theories of labour market segmentation which developed in its wake (Garnsey *et al.*, 1985), pointed out the existence of substantial sectors of non-unionised, low-paid employment characterised by poor working conditions and job insecurity. While white, male workers were not exempt from such conditions, women and ethnic minorities were especially vulnerable to employment conditions of this kind. The 1980s have seen an extension of this type of employment, and the subjection to it of groups who were previously sheltered by the relatively protected internal labour markets of large companies. In their study of redundancy among steelworkers in Port Talbot, for example, Lee and his colleagues have noted not only that one-third of those made redundant had withdrawn from the labour market (chiefly older workers and those suffering ill-health), but that nearly half of those remaining had had 'chequered' employment histories of recurrent movement in and out of work. One important factor in this was the development of an 'ancillary employment structure'—the provision of short-term jobs arising as a result of enterprises contracting out work which in many cases had previously been done by permanent employees (Lee, 1985). In situations such as this informal contacts become of increasing importance in securing access to employment. The consequence of this is that employers are increasingly able to 'screen out' potentially disruptive or troublesome employees, while control of labour within the firm is enhanced by informal pressures on recruits from those on whose recommendation they were hired in the first place (Jenkins *et al.*, 1983).

These trends are part of a wider process. As Jon Clark (Chapter 4) notes, there has been a substantial growth in temporary work, subcontracting and short-term contracts as employers are able to meet their demand for labour without the need to offer the prospects of long-term employment. For some employers, at least, the rise in unemployment and the legislative environment of the 1980s have provided the opportunity to mount an offensive against trade union and shopfloor organisation, and to secure 'slimmed-down' labour forces and a breaking-down of established work practices and manning arrangements (Moran, 1986). The most celebrated instances of this, such as the pit closures leading to the miners' strike and the removal of News International to Wapping, have attracted considerable attention, but there is perhaps a danger of overgeneralising from such cases, just as there was a danger in the 1960s and 1970s of overstating the degree of trade union and shop steward influence from the experience of a relatively limited number of industries. In particular it is by no means clear, even in the circumstances of the 1980s, that the introduction of new technologies has been associated (as the celebrated Braverman thesis would suggest) by a generalised 'deskilling' of the labour force. Empirical research now presents a picture which emphasises the varying effects of technological change on skill distribution, with the outcome depending on a complex interaction of the technology itself, the nature of the product and its market, the strategies of management, the strength of collective identity and organisation among the occupational groups involved, and the state of the local labour market (Braverman, 1974; Jones 1983; Penn and Scattergood, 1985).

While the overall pattern is not entirely clear, there are some grounds for believing that, far from being comprehensively deskilled, the labour force may be undergoing an increasing polarisation. Despite recession and the contraction of employment, demand for certain types of labour remains high. This is particularly true for certain types of skilled labour and for those with expertise in the burgeoning fields of computers and information technology (Connor and Pearson, 1986). Conversely, those who lack skills or formal qualifications, or whose skills are no longer required, are likely to experience increasingly peripheralised forms of employment. This appears to be occurring even in areas of economic prosperity. Boddy *et al.*'s study of the Bristol area, for example, identified a division between technical and professional jobs on the one hand, and semi- and unskilled manual jobs with few prospects of advancement on the other (Boddy *et al.*, 1986). It should, of course, be stressed that we are dealing here with tendencies but they are tendencies which seem likely to grow and to be reflected in a growing diversity of managerial styles and union responses. In this respect the divergent approaches of the EETPU and the GMBATU discussed by Jon Clark (in Chapter 4) can be seen as an expression of these developing divisions within the labour force.

THE POLITICS OF DECLINE?

So far the processes of economic restructuring have been discussed in terms of factors largely internal to the economy itself. Such an analysis is, however, a partial one. Both Cameron and Therborn have shown that the level of unemployment in the period since 1973 has actually varied markedly from one industrial nation to another, and that these variations are due at least as much to political as to economic factors. In particular three countries—Sweden, Norway and Austria—stand out as societies where organised labour has been able to secure fiscal, monetary and labour market policies which have maintained comparatively high levels of employment in return for relative quiescence in the pursuit of its industrial objectives (Cameron, 1984; Therborn, 1986; cf. Rowthorn, 1986). In Britain, in contrast, the commitment to full employment was being eroded from about the mid-1960s onwards, although the process did not reach its full extent until a decade or so later (Edward Heath's celebrated 'U-turn' of economic policy in 1972, for example, was occasioned largely by the desire to avoid the then unacceptable figure of one million out of work.) One important factor in Britain's high level of unemployment then, certainly since 1979, may be the failure to develop some kind of effective 'corporatist' arrangement whereby government, capital and organised labour are drawn into an effectively coordinated strategy to achieve agreed economic objectives. Given Middlemas's analysis of the historical development of 'corporate bias' in the British political system (Middlemas, 1979), and the plethora of analyses of corporatist developments which characterised the 1970s (see Panitch, 1980) this may appear at first sight surprising. However, with the wisdom of hindsight it becomes clear that British trends in the direction of corporatism were much weaker than sometimes appeared to be the case at the time. As John Hall indicates (Chapter 11), the character of the British state, British capital and British labour all militate to a greater or lesser degree against the development of full-blown corporatist arrangements. Consequently British corporatism has shown a consistent tendency to give way in situations of recession to a reversion to more orthodox measures of government policy (Booth, 1982).

At first sight the Thatcher government appears as a clear exemplification of this process. With its commitment to cut public spending, reduce taxation and free economic activity from excessive regulation it appears as a reversion to earlier economic philosophies and practices. In the event, however, it became more constrained by circumstances than either its own rhetoric or that of its opponents might have suggested—a point brought out in several of the discussions of social policy in this volume. In particular the attempt to trim public expenditure was continually frustrated by the government's commitment to increased expenditure on defence and law and order, and by the rapid increase in social security spending resulting from the rise in unemployment. The promise of tax cuts in real terms became increasingly dependent on the selling-off of public assets, a policy elevated from a negligible place in the Party manifesto of 1979 to a central plank of government strategy by the mid-1980s. And the attempt to reduce the share of the public sector in total employment was offset by the effects on the private sector of the 1979–81 recession, so that by 1985 the public sector had been reduced in proportionate terms by only 1 per cent (Dunleavy and Rhodes, 1986). On the principal economic indicators only inflation stands out as a clear 'success', and even here the British achievement was not outstanding by international standards.

It may, however, be mistaken to assess the significance of Thatcherism primarily in terms of its success or failure in meeting its stated objectives. On this criterion almost all post-war governments would be adjudged failures. Rather, the significance of Thatcherism might be held to lie in its more general influence upon the political climate. Christopher Husbands, for example, comments that 'the apparent persuasiveness of the virtues of the market' has become 'an achievement of Thatcherism that will probably long outlive any personal popularity that Mrs Thatcher may have' (Husbands, 1985, p. 15).

One might ask, though, whether Thatcherism should be seen primarily as the cause or the effect of a change in values. The increasing volatility of electoral behaviour over time has been accompanied by arguments to the effect that traditional patterns of class voting are in decline (see Franklin, 1985) and by suggestions that class is giving way as the basis of political alignment to other sources of division, such as housing tenure or consumption locations more generally (Dunleavy, 1979; Saunders, 1984). If housing tenure and consumption cleavages *are* of increasing importance, then we might expect the rise in owner-occupation and 'privatised' forms of consumption, such as car ownership, to be reflected in national politics by an abandonment of commitments to collective provision in favour of measures to facilitate private consumption. More generally, a number of writers have argued that the conditions of the 1970s—and indeed social trends over a longer period—have produced a society increasingly characterised by the pursuit of relatively narrow sectional interests. In 1974 Alan Fox argued that the increasing pervasiveness of 'low trust' relations in British society was leading to an intensification of competition between social groups as each sought to defend its particularistic interests (Fox, 1974, Ch. 8). More recently, Marshall *et al.* have argued that as class situations and processes have become increasingly opaque, so class identity has had a declining relevance and class conflicts have taken the form of sectional distributional struggles: 'Instrumental collectivism, based on sectional self-interest, has become the order of the day' (Marshall *et al.*, 1985, p. 273). Such arguments again suggest the emergence of a significant social base for Thatcherite Conservatism among those able to utilise their market capacities effectively and opposed to government restraints (such as incomes policy) on their doing so.

There is a body of evidence to support the view that social attitudes have changed in the way suggested by these arguments. Alt (1979, Ch. 10) demonstrates that the period of high inflation in the 1970s was associated with a decline in support for 'altruistic' measures and an elevation of dealing with inflation over dealing with unemployment as the main policy priority. More recently, Husbands (1985) has noted the decline in the 1970s of the level of unemployment as a factor linked to government popularity and the increased significance of the level of real wages. This he interprets as a movement away from 'communalistic' attitudes of regard for the welfare of others toward a more 'privatised' concern for one's own immediate well-being. (The revived importance of unemployment in the 1980s can similarly be interpreted as a result of the increasing numbers touched by it, not as a reversion to former attitudes.) Such evidence provides some support for the view that instrumental attitudes and sectional interests have increased in importance, as do the more impressionistic writings of Jeremy Seabrook, for all his tendency to romanticise the degree of communal solidarity which existed in the past (Seabrook, 1978; cf. Pahl, 1984, pp. 95–6). We should, however, be cautious about attempting to relate electoral patterns to such supposed underlying changes in values. It is clear that electoral alignments *are* changing. In some cases these changes may be relatively transitory. The rise of nationalism in Scotland in the 1970s now appears as something of a protest vote against the Labour government, fuelled by the discovery and exploitation of North Sea oil—although at the time of writing the regional effects of unemployment and campaigns against certain government policies have led to a modest revival of nationalist fortunes. Other changes may be more stable in their effects, and have their roots in long-term changes in the electorate. The decline in support for the Labour Party evidenced in the elections of 1979 and 1983, for example, reflects not simply a loss of votes within the working class, but also the continuing decline in the number of manual worker voters due to the occupational changes discussed earlier (Heath *et al.*, 1985, Chs. 2 and 3). The notion that other bases of voting behaviour may be displacing class is, however, more problematic. Housing tenure does appear to differentiate voting behaviour within social classes so that, for example, working-class owner-occupiers are more likely to vote Conservative than working-class council tenants. But this is a pattern which seems to have held for at least twenty years, and if its significance has grown with the increase in working-class owner-occupation this has tended to be offset by the reduction in the numbers in the traditional working class, so that the proportion of working-class owner-occupiers in the electorate as a whole has not increased substantially (Heath *et al.*, 1985, Ch. 4; cf. Dunleavy and Husbands, 1985, Ch. 6).

None the less, directly class-based voting *has* undergone some decline over time, especially among manual workers. This has not, however, been unequivocally to the benefit of the Conservatives. The proportion of working-class voters supporting the Conservatives was higher in 1979 and 1983 than in the two elections of 1974, but lower than in 1970—an election which represents a high-point of cross-class voting

(Heath *et al.*, 1985, pp. 32–3). The principal, if uneven, gains throughout the 1970s and 1980s have been made by the Liberal Party, and latterly the Liberal/SDP Alliance, which have secured support from both blue-collar and white-collar employees. At least until recently the high turnover of the Liberal vote from one election to the next suggested that the Liberal Party was the recipient largely of a protest vote against the perceived lack of competence of the two principal parties. Heath *et al.* suggest that a distinctive Alliance voter may now be emerging among those with 'centrist' views on 'class' issues such as nationalisation and trade union legislation, but distinctively liberal views on such issues as the death penalty and police powers. This combination is particularly found among the highly educated members of the middle class (ibid., pp. 113–16). However, commitment to the Alliance in 1983 remained weaker than that to other parties and, as Harrop notes, these 'core' Alliance voters represented only a minority of the votes cast for the Liberals and SDP (Harrop, 1986, p. 50). This development does, though, hold out the prospect of a longer-term erosion of the 'middle-class liberal' element of the Labour vote, at the same time as its traditional constituency among manual workers is being reduced.

The rise of the Alliance has a further important implication. The Thatcher government's lengthy period of office and the large parliamentary majority it secured in 1983 tend to obscure the fact that in both 1979 and 1983 it secured only between 42 and 44 per cent of the vote—less than any other Conservative government in the post-war period. The dominance of Thatcherite Conservatism therefore owed less to its overwhelming popularity among the electorate than to the decline in support for Labour and the operation of an electoral system which, especially in a three-cornered contest, allocates parliamentary seats with limited regard to the relative degree of popular support for each of the parties. We should accordingly be cautious about seeing the rise of Mrs Thatcher's Conservatism as reflecting a deep-seated shift in social attitudes. Changes are occurring, but these may reflect generational effects rather than a substantial shift in values among established voters. As Harrop notes, the greater volatility in voting patterns has arisen in the main not from existing voters shifting their allegiances, but from the entry of new voters onto the electoral roll who lack the well-defined partisan commitments of their predecessors. Again it is the Labour Party which is the likely loser. Until recently, Labour tended to benefit from the gradual dying-off of those whose political identifications were formed before Labour firmly established itself as one half of a two-party system. But that is inevitably changing: 'Post-1970 cohorts will form a majority of the electorate by the year 2000. These are dealigned generations, unsympathetic to class appeals, for whom the Labour Party has never been an object of strong emotional commitment' (Harrop, 1986, p. 59).

A POLARISED SOCIETY?

The picture presented in this chapter is of a society undergoing processes of substantial economic change and entering—perhaps partly as a consequence—a period of political uncertainty. It should be remembered, however, that for many members of the population the 1970s and 1980s have seen a continuation of the rise in living standards which characterised the 1950s and 1960s. It has become a commonplace to note that the sharp rise in unemployment has been accompanied by a continuing rise in the real incomes of those remaining in employment. This increase is not, however, one which has been shared equally by all those in work. Between 1979 and 1983 the real wages of non-manual workers rose, on average, by 19 per cent, while the pay of manual workers rose by only 10 per cent. As one would anticipate from these figures inequality between top and bottom wage-earners widened (Metcalf and Nickell, 1985). It is therefore not surprising to discover, not only that poverty has substantially increased in the 1980s, but that a substantial proportion of the poor are full-time wage-earners and their dependants (see Chapter 5). As O'Higgins has shown in some detail for the period up to 1983, inequality has increased, but has done so primarily because of a less equal distribution of market incomes, with tax changes operating as a secondary factor and changes in benefit payments having little effect on overall inequality (O'Higgins, 1983).

From evidence such as this, and the earlier discussion of the restructuring of the labour market, it appears that a polarisation is taking place between, as Tony Rees puts it in Chapter 6, 'the comfortable and the established of the middle and skilled working classes and various groups of outsiders, mostly weakly supplied with market capabilities. Included in the latter would be many of the young, a lot of unskilled and semi-skilled older workers, and a disproportionate number of black and brown Britons.' Such polarisation may be reinforced by the pattern of mobility chances. Goldthorpe and Payne, in their updating of the 1972 Oxford Mobility Study using data from the 1983 British General Election Survey, note a continuing expansion of the 'service class', with a consequent continuation of opportunities for upward mobility. At the same time the rise in unemployment between the two surveys had also generated increased possibilities of 'downward mobility' out of paid employment altogether, a risk to which working-class men were much more prone than those in other classes. Manual workers' mobility chances had, in short, polarised (Goldthorpe and Payne, 1986, p. 17). And, of course, the link between wives' and husbands' employment noted earlier also operates in a polarising fashion.

In broadly accepting the thesis of polarisation, however, three points should be borne in mind. Firstly, whatever changes may be occurring in the lower reaches of the class structure, the position of the property-based upper class remains relatively stable. Indeed, cuts in high marginal tax rates, government concessions on capital taxation and the boom in share prices led in the early 1980s to a reversal of the long-term trend for the share of marketable wealth held by the richest 1 per cent of the population to decline (Field, 1983; Huhne, 1986). Secondly, the peripheralisation of sections of the labour force, particularly members of ethnic minorities and many female workers, is by no means a new phenomenon (Daniel, 1968; Smith, D. J., 1974; Wainwright, 1984). What characterises the 1980s is the intensification of this process and its spread to groups of workers who were relatively protected through the 1960s and 1970s. Finally, the actual incidence and effects of polarisation will, as noted earlier, differ significantly between different localities and regions.

This last factor is likely to have significant effects on the political geography of Britain (Heath *et al.*, 1985, Ch. 6; Massey, 1984, Ch. 6). More dramatically, the long-established decline of inner city areas, in terms of both employment and housing, has manifested itself in periodic outbreaks of extensive violence on the streets. Such violence has, of course a diversity of sources, the principal proximate cause probably being the 'unimaginative and inflexible policing' identified by Lord Scarman (see Chapter 9). It is difficult, however, to escape the conclusion that economic factors of continuing deprivation and discrimination underlie much of the violence. There are certain parallels to be drawn here with the situation in Northern Ireland in the late 1960s, on the eve of the present 'troubles'—the division of the community into distinct ethnic groups, high local rates of unemployment disproportionately concentrated in the minority community, discriminatory practices in access to housing and employment, and a structure of political authority and policing substantially un-representative of the minority (Arthur, 1983; Darby, 1983; Jenkins 1984). Such parallels can be overdrawn. The principal differences perhaps lie in the much greater relative size of the minority in Northern Ireland and, more fundamentally, the disputed legitimacy of the state itself. None the less, the principal response to the riots in Britain appears, at least in the immediate future, to lie in the direction of the implementation of techniques and technologies of policing already used in Northern Ireland rather than more fundamental processes of social and political reform. Such responses are part of the general trend to authoritarian state responses discussed by John Hall (Chapter 11), a trend which he identifies as having its roots in Britain's relative economic decline. The nature and causes of that decline provide the subject matter of the following chapter.

2 The Economy

Gordon A. Causer

INTRODUCTION

In the last twenty years the malaise of the British economy has
come to occupy a central place in much academic, as well as
political, debate. The general tenor of that debate may be
gauged from the titles of some of the recent contributions to it:
Britain in Decline (Gamble, 1985), *The Wasting of the British
Economy* (Pollard, 1982), *The British Economic Crisis* (Smith,
K., 1984), *The Economic Decline of Modern Britain* (Coates and
Hillard, 1986), and so on. 'Crisis' and 'decline' have become
the central terms of the debate. Yet there is a paradox here
which must be noted. The period of the late 1950s and the
early 1960s was widely seen as the 'age of affluence',
epitomised by the words attributed to the then Prime Minister,
Harold Macmillan: 'You've never had it so good.' Yet if we
compare the economy of 1960 with the economy of the mid-
1980s we find that in real terms the Gross Domestic Product
per head has increased by something over 50 per cent (Central
Statistical Office, 1986, Table 45). Clearly, if the British people
had 'never had it so good' in 1960, they have had it substantially better since. Why, then, the talk of crisis and decline?
There are, I suggest, three main reasons.

First, and most obviously, there is unemployment. One key
component of the idea of the 'age of affluence' was the notion
that enduring deprivation due to persistent or long-term unemployment had largely become a thing of the past. Today,
with unemployment figures of well over three million, this is a
claim that can no longer be made. Furthermore, as has now

been amply documented, the incidence of unemployment falls unequally on different social classes, ethnic groups, areas and regions (Moon and Richardson, 1985). Of particular importance here is the growth in the number of long-term unemployed—in late 1985 1.35 million had been out of work for over a year—and the emergence of a significant stratum of the semi-permanently unemployed, drawn disproportionately from the unskilled, ethnic minorities, the inner cities, and those regions affected most heavily by the sharp decline in manufacturing industry and manufacturing employment. At the same time, the standard of living of those in employment and in receipt of property incomes has in many—though not all—cases risen, due to rising real wages, cuts in direct taxation and the continuing increase in the employment of the wives of employed men. Thus sustained unemployment does not simply revive the spectre of widespread deprivation, but reopens social cleavages of a kind which post-war commentators had confidently regarded as a thing of the past.

Secondly, there is a growing recognition that, in both the long post-war boom and the succeeding period of recession, the British economy has performed in an inferior fashion to that of most other advanced capitalist societies. This is seen most obviously in growth rates—between 1950 and 1973 Britain's average rate of GDP growth was 3 per cent per annum—high by historical standards, but poor in comparison with the 4.9 per cent growth average of the sixteen leading capitalist nations. In the years of recession after 1973 growth rates in general declined, but the differential between Britain's growth and the sixteen-nation average widened (Smith, K., 1984). On other indicators too, such as the level of inflation and the rate of unemployment, the British economy has tended to perform relatively poorly (Cameron, 1984, pp. 148–54).

Finally, there is the widespread belief that, but for the largely fortuitous and unrepeatable phenomenon of North Sea oil, the problems of the British economy might have been considerably worse. Britain has, historically, been an open economy, dependent on imports of food and raw materials, and paying for these through the export of manufactures and services, together with the earnings from overseas investment. The importance of the latter side of the equation can be gauged from the fact that as recently as 1955 Britain accounted for about 20 per cent of world trade in manufactures and 25 per cent of world trade in services. In the increasingly liberalised conditions of the post-war international economy, however, Britain faced increasing competition, and saw its share of both services and manufacturing eroded. At the same time import penetration of the domestic economy increased (Brown and Sheriff, 1978).

By the early 1960s balance of payments deficits had become a major constraint on economic policy, the effects of the changing pattern of trade being exacerbated by the outflow of funds to pay for overseas military expenditure and by the attempt to maintain what many regarded as an overvaluation of the pound, thus reducing the competitiveness of British exports (Strange, 1971). The devaluation of the pound in 1967 and the abandonment of many overseas commitments eased the immediate pressures, but the balance of trade in manufactures continued to worsen, until in 1983 Britain became a net importer of manufactured goods. That the balance of payments remained in surplus is in part due to a rise in the surplus on services, but in the main to the development of a substantial trade surplus in respect of fuels—a shift which reflects the discovery and exploitation of North Sea oil and gas. This surplus, however, remains highly vulnerable both to short-term movements in oil prices (as the sharp drop in prices in 1986 illustrated) and to the longer-term decline in North Sea output, carrying with it the spectre of a return to recurrent balance of payments deficits (Keegan, 1985).

It is partly for these reasons that so much attention has been devoted to the problem of 'deindustrialisation'—the steady decline in the share of manufacturing in British employment and output. This process has been going on for some time—manufacturing employment as a percentage of total employment reached its peak in the 1960s—but was greatly accelerated in the period 1979–81 by a combination of a sharp world recession and domestic economic policies which led to exceptionally high interest rates (placing increasing burdens on companies which had borrowed money) and a highly valued pound (making British exports increasingly uncompetitive in international markets). Between 1979 and 1981 manufacturing output fell by 20 per cent and by the end of 1985 was still significantly below its 1979 peak. Such a decline may, of course, be compensated for by improved performance in the service sector, but there is little sign that such improvements can be effected in the magnitude necessary to produce either a return to full employment or a resolution of the potential problems of the balance of payments. Over the last decade there has been a growth in service sector employment, but in considerable measure these jobs have gone, not to full-time workers displaced from manufacturing employment, but to married women working on a part-time basis. And while the trade surplus on services and 'invisible earnings' has grown, Britain's share of world trade in this area has continued to decline (Keegan, 1985, p. 77). It therefore appears unlikely that growth in this area can avert the longer-term problems.

These, then, are the problems and challenges facing the British economy in the late 1980s—high levels of unemployment, a persistently declining relative position in the world economy, and a process of deindustrialisation posing significant potential problems for the country's balance of payments in the medium term. It should, however, be noted that these are not new problems. Post-war unemployment reached its lowest annual average level as long ago as 1955, and there has been a steady upward trend since 1967. The relative decline of the British economy has a history going back at least a hundred years (Gamble, 1985), and it is arguable that Britain's relative position was maintained for as long as it was only by its ability to trade substantially in the markets of an empire which it dominated politically. The 'deindustrialisation' process—at least so far as employment is concerned—goes back at least twenty years and, as indicated above, there is nothing particularly new about the British economy being beset by balance of payments problems. None of these difficulties, therefore, can be ascribed simply to the recessions which have afflicted the world economy since 1973. World recession undoubtedly exacerbated these difficulties in a number of respects, but in many ways it has simply thrown into stark relief problems which were already becoming apparent in the 'age of affluence'. Any explanation of these problems must therefore go beyond the immediate past.

EXPLANATIONS OF DECLINE

The problem of Britain's relative decline has generated a substantial and growing literature, many of the contributions to which have advanced particular single-factor explanations. There is not space here to discuss this literature in any detail. I will therefore concentrate attention here on three factors which appear to me to play a particularly important role in explaining the weaknesses of the British economy: lack of investment, levels of innovation, and the political environment within which business activity takes place.

Lack of investment
The low level of investment in the British economy has been extensively documented, e.g. in 1980 the UK investment ratio (gross domestic fixed capital divided by gross domestic product) was 17.4, compared with 21.7 in France, 22.8 in Germany and 32.0 in Japan (Hare, 1985, p. 22). How is this low level of investment, which is by no means a new phenomenon, to be explained? To simplify somewhat (e.g., by leaving government aid out of the picture), we may say that companies may derive investment funds from three main sources: through borrowing from banks and other lenders, through raising capital by the sale of shares in the company, and through the retention of profits. British-based companies have tended to be disadvantaged with respect to all three. Firstly, Britain has tended to lack mechanisms for channelling savings into long-term industrial finance. The greater financial attractiveness (for tax reasons) of building society accounts have tended to draw savings away from banks over the postwar period. But in any case the large clearing banks, where such savings might have been deposited, have until comparatively recently limited their business and commercial lending largely to the provision of short-term finance, and have had greater regard in their lending decisions to the assets against which the loan may be secured than to the long-term prospects of the company in question (Carrington and Edwards, 1981; Williams *et al.*, 1983, pp. 69–70). The specialist merchant banks, on the other hand, which have been concerned with raising business finance, have not themselves possessed sub-

stantial savings resources to invest, and have tended to derive their profits from fees and commissions earned in the process of raising capital, thus limiting their longer-term interest in the firms for which they raise money (Ingham, 1984, pp. 68–74).

Raising money from capital issues has been similarly problematic. The post-war period has been characterised by a rapid expansion of pension funds and insurance business (itself related to the character of the state welfare system—see Chapter 5, this volume). These institutions have in turn become major investors—in 1981 insurance companies and pension funds held nearly half of all listed UK equities. However, a relatively small part of institutional investment goes into new capital issues. The emphasis has rather been on the buying and selling of existing shares. This has been facilitated by the fact that Britain has an exceptionally active secondary market in already issued shares, so that institutions (and indeed other shareholders) may trade shares constantly to realise short-term gains as prices move, and shift between different investments as their perceived prospects change (Coakley and Harris, 1983, Ch. 5; Williams *et al.*, 1983, pp. 70–1; Ingham, 1984, pp. 68–70). This well-developed secondary market in its turn facilitates the process of takeover and acquisition which, even before the boom of 1985–86, had led to exceptionally high levels of concentration in the British economy. Managements wishing to defend themselves against hostile takeover bids are therefore under pressure to emphasise short-term profitability and dividend distribution, with discouraging effects upon longer-term investment.

This brings us to the third source of capital—retained profits. Not only are the above pressures not conducive to the retention of profits for investment, but the very possibility of retaining profits has been reduced over much of the post-war period by the sharp reduction in the level of profits themselves (at least in the manufacturing sector). Not only did this reduction in profitability reduce the volume of internally-generated funds for investment, but it also reduced the incentive for new investment in industry. This was particularly true in the 1970s, when a combination of low profitability and high rates of inflation led to a negative real return on much industrial investment (Martin, 1981; Hawkins, 1983).

Low investment has been an important source of Britain's competitive disadvantage in the post-war period. However, the direction of investment is as important as its absolute level, and therefore attention must be directed to a second factor, the level and nature of innovation.

The level of innovation

In the post-war world economic success has gone predominantly to those countries which could establish an innovative lead with new products, or which could introduce new methods of production. In both respects the British economy has performed poorly. The high rate of import penetration already mentioned was part cause and part consequence of Britain's failure to establish itself in such rapidly expanding fields as consumer electrics, while the decline of such traditional industries as shipbuilding was in substantial measure due to a failure to adapt to the demand for new variations in the traditional product (Williams *et al.*, 1983). (This is not to discount the relevance of the emergence of new sources of competition, notably in the Far East. The point is rather that Britain tended to suffer exceptionally badly from these new challenges in a number of fields). Four factors may be adduced in explanation of this record of adaptation and innovation.

First, as has already been noted, capital for long-term investment has tended to be in short supply. This may be argued to have had particularly adverse effects on research and development, where the return on outlays is necessarily realised in the medium to long term (Rothwell and Zegveld, 1985, pp. 172-9).

Secondly, while British research and development expenditure has historically compared relatively well with that in other countries (although the rate of growth has been slower), an exceptionally high proportion of that expenditure has been provided by government. And within government spending itself an exceptionally high proportion has been directed toward military and military-related uses. This may be held to have had a number of negative consequences, but perhaps the principal one is that it has concentrated much British research and development in areas where it has been difficult to compete with the much greater spending levels of the United

States (e.g. aircraft and military electronics, nuclear power) while neglecting expenditure in such areas as machinery, metal products and chemicals, where Britain increasingly lost market share in the 1950s and 1960s (ibid., pp. 162–72; Pavitt and Soete, 1980).

Thirdly, as well as a relatively poor record in product innovation and development, Britain has a record of a slow rate of introduction of new production technologies dating back to at least the late nineteenth century. One factor in this slow rate of application has been labour resistance to changes in the process of production. This is not to say that technological changes have not been introduced, but that such introduction has tended to be slow, and in part conditional upon the maintenance of established labour demarcations and (to some extent) existing manning levels, which has in its turn limited the productivity gains to be made from technical change. The significance of this factor relative to others has undoubtedly been exaggerated in the past, but it cannot be wholly discounted (Kilpatrick and Lawson, 1980; cf. Batstone, 1984, Ch. 4; Fine and Harris, 1985, pp. 33–7).

Finally, British companies were for many years shielded from the worst rigours of foreign competition—and hence the need to innovate—by their historical dominance of established markets. Indeed, the very dominance of world trade noted earlier may have contributed to the loss of that dominance. Unlike their challengers, British companies felt less pressure to adapt and innovate to win markets. British shipbuilding, for example, accounted in 1950 for about 40 per cent of world output, a position based largely on meeting the specialised and varied needs of British shipping companies. British shipyards continued to serve this traditional market, and hence failed to respond to the expanding demand for more standardised bulk cargo vessels. When British companies themselves switched their demand to this type of vessel in the 1960s British shipbuilders were largely unable to respond. To some extent, then, British failure to innovate may be held to rest on a complacency arising from a traditional dominance in certain markets (Williams *et al.*, 1983, Ch. 2).

The political environment

A variety of theories—emanating from Left, Right and Centre of the political spectrum—have placed much of the blame for Britain's economic problems on its political system. Here I shall argue that the key problem has been a structural dissociation between government and industry, which parallels the dissociation between industry and finance noted earlier. At the most obvious level this has led governments to pursue policies injurious to domestic producers, such as the cycle of expansion and contraction ('stop-go') in the late 1950s and early 1960s, in which sustained economic growth was sacrificed to the maintenance of the value of sterling and overseas military spending (Pollard, 1982). More generally—and more fundamentally—British governments have failed to develop consistent and thoroughgoing strategies for economic development based on an integration of state and enterprise policies such as have characterised, for example, France and Japan in parts of the post-war period (Dyson, 1983). Nor have they been able to develop the kinds of neo-corporatist institutions which in such countries as Austria, Norway and Sweden have been able to secure a relatively high degree of labour peace and low pay increases in return for high levels of state spending and policies which have kept levels of unemployment relatively low (Cameron, 1984). Such failures have been blamed by critics of adversary politics on recurrent reversals of policy and institutional reorganisations introduced by successive governments (see Gamble and Walkland, 1984), but the roots lie deeper. Three factors in particular may be mentioned.

Firstly, in contrast to those countries where the state played a major role in promoting industrialisation, the British state has traditionally seen its role as that of providing the conditions of economic decision-making rather than intervening directly in such decisions. The liberal tradition of the autonomy of the individual is carried over into a belief in the autonomy of the firm. The obverse side of this predominant state position has been a mistrust by companies of state intervention at the microeconomic level—a mistrust reinforced by recurrent fears that such involvement by Labour governments in particular may be the prelude to wholesale nationalisation (ibid., Chapter 4).

Secondly, this split between the state and manufacturing industry has been mirrored at the level of personnel. The British administrative elite has tended to remain separate in training, career path and to some extent, in social origin from those responsible for the running of industry. It has therefore tended to lack the expertise and experience—as well as the inclination—for effective intervention (Dyson, 1983; cf. Chapter 11 this volume).

Finally, we should note the absence of strong, centralised business associations and trade unions with the capacity to integrate their members into a general economic strategy entailing economic trade-offs for political returns. It is this absence which has always rendered quasi-corporatist strategies by government somewhat illusory and essentially temporary expedients (Crouch, 1982, pp. 210–11; Coombes, 1982, Ch. 12).

BRITAIN AND THE WORLD ECONOMY

So far in this paper the British economy has been treated as a 'national' entity, albeit one placed in a context of international trade and competition. However, as is pointed out in Chapter 11, this is a considerable oversimplification, which needs to be corrected by a consideration of the international role of the City of London, and of the role of the multinational company in the British economy.

The City and the international economy
Britain's early dominance in international trade and the need for government revenues in an era of European wars led to the emergence in the seventeenth and eighteenth centuries of the City of London as a major source of finance for both foreign trade and government spending (Ingham, 1984, Ch. 2). In considerable measure the distancing between financial and industrial institutions referred to earlier can be traced back to the way in which, despite Britain's early industrialisation, the City remained largely oriented to foreign investment and loans. This position persisted in some measure until the late 1960s due to the continuing dominance of the pound sterling

as the medium of transactions in the former territories of the Empire. Since the late 1960s, however, the nature of the City has changed substantially, due initially to the development of the market in Eurocurrencies—free-floating units of currency (predominantly, but not exclusively, dollars) which are traded and lent in the international currency markets of the world. London became the major centre of Eurocurrency activities, with an attendant influx of foreign institutions—by 1982 some 450 foreign banks were represented in the City (McRae and Cairncross, 1985, p. 63; Coakley and Harris, 1983, Ch. 6).

These processes of 'internationalisation' have been substantially reinforced by a number of more recent developments. The abolition of exchange controls in 1979 not only led to a substantial exodus of capital from Britain, but opened the way for shares in British companies to be traded in stock exchanges around the world and for foreign shares to be traded in the UK. This in its turn was one of the factors which has led to the so-called 'Big Bang' of October 1986—the dismantling of the traditional restrictive practices of the Stock Exchange and the entry into Exchange membership of former 'outsiders' including large foreign corporations (Clarke, 1986, Ch. 4).

Thus, over the last twenty years, the City has moved from being a distinctively British institution to one which is firmly located within an international economy of loans, share purchase, and so on. It has long been a matter of debate whether, in the past, the government controlled the City or the City controlled the government (Ingham, 1984, esp. Ch. 1). What is clear today, however, is that the internationalisation of the City—and of financial markets in general—has reduced the possibilities of effective governmental control over the activities of financial institutions. It is, for example, difficult to envisage the reintroduction of exchange controls under present circumstances, although a combination of tax incentives and penalties might induce the repatriation of at least some of the capital which has flowed abroad since 1979. The general trend is for governments to be increasingly constrained by the international nature of financial transactions. In the past the ability of the government to determine domestic interest rates and the exchange rate for the currency has been restricted by the fact that higher interest rates elsewhere may lead to a movement of funds out of sterling, causing its relative value to decline. The internationalisation of markets in shares and government equities reinforces this dependence of government on the operation of the financial markets, thus reducing further its capacity to regulate certain of the key decisions affecting the domestic economy.

The multinational company

Although we tend to speak of 'British business' and 'British companies', Britain has become a major location for foreign companies, usually multinational in their scope of operations. Britain in fact now vies with Canada for the place as the second most preferred site for foreign investment after the United States, and around one in seven British workers are now employed by foreign firms. At the same time Britain is the home base for a large number of multinational corporations—in fact Britain has for decades been 'parent' to the second largest national grouping of multinationals, and overseas investments remain approximately double those of West Germany and Japan. However, while the inflow of investment has been concentrated in such areas as oil, motor vehicles and electrical and electronic products, British multinationals are more heavily concentrated in such relatively 'low-tech' fields as tobacco, alcohol, building materials, paper and textiles (Stopford and Turner, 1985, Ch. 1).

The effects of foreign investment on the host economy have been much debated, with fears on the Left especially that foreign firms can undermine the sovereignty of national governments by shifting their production facilities and resources elsewhere. The most recent survey of the effects of multinational investment concludes that, on balance, inward investment has had positive effects in such areas as the provision of employment and the balance of payments. In particular the presence of foreign companies has shifted the British economy toward the possession of a greater proportion of technology-intensive companies than would probably otherwise have been the case (ibid., Chs. 6 and 7). In the longer term, of course, this renders the fate of the British economy increasingly dependent on the decisions of foreign companies, while at the same time the more successful British multinationals may be increasingly locating their activities in other countries. In evaluating the effects of these processes, however, one needs to take account, not only of the consequences of the actions of multinationals, but also—and much more problematically—of whether outcomes would have been better or worse in their absence.

REVIVING THE BRITISH ECONOMY

From the period in the early 1960s when the relative decline of the British economy first came to be widely recognised, successive governments have taken steps to improve the British position—with, it must be said, a general lack of success. We may broadly group these responses under three headings.

Macroeconomic policy
Here the dominant orthodoxy for much of the post-war period was that policies of demand management (primarily through tax measures and government spending) could maintain full or near-full employment by compensating for fluctuations in demand. It may indeed by questioned how effective—or indeed necessary—this was. Throughout the 1950s and the 1960s the British government's current account was typically in surplus, and in the buoyant and apparently self-sustaining post-war boom the problem was typically one of excess rather than deficient demand, leading to a growing concern with the inflationary consequences of this situation (Gamble and Walkland, 1984, Ch. 3). When demand did become substantially deficient, after the sharp oil price rise of 1973, governments which had come to give greatest priority to checking inflation had begun to shift to alternative policy instruments, notably control over the supply of money. The beginnings of a monetarist approach can be traced back to the late 1960s, but it was firmly established by the shift in the Labour government's economic strategy in 1976, and reached its apogee in the early years of the Thatcher government, which saw tight control of the money supply as the key measure in squeezing inflation out of the economic system. By

controlling the amount of money available for the purchase of goods the rate of price increase would be slowed down. In particular workers would no longer be able to secure excessive rises in money wages, for any firm which gave such rises would be prevented by market pressures from recouping the excessive rise. Hence British producers would be rendered more competitive in the international market-place. What this meant in practice was a sharp reduction in government borrowing and an increase in interest rates. The effects of this on manufacturing industry have already been noted, and its effects on the level of unemployment were similarly dramatic, with a rise from 5.1 per cent in 1979 to 11.7 per cent in 1982. The effect on wages and salaries, however, was much more limited, as the average earnings of those remaining in work continued to rise more rapidly than the rate of inflation (Smith, 1984; Keegan, 1984). In any event, it is doubtful if price competitiveness was the main factor in Britain's poor trade performance in the 1970s. High wage rises tended to be offset by the downward movement of the pound, and several studies indicated that non-price factors (quality, delivery dates, etc.) were the principal sources of disadvantage (Stout, 1977). This is not to say that the results of this policy were wholly negative. Some rise in industrial productivity was achieved, and inflation was eventually brought down, although this may be attributed as much to changes in the world economy as to government policy. But of the overall restructuring of the economy on a more competitive basis there was little overall sign, perhaps itself an indication of the general inability of macroeconomic policies alone to achieve these ends.

Incomes policy and labour law
Since the early 1960s there has been a periodic cycle of policy instruments designed to check or regulate the bargaining power of trade unions, either through incomes policies or labour law. This preoccupation with the bargaining power of trade unions requires some explanation, for it is unclear that trade unions and labour relations bear a primary share of the responsibility for Britain's economic ills. Britain's strike-proneness—at least as measured by working days lost—has not been exceptionally high, and while the level of pay

increases has often been abnormally high relative to gains in productivity, the effects of this on international competitiveness tended to be offset for part of the period by changes in the exchange rate (Williams *et al.*, 1983, pp. 44–6). This did, of course, adversely affect domestic consumers and contributed to the decline in profitability which hindered new investment. None the less, the concentration on labour relations as *the* cause of Britain's economic problems by politicians and the media suggests that, in Anthony Barnett's words, 'they were projected into a central symbol of the British crisis in the 1960s and 1970s with an intensity that spoke of displacement, and this fixation on the unions diverted attention from equally critical problems, thereby contributing further to the general malaise' (Barnett, 1982, p. 66).

This is not to say that an enduring compact between unions and government, whereby the former moderated the use of their bargaining power in return for social benefits and policies oriented to maintaining employment might not have had some moderating effect upon Britain's economic problems. But, as the experience of Labour's 'social contract' in the 1970s shows, the possibilities of this are substantially constrained by the difficulty of union leaderships in taking their members with them down routes entailing significant longer-term sacrifices, especially in adverse economic circumstances.

Planning

All governments, however market-oriented in principle, have found themselves compelled to intervene directly in the affairs of the enterprise from time to time. But, as noted earlier, the principal tendency has been, to quote Stephen Wilks, 'to define industrial problems as, *prima facie*, the problems of industry, to be resolved by the market, and with a presumption against government action' (Wilks, 1983, p. 138). The market can, of course, be influenced, as in the mergers promoted by Labour's Industrial Reorganisation Corporation in the 1960s, but the general orientation of industrial policy has been reactive. On two occasions Labour governments have sought to change this pattern. The National Plan of 1964–65, however, was seriously deficient as an attempt to plan the economy as a whole. Among its most central flaws was its failure to translate its target growth figures into specific behavioural objectives for enterprises. Labour's industrial strategy of ten years later sought to overcome this problem with its proposal for planning agreements between government and firms, which would cover such issues as investment and employment. However, in the context of Labour's other policies of 1974 (price controls, the abolition of incomes policy, legislation to strengthen trade union rights, etc.) the possibilities of business cooperation were slight (Hare, 1985, pp. 31–64). Furthermore, throughout the post-war period the issue of planning has operated as a symbolic basis of party conflict, so that Conservative governments—despite extensive economic intervention—have been reluctant to become involved in anything smacking of long-term strategic planning for the economy as a whole. In contrast to other countries—most notably Japan—the conditions for some kind of consensus on planning the economy have not existed in post-war Britain (Gamble and Walkland, 1984, Ch. 4; Smith, K., 1984, Ch. 12).

CONCLUSION

What, then, are the likely prospects for the British economy? The first point to make is that, to some extent, these prospects are shaped by factors external to British society. The fate of the British economy is clearly bound up with the state of the world economy, most obviously in respect of the possibility of maintaining higher general growth rates. More specifically, the competitiveness and profitability of British firms is bound up with the pattern of international interest rates and currency movements, while decisions affecting exports and employment are to a significant degree in the hands of multinational companies whose ultimate loci of decision-making are to be found elsewhere.

Within the British economy the principal problems are, firstly, whether the decline in the oil supply will initiate a new sequence of balance of payments crises and, secondly, whether it will prove possible to return to something approaching full employment. As already indicated, there is little reason to believe that services will grow to fill either the employment or the export gap on the scale needed. Nor can adjustments to interest and exchange rates be expected to do that much. A low exchange rate would enhance the competitiveness of exports, but would also have adverse effects on the balance of payments by raising the cost of imports, which would also inject further inflation into the domestic economy. In the late 1970s one widely canvassed solution to these problems was a return to protectionism, entailing the use of selective import controls, but the problems with this are now fairly clear. Britain's dependence on imports and its high proportion of multinational companies render it particularly vulnerable to retaliatory action, and it is interesting to note that some erstwhile proponents of protectionism are now increasingly oriented to the idea of concerted (often European) reflation as the way out of crisis (see, e.g., Godley, 1986).

The most likely development in the next few years may indeed be the growth of a 'Europeanist' orientation on the part of many companies and policy-makers. In a world where many markets are dominated by a few firms each, it may increasingly cease to be viable to maintain a successful national presence on each industrial area, and pressures will continue to grow for merger or joint ventures with foreign companies. At the same time there may well be growing political antagonism to further penetration by US business, and a growing tendency to seek European partners, especially as British multinationals have had relatively limited success in penetrating European markets. Entry into the European Monetary System may be seen as a way of partially guarding sterling against the effects of currency movements.

Whether this will be enough to arrest Britain's relative decline is a different matter. Remedying the long-standing problems of low investment and poor innovation would require more radical changes in the structure of business financing and government-industry relations. Changes have begun to occur in the former, with investing institutions and banks starting to take a longer-term interest in the companies in which they invest or to which they lend. But short-term orientations persist to a considerable degree, while the history of business–government relations is not such as to encourage hopes of an early development of a Japanese-style industrial policy. Whatever strategy of reindustrialisation is pursued will require a significant financial input, in all probability from public as well as private sources.

In any event it is not clear that large-scale investment to reindustrialise on a competitive basis would necessarily reduce the problem of unemployment. As noted in the introduction to this volume, it appears that job losses in manufacturing due to technological change may be accelerating. Without investment in new technologies the competitiveness of British products is likely to decline further, but such investment itself is likely to increase job opportunities, and may actually reduce them.

In the longer term the best hopes for an increase in employment are likely to lie outside manufacturing, particularly in the expansion of the public sector. (See Chapters 7 and 8 for some indications of where such increases might be made.) In the short term, however, such public sector expansion is likely to founder on a shortage of government revenues already heavily committed to the maintenance of the existing body of unemployed, and needed also to fund the research and investment required to revive the manufacturing base. Thus we return to the paradox with which this chapter began. We are, on average, some 50 per cent better off than we were twenty-five years ago. Despite the talk of crisis and decline many have gained substantially in this period—but increasing numbers have come to lose out. To a considerable extent the cost of sustaining those gains would have to be borne by those who have gained, through higher taxation, income restraint, and so on. Whether this is a politically viable possibility is an open question.

3 Management

J. H. Smith

INTRODUCTION

In the decade immediately following the end of the Second World War, changes in the industrial and commercial structure were believed to have signalled the opening of a new era for British management. Engineering, shipbuilding, electrical goods, vehicles, chemicals, metal goods and building were expanding rapidly. Manufacturing output had increased by more than 40 per cent, while in some industries—notably chemicals and vehicles—it had risen at nearly twice that rate. It was against this background that the large-scale organisation, characterised by hierarchical organisation structures and increasingly sophisticated methods of financial control and technological development, was seen as the ideal form for the successful enterprise.

This belief in bigness as the essential condition of industrial efficiency had been endorsed by the state in the massive programme of nationalisation carried out by the post-war Labour government. Coal, electricity, gas, the greater part of inland and air transport, iron and steel, cable and wireless, the Bank of England were all included. For many Labour supporters these measures were seen as no more than the beginning. One of these, the historian R.H. Tawney, had welcomed nationalisation, among other things, for the opportunity it provided for the emergence of a new managerial class, dedicated to advancing managerial technique rather than financial interests (Tawney, 1937). Professionalism was seen as the key to management's (indeed, the country's) future in both public and private sectors. By the late 1950s, it was possible to identify a rudimentary but none the less developing framework of educational provision and institutional bodies within which managerial professionalism would be sought, but progress generally was slow.

The 1980s imposed an altogether different set of perspectives, into which the ideas and practice of management had to be fitted. A world recession had ended full employment, seemingly forever; many traditional industries (and some not so old) had gone to the wall; new technologies (especially those that were computer-based) were transforming production methods; while the once firm assumptions about the virtues of bigness had been replaced by an emphasis on the need to allow scope for basic entrepreneurial skills in settings which favoured individualistic enterprise. Although a major expansion of management education had taken place in the 1960s, including the establishment of business schools seeking comparability with the best abroad, there was no general sense that as a result the quality of management had decisively improved. Indeed, unsatisfactory management education had quickly become yet another diagnostic factor in the analysis of the British disease, along with 'irresponsible trade unionism' and the 'anti-industrial culture'. There was certainly no awareness that the predicted managerial revolution had taken place; nor any general feeling that the quality of British management could match the needs of an economy and society in crisis.

THE CENTRAL QUESTION

In considering the role of management in meeting the needs of a changing Britain, it is logical to begin with the idea of management itself. A basic question for British management—and perhaps the major challenge—concerns its uncertain sense of identity and purpose. British management is not immediately identifiable as an institution, in the sense that the Civil Service, or local government or even the City can be seen as bodies possessing generally agreed standards of performance and accountability. There appear to be no clear perceptions within our society as to what management is, or should be; yet it is possible when international comparisons are attempted, to argue that our competitors do better because their 'management' is better.

References to the superiority of Japanese or German management suggest that the comparison is focused on industrial management and on sectors where Britain's competitive performance is judged to be poor, e.g. automobiles, microelectronics. To give greater precision to these criticisms requires some consideration of what the management task actually involves and this, as pointed out later, is what the British have traditionally been reluctant to do. The idea of management in Britain does not convey the sense of a unitary entity and it is arguable that the major challenge for management is to create such a sense and to develop standards of performance and accountability appropriate to present needs.

This task is all the more important in the light of the increasing importance of management activity, both quantitatively and qualitatively. The increase in scale can be measured by the growth of managerial employment in industry and commerce and in the public sector. At the same time, the notion that management skills can be developed, transmitted and exchanged across traditional dividing-lines has been widely accepted. The idea that management is an activity to be taken seriously has caught on in the health service, in education, in statutory and voluntary social service and in the armed forces. There has been cross-fertilisation between private industry and the public sector at both the level of ideas and at the level of personnel. Not all of these exchanges have been voluntary: governments have taken a closer interest in deciding what forms of management are best and where possible, how to improve them. The efforts of the Wilson administration of the late 1960s to devise highly centralised organisational panaceas for backward industries were to be counteracted later by the Thatcher policies of privatisation and managerial autonomy. On the whole the contradictory political interventions of the past twenty years have served chiefly to increase the ambiguities which bedevil the role, status and functions of British management.

THE CHALLENGES

Competence

The principal challenges for management may be said to centre on issues of competence, competitiveness (or effectiveness), acceptability (in the promotion of change) and esteem. In summary to fulfil its role in a changing Britain, management must display a basic competence; it must be competitive; it must adapt to changing circumstances and show flexibility but also control the process of change itself; and its activities must command respect or earn esteem.

The question of competence is directly related to the selection, training and type and level of qualification of managers. Census data give an idea of the numerical strength of management as an occupational group, but also highlight the difficulty of generalising. About one in ten of the occupied population holds a management (or quasi-management) position and these posts are predominantly a male preserve. The absolute level of qualification compares unfavourably with other major industrial societies, in that not more than 15 per cent have a degree or similar qualification. The number holding a business-type degree or management qualification is only about 2 per cent. In terms of training for business, taking the output of MBAs (Masters of Business Administration), Britain is currently producing at less than one-tenth of the rate in the United States and one-fifth of that in France. In addition, the far lower proportion staying on at school to the age of eighteen means that the general educational level of British managers is that much lower than among its competitors. This might be expected to stimulate an awareness of the need to invest in management development, updating and retraining but the level of response is no better in that quarter (Forrester, 1985).

The challenge to managerial competence is most commonly understood in terms of the needs of competitive manufacturing. This is the form in which it will be considered here, although there is a considerable and growing overlap with managerial requirements elsewhere, including the service and public sectors. In the manufacturing setting the management task is generally understood in terms of (1) design and development, (2) production management, (3) personnel, (4) marketing, (5) financial control and (6) long-term strategy. The functional specialisations which have grown up around these divisions cannot easily be separated from the rigidities of the British educational system. Premature specialisation in schools reinforced by specialisation in selection and on-the-job training combine to preserve separate managerial interests and enclaves.

The illustrations most frequently given of this separation of interests concern the differing roles and strategies of accountants and engineers. It is widely believed that accountants enjoy a high prestige in industrial and commercial organisations and exert a powerful influence in decision-making. It is also widely believed that engineers have lower prestige than they deserve; furthermore that insufficient weight is given to areas of management for which their expertise is especially relevant e.g. R & D, design, production management.

These beliefs may be supported by international comparisons. In West Germany, for example, engineers are both absolutely and relatively more numerous and they dominate industrial management. They monopolise the technical functions in industry, spill over into the non-technical functions (such as sales and advertising) and they are very well represented in higher management. The result, not surprisingly, is a powerful emphasis on design, production and quality (Hutton and Lawrence, 1981). While it might be argued that these are not the sole criteria for appraising managerial competence they are inescapably important elements in manufacturing and they are inherent in the objectives and procedures of a well-founded profession. At least part of the ambiguous position of British management and a major factor contributing to doubts about its competence is the absence of any single dominant professional group within its ranks.

Competitiveness

Competitiveness, or the lack of it as applied to market opportunities and performance, is widely regarded as a principal challenge for British management. The factors judged to be important in competitiveness are for the most part specific instances of the question of competence and can be related to the management tasks already listed. They include (1) product design, (2) productive efficiency, (3) cost control, including control over labour, (4) marketing, and (5) company strategy in general. Much of the criticism of British management hinges on an alleged lack of thrust and poor coordination of effort in seeking to achieve high standards in these areas.

Yet the UK economic base possesses strengths as well as weaknesses. It is relatively strong in its base of large companies (over half the largest European companies are UK-based). It attracts substantial foreign investment which, although not without drawbacks, promotes economic development and employment—about one British worker in seven is employed by a foreign firm (Stopford and Turner, 1985). However, investment in the UK economy remains at a lower level than that of its main competitors and, unlike them, is concentrated more in the service than in the manufacturing sector.

From the point of view of future development, there are two particularly serious concerns. One is the relatively low number of smaller firms by international standards, since it is at this level that much of the potential for development and responsiveness to change may well be located. The other is a more familiar and indeed thoroughly rehearsed concern. While research and development is one of the great strengths of British industry—especially in basic research—the capacity to turn this to advantage in developing marketable products is weak. A related difficulty is the high proportion of R & D spending attributable to defence (Confederation of British Industry, 1985).

Although the UK share of world markets has fallen, it is still one of the world's major exporters and retains a considerable measure of control over its domestic markets. But it has been less successful than its competitors at anticipating customer needs and identifying new sources of custom.

The challenge of competitiveness for British management has to be understood in terms of world markets which are increasingly dominated by international business and rapid developments in customer needs and awareness. The main criticisms of British managerial performance centre on its lack of coordination and forward planning and its inability to

identify and meet new demands. Here the potential of technological advance is a prime factor and one of such importance
that it deserves separate consideration as part of the challenge
of the management of change.

The management of change

The advent of the microchip and the apparent lack of limits to
its application in all sections of employment has given a new
and sharper focus to the management of technological change.
The economic and social implications of changing technology
are not new considerations for industrial societies. As matters
for public concern and political response they are almost as
old as the industrial revolution itself, but the accelerating pace
of technological change means that the capacity to handle not
just one but a continuing series of changes in products and
processes now ranks as a fundamental test of managerial competence. The computer has been harnessed to all aspects of the
production and distribution process from materials handling
to information handling. While management has been given
increased control over the means at its disposal for the control
of products and personnel, its own position—and especially
that of middle management—has become increasingly susceptible to central monitoring and control. For the first time,
groups previously immune to the displacement effects of new
technology—managers, supervisors, clerical workers—have
experienced both the threat and the reality of loss of employment. A whole series of organisational revolutions, characterised by smaller workforces and more flexible administrative
structures, have affected industry and commerce and the
private and public sectors in equal measure. All this has presented a major challenge to management's skill in initiating
and implementing change.

An important element in the management of technological
change is the perception of it held by managers and employees.
At one time, the greatest attention was directed towards
specific items of technology and their consequences as 'labour-
saving devices'. Negotiations and worker resistance tended to
treat every introduction of new technology as a unique event,
for which a specific bargain had to be struck. The result was
often prolonged delays amid a reputation for obstruction or

Luddite mentality on the part of the unions. As is made clear in the discussion of trade unions in Chapter 4, the reality is some way from this. The pace of technological change is now such that single events are difficult to identify and manage in isolation from a general process of change directed towards the improvement of business efficiency. This is likely to become even more marked with improvements in business confidence and increased competition from Third World producers.

Too great an emphasis on the management of technological change may minimise or overlook altogether other changes in the nature of work of no lesser importance. It has already been noted that there has been something of a retreat from size, in the sense that there is less confidence than there was twenty or thirty years ago in the merits of very large organisations. To a considerable extent, some of the psychological and social disadvantages of bigness from a managerial viewpoint have been lessened by conscious efforts to delegate and decentralise. In this regard, the application of computers in developing and operating new systems of management information and control have tended to simplify management structures by collapsing hierarchies and generally de-bureaucratising large enterprises (Buchanan and Huczynski, 1985). But it remains the case that British managerial expertise has typically been developed within large organisations, with a reduced capacity to innovate and to respond to changing market conditions. This tendency has been greatly strengthened by the strong appetite in British industry and commerce for mergers and takeovers. The creation of these very large organisations, largely determined by financial considerations, poses a special challenge by creating a need for effective all-round management systems operating across a number of sectoral boundaries.

At the other end of the scale, new types of small-scale organisations have emerged with developments in subcontracting, franchising and the general emphasis on small business formation. How these developments may affect management recruitment and performance is difficult to assess. Some, of course, are the direct result of the efforts of managers whose expertise was acquired in the setting of the larger-scale enterprise: in the establishment of subcontracting, for example, there may have been encouragement from the manager's previous firm to hive off an activity for organisational and economic reasons. Others result from the traditional desire to set up on one's own, but it is here, as the statistics of business failure confirm, that inadequate levels of managerial competence and commitment are most common (or most commonly made public). In their study of small businesses, Scase and Goffee (1980) found that a reluctance to take responsibility for employees was often given as a reason for unwillingness to expand. The challenge of responsibility for employees, including concern for their motivation, training and personal development is a longstanding one for management in all enterprises. It is not a responsibility for which British management seems to have a special enthusiasm, yet it is one of special importance in the context of a rapidly changing economy.

Status and esteem

Popular views of the status of management must be taken as a general reflection of management's competence in meeting the challenges outlined in the previous sections. If management is believed to be doing a good job, then its status *vis-à-vis* other occupational groups will be relatively high. This is more than a question of differential rewards, although the British tendency to hang on to managerial perks, such as company cars, separate dining rooms and other privileges, suggests that managements remain very dependent on these as symbols of status.

The question of 'esteem', in the sense of the value placed on management activities by the community, is more difficult. Here the comparison tends to be made—and unfavourably— with the Civil Service and the older established professions. The supporters of the 'anti-industrial culture' argument take the view that low esteem puts a brake on the rate and quality of industrial recruitment, but it is difficult to attach much weight to this if one takes the recruitment of good university graduates as a measure. The growth of British management must be seen as part of the general expansion of Goldthorpe's 'service class' and of the educational provisions related to it. This process provides fresh avenues of social mobility as well as significant opportunities for others to consolidate their class position of birth (Goldthorpe, 1982). The ranks of management would appear to be getting (and to be likely to continue to get) a continuous infusion of new blood. The problems of managerial effectiveness in the workplace and of managerial acceptance in the society are certainly social, in that they have their roots in social attitudes and relationships; but the solution calls for much more than improving the managerial or industrial image in schools, however worthwhile that may be as an educational objective.

RESPONSES

'We're not doing too badly, are we?'
Before considering what responses have been made or might be expected to the specific challenges just described, it is important to retain some sense of proportion concerning British managerial performance. The situation may not be quite as desperate, nor are the international comparisons necessarily as unfavourable, as is often made out. There are many very successful British firms, whose managements are committed to and achieve excellence. It can be argued that despite its falling share of world trade, Britain exports more per capita than the Japanese, and as an exporter is second only to West Germany among the EEC countries (Confederation of British Industry, 1985). Britain has a very strong international customer base, with highly diversified exports, both by product and by market. This position could not have been maintained, in the face of keen international competition, without the exercise of well-developed managerial skills.

Unfortunately, these considerations, supported by patriotic enthusiasms (which do not always reflect as favourably as intended on the British image) gloss over persistent weaknesses in the scope and character of British management. It is only a partial response to point to the high quality of management in firms like ICI or BP, whose success and survival depends on their competitiveness with the very best of foreign enterprises. Again the performance of the one in seven of British workers who are employed by foreign firms directly reflects what *can* be done. It is what happens outside these special circumstances and what management could be doing there which needs to be more closely examined. In doing that, it makes no sense to take the complacent view, that 'we're not doing too badly'. That may be true in specific instances, but it is no truer than the statement 'we're not doing very well'. It is certainly not the appropriate response to the questions put earlier in this chapter. To answer these it is useful to take note not only of current initiatives by government, employers and unions, but also to consider some recent research findings, especially on competitiveness and the management of change.

Improving competence
The key to improved managerial performance is to be found in the capacity to recruit people of high potential to management jobs and to train them to meet present and future needs. In management education, there is a far greater emphasis on purpose and effectiveness (at least from the educational sector). The settled confidence of twenty-five years ago that the creation of two elite business schools (London and Manchester) would suffice to set standards for the whole of British management has been replaced by a highly localised grassroots approach in which the principal emphasis is on ties between local industry and local institutions of higher education. Universities, polytechnics and further education colleges are reaching out to establish links with industry and commerce. Management education, both of a formal and informal kind, is a central feature of these initiatives.

Unfortunately, the (to some quite surprising) aggressive marketing style of the educational institutions does not seem generally to be matched by enthusiasm on the part of employers. It is a longstanding criticism of British employers that they lack enthusiasm for training, at least when they are required to bear some of the cost themselves. A recent report by management consultants for the Manpower Services Commission and National Economic Development Office found that most British employers did not regard training as a particularly important issue. Furthermore, top managers were surprisingly ignorant of how their company's training record compared with the efforts of competitors. Statistics not only support these conclusions but reveal an alarming trend: the number of trainees in all sections of manufacturing industry has more than halved during the 1980s (Institute of Manpower Studies, 1985).

This lack of awareness has to be set against the official expressions of employers' views on management questions by bodies such as the Confederation of British Industry, (CBI), the British Institute of Management (BIM), and the Institute of Personnel Management (IPM). These organisations aim to issue public statements of an authoritative, professional kind and make important contributions to public debates. But what they have to say is rarely representative of the general quality of managerial thought and action. They take the view, not surprisingly, that when they say 'management' they are referring to a body of professionals who can be expected to think and perform like themselves. Although there are grounds for believing that this is now more likely to be the case, there is still a very considerable gap between rhetoric and reality.

Some part of the gap may well be closed by the development of new forms of training, especially distance learning. For example, the Open University is in the process of developing the Open Business School. The OU based its scheme on the assumption that most managers could not contemplate taking time off for conventional full-time study for any extended period. Even where training is seen as particularly desirable, the majority can do very little about it because courses are not accessible to them. The first course of this type, 'The Effective Manager', was offered by the OU in 1983 and achieved an initial intake of 1500.

The scope of these initiatives and the level of response indicates the sense of 'room for improvement' held both by employers and by those in education. But the essential contribution of education to managerial competence still seems to be imperfectly understood by employers. There is a sense in which this problem will only be overcome in a world in which most managers will have had the kind of training which makes them aware of the need to train others. But management competence needs to be consciously improved in the short term and the principal obstacle to achieving this appears to be the attitudes of managers themselves.

Increasing competitiveness

At its national conference in November 1985, the CBI presented a report, *Change to Succeed*, which takes the form of a business plan for the UK (Confederation of British Industry, 1985). The report is unusually frank in identifying shortcomings in managerial thinking and performance, and places its chief emphasis on the role of management and leadership in the improvement of organisational performance. The improvement of managerial goals was seen as essential to increasing the competitive spirit within the company. The two areas in which CBI members felt managers could most improve their goals were (1) to move away from short-term profit objectives to longer-term considerations, such as investment in innovation, marketing and training; (2) to pay more attention to the needs and opinions of customers. Particular problems in the determination of profit objectives were identified as the imposition of accounting conventions on management perspectives and the attitude of financial institutions. Other factors identified as important included the involvement and motivation of employees and the need for government decisions to be more closely targeted towards improving business competitiveness.

In this connection, attitudes to customers were seen, as already noted, as an area in which there was a need for immediate improvement. The CBI view is that UK companies as a rule do not really know where to look for new customers, or to find out what those customers want, or will want. There is a low commitment to creating products and services to meet new demands and a complacency about the selling of existing products. A study by the Institute of Marketing of over 1500 firms showed 13 per cent admitting that 'we make what we can and sell to whoever will buy' (Institute of Marketing, 1984). A common attitude was that advertising and selling were more important than market analysis. Marketing, as well as product development, was seen as an activity which required greater encouragement and coordination by management.

Coordination of management effort is a general theme of the CBI report. Its relevance to competitiveness is well brought out in an independent study *Managing for Success* carried out for the CBI in 1985 (Matthews, 1985). Although modest in scope and method, this survey of British business performance provides some useful insights into the factors which business-men who were themselves successful think vital to success. The principal factors to emerge were cost control and decentralisa-tion of decision-taking; attention to customers; attention to products; motivation of employees. The most important changes seen as having taken place were in controlling costs, in developing more professional systems of financial manage-ment and in decentralising decision-making. Improvements in financial management were regarded as the essential condition for decentralised decision-making.

The following aspects of company operation were con-sidered: company organisation and financial control, strategic planning, employee relations, technology, marketing. A common element in recent developments was the impact of computerisation. It was generally felt that computerisation had simultaneously reduced the cost of financial management and the time needed to provide relevant financial data for senior management, especially for strategic planning. This enhanced quality of financial managerial techniques was be-lieved to have encouraged major steps in decentralisation and the devolution of decision-making and financial responsibility to operational management.

Computerisation is widely regarded as the most important single advance in managerial technique and its implications for organisational theory and practice are given further consider-ation in the following section. At this point, attention can be focused on the contribution made by the computer, not only to decentralisation, but to a general emphasis on the need to establish a clearly understood strategy within a company. Effective management was believed to be dependent on the setting of common goals and a sense of team effort.

Most strategic plans included an intention to move up-market and to improve international strength, while reducing dependence on the UK economy. Most also included plans for acquisitions. Although acquisitions and 'merger mania' often seem in the British economy to be ends in themselves, the study suggests that the desire to acquire other businesses is part of a coherent management strategy, e.g. to use strengths of existing managements and technologies, to gain entry to new markets, to acquire new technology. But acquisitions were only one feature of strategic planning, which called for both the centre and the lower tiers to exploit the possible effects of technological change, the activity of competitors, shifts in market demand and changes in resource costs. The picture which emerges from this study is of managerial coherence arising from a pooling of expertise and a successful co-ordination of interests and objectives. This perspective is underlined by the views of the managers in the study on employee relations, communications and motivation. While most of these interviewed believed that adversarial attitudes prevail within the British economy, only a small proportion believed such attitudes were characteristic of their own firms. The study found that the most successful firms were those devoting the greatest effort to employee relations. Overall, the quality of management was believed to be the prime factor in company success, operating a coherent strategy embracing technological motivation, marketing and employee motivation and communicating this to the organisation as a whole.

It has to be said, however, that the concern with the communication of goals as a factor in company success remains one of the most substantial points of disagreement between employers and unions. Unions are in favour of communication and participation, but argue that British managements are unnecessarily secretive, seeking to restrict the supply of information to employees and their representatives. They further insist that such behaviour inhibits collective bargaining and creative personnel policy-making and so encourages the adversarial attitudes complained of by so many managers. The challenge here is for management to find a more appropriate response than simply insisting that employers and employees are really 'part of one team'. As the study *Managing for Success* shows, the effort called for here is exceptional, but it is directly related to the greatest competitiveness and the most effective performance.

Managing change
It has already been noted that the approach to change—and in particular to technological change—is a severe test of managerial strategy and adaptability. How is British manage-

ment responding to this challenge? As in the previous section, this question can be answered by drawing on the growing body of research findings available. In this case the source is the work of the New Technology Research Group at the University of Southampton. This interdisciplinary research unit was founded in 1979 by members of the Department of Electronics and of the Department of Sociology and Social Administration. Studies carried out by members of the Group include the adoption of a computerised freight information system in British Rail, the introduction of electronic news-gathering equipment in a television company (TVS), and telephone exchange modernisation in British Telecom. Each of these cases could be regarded as examples of major new technologies being introduced successfully. While there were naturally many differences in detail, certain basic features were found to be common in respect of the implementation of change.

Faced with new technologies, managements had to choose one of two strategies: either they placed the principal emphasis on the maintenance of existing operational concerns or they gave absolute priority to the requirements of change. Successful implementation is shown to be closely related to the second option, which involves far more adaptation than simply to the requirements of the new technology itself. As in the promotion of competitiveness, a whole range of considerations need to be identified and drawn into a coherent strategy. In the British Rail case, which called for the replacement in freight management of what were still in essence Victorian operating and reporting techniques by a centralised computer network, these considerations extended from the design and practical operation of training packages to the development of new organisational and supervisory structures. In all cases, management had to devise means for ensuring the continuity of managerial responsibility for each stage in the process of change. This was coupled with the anticipation and (for the most part) avoidance of industrial relations problems by welcoming participation by local trade union representatives in establishing new processes, e.g. in selection for training, staffing levels, and working practices. Finally, 'key individuals', through their motivation, personality and roles,

had a significant effect on the way in which the new technology
was introduced and on its outcomes (McLoughlin *et al.*, 1983).

The clear evidence provided by these studies of the influence
of individuals and of the exercise of choice contradicts the
popular view that technology is an all-powerful and irresistible
determinant and that its introduction should simply be
accepted. The scope for creative interpretation of the role of
technology in the work situation is considerable. That technological change is not an inevitable or immutable process is
demonstrated by management's many errors of judgement or
failures of foresight in handling it. Managements need to
invest far more effort in the understanding of the processes of
change as an essential preliminary to controlling them. For
example, in the British Telecom case, the implications of
exchange modernisation for existing supervisory roles were
not foreseen, which contributed to the erosion of some supervisors' roles as a result of the introduction of new systems.

Management's response to the challenge of technological
change has generally been welcoming, but perhaps for the
wrong reasons. New technology is seen as a means of introducing more effective control over labour and there are
respects in which this perception cannot really be questioned.
For example, figures for settlements in UK manufacturing
between 1980–84 show that settlements involving new technology achieved in 39 per cent of the cases the removal of
restrictive practices, a reduction in numbers employed also in
39 per cent of the cases and other productivity improvements
in 48 per cent of the cases (Northcott and Rogers, 1985).

Yet new technology—especially information technology—opens up possibilities in the sphere of communication
and participation which managements are only now beginning
to sense. The demise of the large-scale organisation as the preferred formal structure means that management can be much
closer to the work setting and in closer contact with
employees. In particular the possibility of new organisational
forms is beginning to be recognised. Management structures
generally have become more devolved and have begun to
assume a more fluid form. Information technology has greatly
stimulated these developments, not least by rendering obsolete
the accepted middle-management function of interpreting data

from and monitoring performance at the operational level and directly transmitting instructions from the corporate head office. Both individual units and specialist functions can now be in immediate and continuous contact via computer networks: old organisational maps are being rolled up as the traditional management hierarchies are dismantled. Computer information and control systems are introducing a new and dramatic potential for the integration or consolidation of previously disparate activities within organisations. These developments present a major challenge but also perhaps the best opportunity for many years for British management to improve its competitive strategies and its overall level of performance.

CONCLUSION: IMPROVING THE MANAGERIAL IMAGE AND IDENTITY

Skills in the management of human and material resources are as vital as any in meeting the economic and social challenges facing Britain. Here the recruitment of the best talent and its proper use are prime requirements. It is suggested that industry misses the best products of the British educational system because of an unfavourable image (especially in schools) and a lack of interest in wealth creation as a form of service to society. Whether an improvement in the managerial image will regenerate economy and society is a matter of opinion, but managerial performance can be counted as an important factor in maintaining and improving living standards and, some would add, the quality of life. For this reason, improved managerial professionalism to raise standards of performance is an important goal, but this also calls for a commitment to the broadening of facilities for management education and training, including updating.

Two aspects of managerial professionalism are particularly relevant to the theme of this book in that they are directly related to the potential for change. The first is the recognition that change includes change for management itself—indeed, that management should display a readiness to seek change for itself, before attempting to impose it on others. This might well include the adoption of imported management practices, such as the Japanese use of quality circles. At the same time, an emphasis on identifying a distinctive British style for managerial success is long overdue.

The second aspect is of special importance in determining the managerial image and is concerned with management's ability to secure the collaboration of its workforce. Employee involvement in and commitment to managerial objectives is a more solid testimony to managerial status than a company car or a separate dining room. Yet much of British management is still marked off from the general body of workers by sharp differences in status and imperfect communication systems.

In noting the problems facing British management in the way it handles human resources, some consideration of the anti-industrial culture thesis is useful. As yet there appears to be no independent realm of judgement for British management, no self-contained frame of reference within which meaningful assessments of its performance can be made. A pointer to this is the deferential attitude of British businessmen to the Civil Service. A particularly marked characteristic is the wish to imitate higher civil servants, and to recruit them to top positions after their retirement from the public service. Apart from their obvious value as sources of inside information, appointments of this type contribute a form of symbolic deference and an admission of intellectual and administrative inferiority, which does no good at all to the managerial image.

On the whole the idea of management remains a somewhat vague one in British society and the belief in management as an essential element in economic and social life lacks assurance. As has been shown, its position is changing, but it is still hampered by ambiguities and uncertainties which reduce its effectiveness. Some of these are the result of government (and Civil Service) attitudes. Britain does not achieve the close strategic integration of government, employees and unions which some of its international competitors bring to bear on specific aspects of economic growth. Government intervention in British business, both from the Left and the Right, often demonstrates low regard for home-based talent. The more spectacular management tasks are entrusted to overseas recruits, such as Michael Edwardes (British Leyland), Ian

McGregor (British Coal) or Graham Day (British Shipbuilders). Each of these was an outsider, or strictly speaking
someone who had acquired or proved his managerial skills in
another culture. The final challenge for British management is
to assert its cultural independence as well as its professional
strength and identity.

4 Trade Unions

Jon Clark

INTRODUCTION

Between 1969 and 1979 trade union membership in Britain increased by 28 per cent. Between 1979 and 1985 it declined by 19 per cent. These figures provide an immediate starting point when looking at the challenges facing British trade unions in the late 1980s. Considering that employment declined by around 8 per cent between 1979 and 1985, it appears that getting on for half the decline in union membership is directly attributable to unemployment. But this is clearly only part of the story. Job losses have hit disproportionately those sectors of the economy, such as manufacturing and nationalised industries, where union membership has been traditionally high. Between 1979 and 1985, for example, the number of manufacturing jobs in Britain declined by more than 1.5 million We cannot simply look at unemployment in the generality, we must also explore its links with longer-term changes in employment and industrial structure. This chapter will begin by looking at two of the main economic causes of the recent decline in union membership, unemployment and changes in industrial and employment structure.

Perhaps a more powerful and lasting challenge to British trade unionism, though, is a political one, represented by the policies of governments or (more widely) the state. Since the early 1960s, government policies have ranged from restrictive legal interventions limiting the freedoms of trade unions to supportive measures promoting their activities. Both types of policy have important implications for collective bargaining, the main method by which British unions seek to achieve their objectives. We shall therefore follow our discussion of some of the economic causes of declining union membership with an examination of the political challenges facing unions, and whether these and other factors call into question the sufficiency of traditional collective bargaining.

The responses of British unions to these challenges and opportunities have been uneven and fragmented. In the central section of this chapter, we shall look at a number of recent positive union initiatives. These include moves towards a greater professionalisation of union activity, the development of a more market-based trade unionism, and new policies in areas such as job security, working time and positive discrimination in favour of women trade unionists. In the conclusion, we shall go back to first principles and re-examine the basic reasons for trade unionism. We shall suggest that the future of unions will depend partly on factors beyond their control, particularly management behaviour and attitudes, but also on the extent to which they can provide an effective vehicle for employee protection and participation in the changed circumstances of the 1990s.

THE MAIN CHALLENGES

Unemployment

Unemployment represents a challenge to trade unions in two main ways. Most obviously, as we have seen, it reduces the potential number of trade union members. This is why, among other reasons, trade unions have a vested interest in reducing unemployment. Perhaps more fundamentally, unemployment alters the balance of power between trade unions, managements and government. If trade unionists live in fear of dismissal because they can be easily replaced and find it difficult to get alternative work, this can reduce their willingness to question management decisions and ultimately their capacity to strike.

In essence the effectiveness of trade unions depends on their ability to represent the interests of employees to employers and governments and to mobilise the occupational power of their

members in the labour market. As a result, the effect of unemployment on trade unions is likely to be uneven. Those
unions operating in profitable companies and expanding
sectors of the economy, perhaps organising occupational
groups such as computer staff whose skills are in great
demand, are likely to be less hit than unions with large
numbers of members in declining industries who possess skills
which are less marketable. The Transport and General
Workers Union in Britain belongs to this latter category, and
has seen its membership decline, despite amalgamations and
mergers, from nearly 2.1 million in 1979 to around 1.4 million
in 1985. At an aggregate level, therefore, unemployment
represents a major challenge to trade union membership. At a
disaggregated level, it can have an extremely uneven impact
and may well accentuate differences between different types of
unions.

Changes in industrial and employment structure

If we turn now to the challenge to trade unions resulting from
changes in industrial and employment structure, a similar
uneven picture emerges. The most important indicator of the
challenge here is trade union density, that is, the number of
union members in a particular sector or occupation as a percentage of potential union members. Looking first at the distribution of union membership across the three main
industrial sectors in Britain, the figures in Table 4.1 tell a clear

Table 4.1: Union membership and density by sector in Britain, 1948–85

Sector	Potential union membership (millions)				Union density (%)			
	1948	1968	1979	1985	1948	1968	1979	1985
Public	4.6	5.5	6.3	6.2	71	66	82	81
Manufacturing	7.3	8.3	7.4	5.5	51	50	70	73
Private services	4.6	6.0	7.3	7.9	15	13	17	15

Source: Bain and Price, in Bain (1983, p. 11). Figures for 1985 have been provided by
Robert Price. The 1948–79 figures include the unemployed in potential union
membership, the 1985 figures do not. This is due to a change in the way the
government presents the statistics in the official *Employment Gazette*.

story. The only sector which has shown a consistent increase in employment since 1948 is private services, the one with traditionally low levels of union membership (and pay). Manufacturing employment has been in decline since the early 1970s, and the public sector since 1979. These have been the two main bastions of trade union membership since the end of the Second World War.

Next, if we look at the size of workplace and its correlation with union activity, we find employer recognition of trade unions in 94 per cent of workplaces with over 1000 employees, but in under 50 per cent of workplaces with between 25 and 49 employees (see Daniel and Millward, 1983, p. 22). The significance of these figures can be better appreciated if we consider the present general trend, with some obvious notable exceptions in commerce and administration, in favour of smaller employment units. Interestingly, this trend often goes hand in hand with an increase in company mergers and takeovers and the growth in large, multi-plant, multi-product, multinational companies.

In terms of broad occupation, too, the traditional pattern of trade union membership is changing. At the beginning of the twentieth century, manual workers constituted around 80 per cent of all employees and 90 per cent of trade union members. By the early 1980s, white-collar workers constituted over 50 per cent of employees and nearly 40 per cent of all union members. Traditionally, of course, trade unionism has been much higher amongst manual than white-collar workers.

Before we try and summarise the overall effect of these changes, two other comparatively recent developments in employment structure should be mentioned. First, as Table 4.2 shows, female participation in the labour force in Britain increased by almost three million between 1948 and 1979. By 1979, women made up around 40 per cent of potential trade union membership. Traditionally, union membership has been lower amongst women than men, although this is largely the result of the type and location of jobs women do. They are disproportionately concentrated in white-collar occupations, the private service sector and smaller workplaces, and in part-time jobs with comparatively high labour turnover.

Finally, mention should be made of the increasing

Table 4.2: Union membership and density by sex in Britain, 1948–79

| | Male | | | Female | | |
	Union member-ship (000s)	Potential union member-ship (000s)	Union density (%)	Union member-ship (000s)	Potential union member-ship (000s)	Union density (%)
1948	7468	13,485	55.4	1650	6785	24.3
1968	7428	14,452	51.4	2265	8251	27.5
1979	8866	13,979	63.4	3837	9708	39.5

Source: Bain and Price, in Bain (1983, p. 7).

fragmentation of the full-time continuous employment relationship and of the traditional fixed workplace in factory or office. This recent trend covers a number of interrelated phenomena, including part-time employment, self-employment, subcontracting, temporary employment, youth training schemes, short-term contracts, job-splitting and homeworking (the latter not just in the old cottage industries, but also 'telecommuting' in the aptly named 'electronic cottage'). Such types of work are not carried out in workplaces or under employment conditions which are conducive to collective organisation or collective action, and these groups of workers are typically not members of trade unions. Also, they are often excluded from employment protection legislation.

All these changes in industrial and employment structure, some of recent origin, others going back many years, represent a multitude of challenges to trade unions, to their existing structures, recruitment methods, organisation and bargaining activities. Perhaps the clearest way to illustrate the challenge is to contrast what is often held to be the typical trade union environment of the 1960s with its most likely counterpart in the 1990s. To quote John Edmonds, General Secretary (since 1986) of one of Britain's largest unions, the GMBATU:

In the 1960s many academics regarded a large engineering works as a model environment for the study of industrial relations. People who want to understand the problems of the 1990s would do well to find a medium-size hotel owned by a large and diverse company. (Edmonds, 1984, p. 19).

What Edmonds is highlighting here is a fundamental change in the structural basis of trade union organisation and the fragmentation of workplaces and employment likely to result from it. A number of possible responses to these developments will be discussed below.

The political challenge

The changes in employment and industrial structure discussed above are in some respects connected with the political challenge facing British trade unions. In an age of mass media and instant news reporting, trade unions are no longer (if they ever were) isolated from the wider society, and their place within it is strongly shaped and expressed by the policies of governments and the main political parties. There have been wide fluctuations in the degree of legitimacy accorded to trade unions since the beginning of their modern history at the end of the eighteenth century. In the past fifty years in particular, their treatment by governments has oscillated between some kind of incorporation into the affairs of state (e.g. 1940–48, 1964–66, 1974–77) and vilification as usurpers of government power (e.g. 1970–72) or even as the 'enemy within' (Prime Minister Thatcher in 1984). The broad policies of governments and political parties, and of state agencies more generally, will clearly continue to exert a powerful influence on the general climate within which British trade unions operate.

There are two particular areas, though, where the effects of state policy on trade unions have been, and are likely to continue to be, strongly marked: the determination of wages and salaries, and the law governing employment. Although real disposable incomes are affected by many factors such as taxation, social security benefits and the number and type of wage-earners in individual households (see Chapters 5 and 7), income from paid employment still represents the main element in the budget of the majority of British households. In their effect on economic demand, prices and general competitiveness, wages and salaries are also important, if not necessarily decisive, factors affecting the overall performance of the British economy (see Chapter 2). Since the late 1940s, governments of all political persuasions have rejected leaving the regulation of wages to autonomous collective bargaining and sought to influence, directly or indirectly, the general levels of income from employment. Indeed, the three main political parties in Britain in the mid-1980s envisage some kind of continued state involvement in pay determination. This ranges from a fully-fledged incomes policy in the case of the Liberal/SDP Alliance, via a national economic assessment and national agreement on pay guidelines in the case of the Labour Party, through to strict monetary controls for the public sector by the Conservatives.

As for government intervention via employment or labour law, British industrial relations have traditionally stood out from those of other industrialised countries 'because they are so little regulated by law' (Phelps Brown, 1959, p. 355). Since the early 1960s, however, there has been a steady increase in the number and scope of laws establishing rights for individual employees in areas such as unfair dismissal, race and sex discrimination, and redundancy. How effective these laws are in influencing day-to-day industrial relations remains a much disputed question (see Clark and Wedderburn, 1983, pp. 127–242; Clark and Wedderburn, 1987; Lewis, 1986, pp. 1–43). More controversial still is the question of the role and influence of the law in shaping the relations between unions and employers. In Britain, where collective agreements have traditionally not been legally enforceable (except through individual employment contracts) and where there is no legally established system of employee representation in the enterprise, collective labour law has meant essentially trade union law and strike law. Here, too, government policies have fluctuated widely, ranging from the imposition of severe legal restrictions on strike action and the freedom of unions to establish their own rules (on electing their executives and calling strikes) to the legal promotion of union organisation and activities.

The ability of trade unions to achieve their objectives in the 1990s will in part depend on how far they can shape government approaches to pay determination and labour law in ways which promote, or at least tolerate, effective trade union and collective bargaining activity. Whether this is via national understandings with governments on pay, or more decentralised autonomous bargaining, via the introduction of positive legal rights to organise and strike, or the retention of the traditional union immunities from common law liabilities, must remain an open question (see on this Wedderburn, 1986, Chs. 1 and 10).

Collective bargaining

Collective bargaining, the 'central method of joint regulation in industry and the public services' (TUC, 1974, p. 292), deserves special consideration at this point. Although it is not a source of challenge to trade unions in itself, its sufficiency as a method of achieving union objectives is certainly called into question by the economic and political developments so far discussed. Unlike these developments, though, which are beyond direct union influence, the form, scope and spirit of collective bargaining are matters which trade unions, together with managements and employees, are in a position to influence directly.

Around 75 per cent of employees in Britain are estimated to have their basic terms and conditions of employment determined by collective bargaining. In the public sector (apart from public nationalised industries such as mining, rail and steel), bargaining in the post-war period has traditionally been both highly centralised and stable. Most governments have been committed to 'good' industrial relations practices and, in return, unions and employees have worked to avoid industrial conflict where possible. Since the 1970s, though, the public service and utility sectors have been subject to continuous political interference, often being used as tools of government monetary and social policy (see Winchester, 1983). For the trade unions concerned, such political interference has challenged the status of public service occupations, and led to a periodic deterioration in the relative pay of their members. For this reason, the first priority of public sector unions has been to achieve better recognition for public service workers, and a return to an independent system of pay determination which would make it less subservient to the vagaries of short-term political requirements.

Bargaining in the private sector, which accounts for around 75 per cent of the employed labour force, is more complex and fragmented than in the public sector. Between the 1950s and the 1970s, bargaining in manufacturing industry, the heartland of private sector trade unionism, became increasingly decentralised, with semi-autonomous shop stewards often developing their own policies and practices in response to the demands of their members in the workplace. The range of demands or issues covered by this kind of collective bargaining was relatively narrow in scope, and its effectiveness as a method of achieving union objectives depended mainly on the militancy of union members expressed in the use or threatened use of industrial action. The philosophy underlying this type of bargaining, and also the view of management it implied, is well captured in the words of the leader of the mineworkers' union in the 1970s, Joe Gormley (the formulation is sometimes attributed to US President John Kennedy, too): 'If you've got them by the balls, their hearts and minds will follow.'

This approach, developed during a period of relatively full employment, fed off a top management which, with notable exceptions, was among the most secretive in the western world and among the most cut off from its workforce. Thus was a vicious circle created, which many would argue lives on in the 1980s, fostering a climate of 'low trust' relations (Fox, A., 1974) between managements, unions and employees. Managements, fearing an increase in union power, were reluctant to give employees detailed information about company plans, manpower projections and training requirements, and were decidedly lukewarm about advances in employee participation. In response, unions continued to treat managements with distrust, and employees often exhibited a low commitment to their job.

This rather crude characterisation of traditional collective bargaining is not meant to question fundamentally its validity. As the Donovan Commission on Trade Unions and Employers' Associations wrote in 1968, 'properly conducted, collective bargaining is the most effective means of giving workers the right to representation in decisions affecting their working lives, a right which is or should be the prerogative of every worker in a democratic society' (Royal Commission on Trade Unions and Employers' Associations, 1968, p. 54). However, much depends on what is meant by 'properly conducted', in particular whether 1960s collective bargaining with its low trust and limited scope will be sufficient to achieve union (and management) objectives in the 1990s. In the next section we shall examine a number of recent responses of British trade unions which suggest directly or indirectly that it is not.

TRADE UNION RESPONSES

Some British trade unions have responded to the challenges discussed above by simply reaffirming the appropriateness of existing approaches and practices. In this section, however, we shall look at two positive strategic responses, and a number of more specific initiatives to deal with particular issues.

The professionalisation of trade unions

One strategic response to the challenges outlined above has been the call for what might be called a greater professionalisation of trade union organisation and activity. One of the foremost advocates of such an approach has been John Edmonds, General Secretary of the General, Municipal, Boilermakers and Allied Trade Union (GMBATU) since 1986. In a series of speeches and articles in the mid-1980s, he justified his response by pointing to the changed conditions which are likely to face many British trade unions in the 1990s. In his view, as we have seen, the typical workplace is more likely to be a medium-sized hotel than a large engineering works, the typical trade unionist will probably be part of a fragmented workforce, with limited bargaining power, no representation by a full-time experienced shop steward, and a management neither trained nor specialising in personnel or industrial relations. Against this background, which is very much that of the membership within his own union, Edmonds has argued that trade unions need to upgrade substantially the professional support provided to trade union members by full time paid union officials. This would entail a shift of emphasis in the role of full-time officials, away from being mainly fire-fighters in individual disputes and wider industrial relations conflicts, and towards becoming a resource, a source of professional advice, expertise and information for their members and workplace representatives.

A second aspect of Edmonds' view is that trade unions and their full-time officials will need to demonstrate to their members that there are a variety of ways in which trade unions can pursue their aims in addition to traditional collective bargaining. This is in recognition of the fact that the legitimacy of some aspects of British trade union activity is under challenge, not just from governments, employers and public opinion, but also from trade union members themselves. As possible new forms of action he cites publicity campaigns and techniques, the forging of alliances with other pressure groups, the more selective use of the strike weapon, the provision of financial information and analysis to members, and, perhaps more controversially, a more extensive use of the law (and the introduction of new laws) to promote union objectives and protect the rights of individual workers.

Third, Edmonds argues that trade unions will need to broaden the range of services they provide to their members to include surveys of salaries and conditions across British industry, pensions expertise, advice on social security and insurance, and guidance in areas such as careers and training. Trade unions in the 1990s should be, in his words, 'an independent centre for authoritative advice on all work-related matters' (1984, p. 19). How far this programme will be implemented within Edmonds' own union, or more widely, is not yet clear. It could signal, though, as Edmonds admits, the end of 'the era of cheap post-war trade unionism' and the advent of a different kind of professionalised trade union organisation.

Market-based trade unionism

The trade union which has so far gone furthest in breaking with traditional practice is the Electrical, Electronic, Telecommunication and Plumbing Union (EETPU). Its new philosophy of 'market-based unionism' (Lloyd, 1986), particularly identified with Eric Hammond, its General Secretary since 1985, has a number of interrelated strands. It preaches active acceptance, rather than tolerance or even total rejection, of free competition and the market environment, and a commitment to peaceful cooperation with employers. This is often expressed in a number of relatively new industrial relations institutions, such as no-strike procedure agreements and binding arbitration in cases of failure to agree. In return, the priority demands of the EETPU are single-status employment for all, that is, the abolition of status distinctions between the employment conditions of manual and non-manual workers; increased information and employee involvement at workplace level; and some agreement on job security. While all these objectives are common to most British trade unions, few have achieved them in practice. The distinctiveness of the EETPU strategy, and the main cause of the criticism of the union from within the wider trade union movement in Britain, is that it is prepared to make major concessions to employers in order to achieve them, concessions regarded by many as irreconcilable with the principles of free and independent trade unionism.

Another cornerstone of the EETPU approach is the belief in the outdatedness of traditional trade union structure, particularly when confronted with new information technologies and management demands for more flexible working arrangements and career structures. Recent studies (e.g. by Moore and Levie, 1985) have shown that new technologies challenge rigid occupational demarcations, for example between engineering and clerical, or manual and non-manual jobs, and that union structures which are based on these demarcations often weaken their effectiveness in the face of new technologies. Indeed, there is strong evidence that fragmented union organisation fosters a purely reactive, fragmented response to technological change. Against this background the EETPU argues that the survival of trade unionism in high-technology industry, where unlike GMBATU its membership is increasingly concentrated, requires a move towards single-union agreements with exclusive rights for one union to represent all grades of worker in one workplace.

Where high-technology companies decide to establish completely new 'greenfield' sites, the EETPU actively goes out to sell itself to the employers and to persuade them of the advantages of concluding a single-union agreement. The most well-known examples of such agreements made by the EETPU, but also by the Amalgamated Engineering Union (with whom it is engaged in informal merger talks), are with high-technology Japanese companies in Britain. However these are by no means the only such agreements, which are particularly controversial when they involve the recruitment of workers who would have traditionally belonged to another TUC-affiliated trade union. Although disavowed by the EETPU executive, the recruitment of print workers by two local full-time EETPU officials for the Wapping works of Rupert Murdoch's News International Group in 1986 is an extreme example of the kind of future inter-union conflicts which could result from this new strategy. The market-based logic of the EETPU carries with it an implicit rejection of traditional union spheres of influence agreements and of multi-unionism in the workplace. If put into practice across British industry, it could usher in an era of unrestricted competition between unions in recruiting workers and fighting for employer recognition.

Finally, as part of its active campaign to increase recruitment, the EETPU has massively expanded its services to its members. It now provides not just shop steward training in its own training college, but also retraining of its members in subjects such as electronics and computing. It even sells its courses on a commercial basis to private companies seeking to retrain their staff. It also offers financial concessions and advice to its members on matters as diverse as car insurance, mortgages, private health care, and even stock market investments.

For many within the British trade union movement, this philosophy and practice represents a move away from free independent trade unionism towards a kind of business unionism. For others, particularly within the EETPU, it is the only way that trade unions will be able to survive at a time of intense international competition and union weakness in the face of unemployment, new technologies and enhanced management power. The EETPU response has been discussed at some length. This is not because it necessarily offers the best way forward for British trade unions, but because it highlights so many of the challenges facing them. For those who reject the philosophy underlying market-based trade unionism, the task is to provide alternative strategies to meet the real challenges the EETPU itself is attempting to confront in its sphere of operation. In the words of the one time Labour Editor of the *Financial Times*, it is possible that the approach of the EETPU 'may well be...more in tune with long-run trends in the labour market, and even with emerging positions taken up by the Labour leadership, than anything else on offer' (Lloyd, 1986, p. 15).

Job security and the reform of union structure

The twin challenges of unemployment and redundancy have led many unions to develop particular policy initiatives on what has become for many the first priority in industrial relations, the achievement of job security. One of the first British trade unions to make a breakthrough in this area (in the late 1970s) was the Post Office Engineering Union, which, after prolonged industrial action, eventually achieved a reduction in the working week from 40 to $37\frac{1}{2}$ hours. This was followed in 1979 by the conclusion of a job security agreement with management, aimed at avoiding compulsory redundancy and including detailed procedures for the redeployment and retraining of displaced staff.

By 1984, against a background of increased competition, rapid technological advances, and a now privatised employer (British Telecom), the POEU decided that the achievements of the late 1970s were inadequate to meet the challenges of the late 1980s and called a special union conference to agree a new 'broad strategy'. At this conference union members decided to press for a four-day, 32-hour week for all staff, and (more controversially) to take a unilateral initiative to persuade its members to reduce overtime. This initiative on overtime was something relatively new for British trade unions, and is not likely to be popular with those union members who have in many cases come to rely on systematic overtime to boost overall earnings. But the POEU's decision is evidence of a union prepared to campaign actively for an unpopular short-term measure in order to achieve what it sees as the longer-term objective of greater job security for its members and, perhaps more improbably, of creating new jobs.

On top of this, in 1985 40,000 clerical workers within British Telecom transferred membership from the civil service union, the CPSA, to the POEU, thus creating in the renamed National Communications Union one organisation to cover all clerical and engineering grades within the business (the telephonists remained outside in the Union of Communication Workers). Many new technological systems being introduced within British Telecom and elsewhere are already blurring the differences between engineering and clerical jobs (see Clark *et al.*, 1984), and while conflicts might still arise over the distribution of work between these different occupational groups, the creation of the NCU will at least avoid the kind of inter-union conflict and resistance which might have occurred if the competing groups had still belonged to competing unions. How effective the NCU's initiatives on job security, overtime and union organisation will be, must remain an open question.

Female participation in trade unions

Rationalising union structures and adopting new policies to meet the challenges of technological change and unemployment are initiatives which are being widely adopted across the British trade union movement. Another challenge to which a number of unions have responded positively in recent years is that presented by the growing number of women in the labour force who are joining traditionally male-dominated unions. In the mid-1980s the participation of women (and of ethnic and racial minorities) in unions still remains disproportionately low. To this extent, trade unions are typical of many other British institutions, including political parties, top management, the Houses of Parliament, the legal, engineering and medical professions, and the universities. However, a number of unions, led by the pioneering initiative of the National Union of Public Employees in the late 1970s (see Fryer *et al.*, 1978), have introduced forms of positive discrimination and other measures, such as changing the time and location of branch meetings, to encourage greater female participation at all levels within unions. More recently, in the light of legal changes which allow women to claim equal pay with men for work of equal value, a number of unions, particularly in white-collar areas, have become much more active in encouraging their female members to claim equal pay with their male colleagues. Positive initiatives to encourage female participation in unions and support equal pay claims could do much to make unions more attractive to women workers.

The Trades Union Congress

When discussing new union initiatives to meet the challenges of the 1990s, mention should also be made of the role of the umbrella organisation of the British trade union movement, the Trades Union Congress. From its high point of involvement in national economic and social policy in the mid-1970s, the TUC appears in the mid-1980s to be a much less significant force, both within the trade union movement and in national economic and political life. However, a change in political climate could present the TUC with the opportunity of becoming once again the main focus and channel for the trade union response to many of the most deep-seated challenges facing British society. At present, it has a wide range of potentially influential policies: to reform the framework of labour law, to negotiate with government a legally enforceable national minimum wage, expand the education and training system to deal with unemployment and skill shortages, and to participate in establishing nationally agreed guidelines on incomes, prices and social security benefits. However unlikely it may appear from the vantage point of the mid-1980s, whether we meet many of the challenges of the 1990s may well depend on the effectiveness and resources of the TUC as the representative of the general interests of organised labour.

CONCLUSION: WHAT ARE TRADE UNIONS FOR?

Having concentrated so far on the key challenges to trade unions and on new union responses, it is perhaps worth reflecting by way of conclusion on why trade unions exist and have existed over the past two or three centuries in Britain (see on this Flanders, 1975, pp. 42–3; also McCarthy, 1985). The reasons for the existence of trade unions are essentially threefold: to protect employees and their employment conditions, to improve employment conditions, and to enable employees to participate in the decisions which affect their working lives. In short, protection, improvement and participation. While these reasons may appear to be relatively straightforward, they do repay closer attention.

Protection and improvement involve in the first instance the defence and advancement of employees' basic economic terms and conditions of employment: pay, hours, holidays and working conditions. However, protection also involves the less tangible objective of defending employees against arbitrary management decisions and the vagaries of the labour market, what Allan Flanders called 'their security, status, and dignity as human beings' (ibid., 41–2). This less well-publicised, but none the less extremely important objective is clearly illustrated in a recent survey (Clark *et al.*, 1985) by the responses of trade unionists to the question: 'What are the most important things your trade union does for you?' Unsurprisingly, the answer most often given in reply (22 out of 30 responses) was connected with pay—its overall level, annual increases, the grading structure, and so on. Perhaps more surprisingly, conditions of work such as hours and health and safety facilities came a clear third (13 out of 30) behind protection in cases of individual grievances and difficulties at work (17 out of 30). The following excerpts give a flavour of what the respondents meant by 'protection' in this context:

The fact that they're there. If anything does happen you can just go along and report it to the union and someone will help you.

It is an umbrella of protection against wrongful dismissal, legal representation if you get into trouble internally.

...that the managers are treating me fairly, aren't doing something I'm not aware of.

The most important things they've done for me is when there's been any hassle...they step in and instantly the water seems to calm. Management seems to think a little before they put their mouth into gear.

It should be emphasised that the survey was conducted in an organisation which was regarded by most of the trade unionists interviewed as a good employer: how much more important would be the protective function where the employer was not so well regarded.

As far as the third objective is concerned, trade unions provide a mechanism, both internally through their own structures of policy- and decision-making, and externally through representing their members' interests to management and public agencies, through which employees can participate in processes and decisions which affect their working lives. In this sense, protection, advancement and participation constitute the democratic functions of free trade unions. Much public and government interest was concentrated in the early 1980s on internal union democracy, more particularly on the rights of union members to participate via workplace or postal ballots in decisions concerning strikes and the election of union governing bodies. Sometimes under pressure from union members, and more often as a result of recent legislation (e.g. the Trade Union Act 1984), large numbers of British unions have recently revised their rule-books to allow for greater formal participation of members. Nevertheless, it is likely in the future that elected shop stewards will remain the most important mechanism and guarantee of democracy within trade unions, as they have been in the past.

However, in contrast to moves on internal trade union democracy, there have been few recent management initiatives to increase employee participation and involvement in the work organisation. Some companies, it is true, have attempted to provide an environment, particularly for management employees, but also in some cases for non-managers, in which the company itself protects and improves the position of employees and encourages their participation without the involvement of trade unions. But in Britain in the mid-1980s, this is still the exception rather than the rule. As a senior manager in a British multinational company wrote in 1986: 'For every company which is properly operating employee involvement, there are ten who are doing nothing at all' (Long, 1986). In fact, proper or genuine involvement, giving employees a real influence on the decisions which affect their working lives, may not only be in the interests of employees and trade unions, but also of management. As the same manager has argued:

The advantages of employee involvement for management are obvious: greater flexibility, acceptance of radical change, better productivity, higher quality, improved reliability, commitment to success and, at the end of the day, greater profitability. But what are the advantages for the employee?
There is certainly greater job satisfaction, perhaps improved career prospects, more security and the benefits that flow from higher morale. But

the most significant advantage must be the ability to influence decisions in advance of them being made. They are going to be better decisions if all the voices have been heard, because we must never lose sight of the fact that out there on the shopfloor is a tremendous reservoir of experience and expertise which for too long in this country has been allowed to run waste. (Long, 1986).

Ultimately, of course, future developments in work and industrial relations will depend to a great extent on management commitment and action. But new union strategies and initiatives, not only to increase employee participation, but also to protect and improve the conditions of their employment, are likely to influence the eventual outcome.

5   Social Security and the Division of Welfare

Roger Lawson

INTRODUCTION

Following the Beveridge Report of 1942 Britain appeared to be in advance of many other western nations in developing social security into a major social institution with potentially far-reaching consequences for society. The legislation based on the Report created a more all-embracing and comprehensive programme of income support than in other countries, and one which seemed to express a new sense of national solidarity and will to achieve a fairer and more equal society. This was a theme developed by T.H. Marshall in a famous series of lectures on 'Citizenship and Social Class', delivered at Cambridge at the end of the 1940s. Marshall argued that the new principles of social justice embodied in the reforms, particularly the emphasis on a universal right to income based on the status of citizenship, had profound implications for class divisions and the whole pattern of social inequality in Britain. In essence, he claimed, the aim of the new social rights 'is no longer merely an attempt to abate the obvious nuisance of destitution in the lowest ranks of society ... It is no longer content to raise the floor-level in the basement of the social edifice, leaving the superstructure as it was. It has begun to remodel the whole building' (Marshall, 1963, p. 100).

Forty years later the building has undoubtedly changed in appearance, though mainly because of structural modifications in the middle rather than at the lower levels. Moreover, in so far as 'social security' has contributed to social change, this has occurred less as a result of the expansion of state benefits than through the rapid post-war growth of alternative forms of welfare, particularly occupational benefits provided by private and state-owned companies and organisations for their employees. As a result of this development, what nowadays most distinguishes Britain's approach to social security, by comparison with other European countries, is the extent to which the middle classes and better-off workers have come to look primarily for security to their employers or other private insurance arrangements, and the consequent emphasis in much of the state system on residual care for the poorer sections of society. A closer analysis reveals, however, not so much a dual social security system, but one which has become highly stratified and segmented and produces the very reverse of what was envisaged in the 1940s. Thus, like the wage system, there are gradations in the scope and value of work-based welfare corresponding with occupational class and conceptions of social honour and esteem. A similar process of 'differential recognition of needs' (Sinfield, 1978) has been evident in the state sector, especially with the growing reliance on means-tested programmes and tendency to classify and treat differently various groups among the poor.

These 'social divisions of welfare' are the subject of this chapter. It begins by tracing briefly how and why they developed in the wake of the Beveridge reforms, and then looks more closely at some of the different ways in which they have influenced social security and its relationship to other spheres of public activity. The chapter argues that perceptions of the 'crisis' of social security in the 1980s and responses like the Fowler reforms to a large extent reflect the consequences of a socially divisive and fragmented approach to social security. This is true not only of attitudes to the public spending 'problem' and other 'burdens' of welfare, but, more fundamentally, to the challenges posed by high unemployment and poverty.

THE BEVERIDGE REFORMS IN RETROSPECT

Views like those expressed by T.H. Marshall in his Cambridge lectures rested on a belief that an important threshold had been crossed during the 1940s, with the emergence of a more consensual and depoliticised approach to social security. The enormous popular interest generated by the Beveridge Plan had seemed to indicate far more public willingness to accept egalitarian reforms and, more generally, a new confidence in the beneficent role of the state (Deacon, 1984). In retrospect, however, it is clear that the welfare consensus of the 1940s was a consensus of an unusual kind and was less stable and deep-rooted than many at the time believed. As José Harris has argued, it owed much to the artificial circumstances of the war, such as the sense of unanimity created by the menace of Hitler and the shared experiences of vulnerability and sacrifice. But it was based 'not upon a reconciliation or compromise between conflicting ideas, but rather upon the falling away of certain interests and opinions that were powerful features of the normal peacetime spectrum of opinion in British political life' (Harris, 1981, p. 258). Many Conservative MPs, for example, seem privately to have had misgivings about the Beveridge Plan. In 1943 a secret Party document declared that social security could only be provided by the state 'at the expense of personal freedom and by sacrificing the right of an individual to choose what life he wishes to lead' (Deacon, 1984). However, such views were rarely aired in public during and immediately after the war and officially the Party appeared to identify increasingly with Beveridge's ideas.

A similar muffling of conflict and controversy over welfare was evident on the Left and amongst more 'middle of the road' opinion. With the benefit of hindsight we can see how this had a paradoxical effect on welfare developments, particularly in social security. It meant that the Beveridge reforms were enacted with relative speed both by the wartime Coalition Government and by Labour after 1945, which in turn gave the impression that Britain's wartime experience was enabling it to forge ahead of other countries in the longer-term reconstruction of society. Elsewhere in Europe, immediate post-war policies were more a crisis response to the wartime devastation and conflicts arising from occupation and defeat. However, the peculiar circumstances in Britain meant also, as Harris suggests, that the kind of welfare state policies designed in the 1940s were ill-equipped to meet the criticisms, either of free marketeers or of theoretical socialists or simply of moderate people who disliked paying taxes or who disliked excessive officialdom, when all these groups began gradually to resurface in the years after the war. (Harris, 1981, p. 259)

This uncertainty about the stability and strength of the wartime commitment to social security also reflected an important difference between the reforms in social security and health care. With the creation of the National Health Service the middle classes and more skilled workers gained substantial personal benefits compared with the pre-war provisions, and this was to play a significant role in reducing pressures for alternative private provisions. It led also to a broad coalition of interests which has helped support and defend the essential principles of the health service over much of the post-war period. With social security, by contrast, the Beveridge reforms, while introducing the new principles of universal coverage and equal treatment of citizens, were primarily concerned to guarantee a national minimum income set at levels designed to meet the basic subsistence needs identified by Rowntree in his poverty surveys. In the circumstances of the time this was perhaps the most realistic way of making an immediate impact on the poverty and human misery revealed by the surveys of the 1930s and, as an important part of this, of reducing dependence on the much despised means-tested relief of the pre-war period (see, e.g., Lynes, 1984; Deacon and Bradshaw, 1984). Raising insurance benefits even to subsistence levels meant considerable and costly improvements in most benefits; and, as Rowntree's final poverty survey in 1950 showed, it did achieve quick results.

However, the emphasis on poverty and subsistence meant that, unlike the NHS, the social security reforms left considerable scope for an 'us and them' division in welfare, with the more fortunate sections of society relying heavily on private or voluntary action and regarding state benefits more as an expression of benevolence towards the weak and needy. This in turn meant a conflict between the principles of universality and the national minimum which was not necessarily to be resolved, as Marshall implied, in favour of more generous universal benefits. On the contrary, after the Conservatives returned to office in 1951, there were already growing pressures for more selectivity in the distribution of public benefits. *The Times*, for example, carried a series of articles in 1952 headed 'Crisis in the Welfare State' demanding a reappraisal of the Beveridge principles, while the *Daily Telegraph* was arguing in the same year that 'the most prolific source of waste is the provision of social security for the socially secure' (Golding and Middleton, 1982, p. 228).

A major weakness of the Beveridge reforms was that they left unresolved important issues like this involving the balance and relationship between public and private welfare. Beveridge was particularly anxious to promote voluntary action above the minimum. However, his proposals focused mainly on traditional working-class forms of mutual aid, such as friendly societies, trade union benefit funds, and the numerous clubs and savings schemes. To encourage these and also to prevent excessive state bureaucracy he wanted friendly societies and trade unions to cooperate in the management of the new state scheme and become the agencies from which people received at least some of their state benefits. He also placed great stress on reducing the role of large commercial insurance interests in this field, particularly industrial life insurance companies. These companies had built up a hugely profitable business based on door-to-door collections from more than three-quarters of working-class homes, but were widely accused of swelling their books by high-powered salesmanship to families unable to meet their commitments. Beveridge's response was to propose that the state took over these aspects of the insurance business, converted them into a new non-profit-making public service, and thereby released substantial working-class funds for national investment purposes.

Even with these proposals the Beveridge Report gave too little thought to the interaction of state and voluntary action. Beveridge totally miscalculated the future shape and influence of the voluntary sector, by largely neglecting the expectations of the middle classes and more skilled workers and the growing role in their welfare of employers and occupational benefits. However, much of the blame also lay with the post-war Labour government, which rejected Beveridge's proposals for including friendly societies and trade unions in the administration of social security and then delayed until too late the plan for nationalising industrial insurance. It was only at the end of the 1940s that Labour seriously considered implementing this. But this then produced what Michael Foot (1982, p. 258) has called a 'titanic struggle' within the Party between those who saw the possibility of extending public control over investment and completing the Beveridge reforms, and others who warned against electoral consequences, especially since the insurance agents might become door-to-door canvassers for the Tories. The commitment to nationalisation or 'mutualisation' of insurance did appear in the 1950 election programme but the outcome made any progress on this controversial issue impractical.

ECONOMIC GROWTH AND THE SOCIAL DIVISION OF WELFARE

By the end of the 1950s T.H. Marshall was expressing the disillusionment of many of those associated with the Beveridge reforms at the subsequent course of events. Writing about social policy in the affluent society (1963, esp. Ch. XIII), he was highly critical of the new atmosphere of self-enrichment and competitive consumption which was encouraging people to think of the welfare state as conceived in the 1940s as 'a back number'. Hence, while its institutions and procedures were still evident, they were 'operating in a different setting and without the original consensus which welded them together into a social system with a distinctive spirit of its own'. While Marshall seemed to blame this on the values of the affluent society, others pointed to more specifically British problems. In his study of *Modern Capitalism*, Andrew Shonfield (1965) compared Britain's 'disappointing performance' in welfare in the 1950s and 1960s with the speed with which advances in national income elsewhere in Europe were being translated into more generous standards of social security. But he saw this as part of a more general failure in Britain to consolidate and build further on the institutional changes in capitalism begun in the 1940s. The outstanding feature of the 1950s, Shonfield argued, was 'a kind of vigorous spiritual back-pedalling, the expression of a nostalgia for some bygone age when market forces produced the important economic decisions, while governments merely registered them'. Hence, while other European countries were now mastering new techniques of planning and cooperation between government, industry and labour, and pushing ahead in the field of welfare, what characterised British policies was a return to 'arm's length government'.

It is important to look more closely at how this affected social security if we are to see today's problems and challenges in clear perspective. There is a tendency to associate economic growth and full employment with relatively uncontroversial years of 'Butskellite' consensus when there were only minor policy changes. It is certainly true that public expenditures on social security rose significantly in this period, partly as a result of population ageing and changes in retirement patterns, but also because of increases in benefits. In fact, the highest uprating in benefits in real terms during the whole post-war period occurred in 1958, when Beveridge's idea of a minimum based on subsistence needs was formally abandoned in favour of a more flexible minimum reflecting the general improvement in living standards. Nevertheless, state benefits remained at modest levels and, as Shonfield emphasised, what seemed to be missing in Britain was 'the impulse to extend the depth of public intervention' beyond assuring a barely adequate minimum standard. On the contrary, Conservative policies between 1951 and 1964 always gave priority to tax reduction over welfare expansion and tended to see rising prosperity as providing the opportunity for reducing dependence on state welfare and promoting the free market ideal of the self-reliant, self-interested individual.

This was almost the reverse of what was happening in many other European countries at the time (George and Lawson (eds.), 1980; Walker *et al.*, 1984). In West Germany the rate of increase in the national product between 1950 and 1960 was three times as great as in Britain, but it was not seized upon to cut taxation or to limit government responsibilities in welfare. Instead, by the early 1960s the Germans were regularly taking in taxation more of the nation's output than any other major western nation, and were using this both to fund a major expansion of social security and at the same time to support industry and maintain an exceptionally high level of capital investment. The social reforms were explicitly designed to foster good industrial relations by reducing the kind of 'works and staff' divisions in working conditions and social security evident in British industry. Unlike British policies, they thus involved close cooperation between government, employers and trade unions in the public sector of social security, a factor which has raised its status and esteem as a major social institution. Similar aims were evident in Scandinavian and Dutch policies, though these countries placed more priority on raising minimum benefits to levels much higher than in Britain and complemented this with policies aimed at reducing wage differentials. Moreover, the core component of the Swedish welfare state has been a vast network of 'active labour market policies' (i.e. training and job-creation schemes), which have been designed where possible to reduce dependence on expensive, 'passive' social security benefits. With these measures the Swedes have maintained a remarkable record of virtually full employment, even in the present recession. This in turn has helped strengthen and consolidate public support for generous social provisions for those unable to work (see e.g. Goldthorpe (ed.), 1984; Therborn, 1986).

By contrast, developments in Britain embodied a paradox which was to remain evident under Labour as well as Conservative governments. On the one hand, the importance of the public sector in social security appeared to increase as expenditures rose and benefits became a more widespread source of income, mainly because of the growing number of pensioners. On the other hand, however, the policies pursued in Britain led to a shift in emphasis towards alternative systems of welfare, so that the modest benefits provided by the state began to play a more marginal or residual role in the distribution of welfare. Moreover, contrary to Beveridge's ideas, the new developments involved a revival of the power and influence of the large commercial insurance interests in this field and, closely connected with this, a great expansion of occupational welfare (Titmuss, 1963; Field, 1980; Reddin, 1982). Some of these benefits are still rather dismissively called fringe benefits, which perhaps gives the impression that they are frills added to salaries and wages. However, already in the 1950s the 'company welfare state', which had warranted only a brief paragraph in the Beveridge Report, was providing a wider range of benefits—from company cars and expenses for travel and entertainment to pensions, family benefits and medical support—than the state itself, with far-reaching consequences for the economy as well as social policy. The costs of these benefits also fell heavily on the Exchequer, since successive Budgets in the 1950s had greatly extended employers' tax advantages in setting up welfare schemes, while reducing the government's contribution to the costs of national insurance to less than a quarter of that proposed by Beveridge. Thus in 1955 occupational pensions alone were costing the Exchequer £100 million, whereas the government was paying little more than £45 million towards state retirement pensions.

One of the more curious features of this development was that it was not at the time the subject of extensive public debate or parliamentary scrutiny. Many politicians and civil servants seem also to have separated occupational welfare, conceptually as well as administratively, from social security and seen it more as an expression of 'good human relations' in industry. It was left mainly to a small group of academics led by Professor Richard Titmuss of the London School of Economics to suggest a very different interpretation. Titmuss (1963, Ch. 2) showed how occupational benefits were 'in effect, if not in administrative method, "social services"': they duplicated, overlapped and enlarged upon state provisions. His main concern, however, was with the divisions and con-flicts accompanying this. While conceding that occupational benefits were part of the model of the good employer, he argued that as they grew and multiplied they came into conflict with the aims and unity of social policy, by acting as 'concealed multipliers of occupational success' rather than reducing inequalities of treatment between employees. In his essay on *The Irresponsible Society* (1963, Ch.11), Titmuss set these arguments in a much broader context, by linking the rapid growth of occupational welfare with a major shift in economic power in favour of 'the anonymous authority of the City'. By the end of the 1950s the immense funds generated by company pension schemes and group and life insurance constituted by far the largest single source of new capital. This in turn meant an unparalleled concentration of power in relatively few hands: company pension funds were mostly managed or controlled by insurance companies, merchant banks, stockbroking firms, etc., often with interlocking directorates or close business or social connections. But it was also a power that was subject to less public accountability than in any other advanced western country. Britain was virtually alone in allowing insurance companies and pension funds to refuse to disclose even to official committees information about their sales or purchases of assets.

Since the end of the 1950s the growth of occupational welfare, especially of pension funds, has been even more spectacular. The assets of company pension funds grew from £2 billion in 1957 to almost £65 billion in 1981, when together with related insurance assets they amounted to more than Britain's total national debt. By the 1980s cash was flowing into these funds at an annual rate which would have covered the costs of developing the Concorde aircraft several times over (Plender, 1982). As a result, pension funds and insurance companies have become the principal owners of ordinary shares in companies quoted on the Stock Exchange (in 1939 80 per cent of the shares were owned by private individuals), the main lenders of money to government, and increasingly investors in property as well as works of art (Coakley and Harris, 1983). But, more significantly, the effective control of much of the pensions business has passed over the years, as Titmuss foresaw, into the hands of the banks, large insurance corporations and pension fund managers. As far as the economy is concerned, recent studies have suggested that these institutions have remained in some ways a 'sleeping giant': they appear to have intervened directly only to a limited extent in company affairs and takeovers (ibid; cf. Minns, 1980). Nevertheless they have created some serious problems. There is evidence that the lack of accountability has led to haphazard investment judgements and more generally of a failure to provide long-term finance for the economy's new growth points, partly because of the avoidance of 'risky ventures' but also because overseas investments have proved increasingly attractive. All this is a far cry from Beveridge's visions of a voluntary sector in social security generating funds for national economic development, or from the practices in a number of other countries. In Sweden, for example, the huge amount of savings resulting from pensions has been used explicitly to strengthen public steering of the credit market and direct investment towards growing, job-creating sectors of the economy, as well as a massive house-building programme (Esping-Andersen and Korpi, 1984).

The importance attached to company welfare also helps in other ways to explain the failure in Britain to establish the kind of institutional links between social security, labour market and wages or industrial relations policies found in a number of countries. For many British companies pensions and other benefits have been seen primarily in domestic competitive terms, as a means of enabling them to compete with others in the labour market, rather than promoting national interests in labour mobility or coherent employment policies. Indeed, one of the most controversial features of the company welfare state has been the severe financial penalties, in terms of loss of pensions, etc. for those changing jobs. To add to these problems, many trade unions have also come to see occupational welfare in competitive terms, as an acceptable face of privatisation to be exploited for their individual members. The decentralised structure of the trade unions has in turn produced fragmented, separate negotiations with each firm or employer, with little attempt at a coordinated national policy. This contrasts, for example, with the French situation, where the TUC's equivalent has negotiated national collective agreements on pensions and other benefits which cover the entire workforce and where firms and industries pool risks (Walker *et al.*, 1984).

COMPETITION BETWEEN THE PRIVATE AND PUBLIC SECTORS

Problems like these have been further exacerbated by the failure of successive governments since the 1950s to achieve a stable 'working relationship' between the public and private sectors in social security. This is again most vividly illustrated in the pensions field, but by no means confined to it. A particular problem has been the substantial number of workers with no access to occupational pensions or only limited entitlements. Although the proportion of the workforce building up private pensions advanced rapidly in the 1950s and 1960s, since then there have been more pressures to improve existing pension rights while the coverage of the schemes has actually declined. Thus still today only about half the workforce have occupational or other private pension arrangements, and overwhelmingly those most disadvantaged are lower paid manual workers in private industry and commerce as well as the vast majority of women workers (Silburn, (ed.), 1985). But numerous other disparities of treatment exist, including the financial penalties for those changing jobs or unemployed even for a short period. Indeed the funding of many occupational schemes seems to be based on 'the principle of robbing job-changing Peter to pay time-serving Paul' (Plender, 1982, p. 202).

In Britain the first serious attempt to tackle these problems was the national superannuation plan, which Labour produced when it was in opposition in 1957. Significantly, however, this was accompanied by a sudden burst of activity by the private pensions industry, which the Conservatives then strongly encouraged by introducing a limited state graduated pension scheme with big incentives to 'contract out'. It has been claimed, though the evidence is by no means conclusive, that the pension funds deliberately made a pre-emptive strike 'to forestall or constrain the possibility of major state expansion in this field' (O'Higgins, 1986). What is beyond doubt, however, is that they played a decisive role when Labour was in office in the 1960s in ensuring that even a modified version of the 1957 plan failed to reach the statute book. Harold Wilson (1971, p. 605) in his memoirs described the pension funds, backed by the Conservative Party, as 'declaring war on the state scheme'. When eventually a settlement appeared to be reached under the 1975 Pension Act, the new SERPS scheme was widely heralded as at last resolving the problems of those without occupational provision and laying the basis for a new partnership between the state and the private sector. However, in reality the 1975 Act merely reinforced the unstable and competitive nature of pensions policy. O'Higgins (1986) has characterised it as 'subsidised competition', in which Labour in its anxiety to reach a settlement created a new structure 'within which private provision could compete with state provision on terms which were more than equal'. Under the Act the state guaranteed for the first time to pay in full a basic component of each occupational pension, in return for improvements in benefits, and it also continued the elaborate tax concessions to the occupational schemes and life insurance. Moreover, the changes under the 1975 Act were to take more than twenty years to come fully into effect, and in the intervening years the reform intensified inequalities between pensioners. By the early 1980s, for example, only about four million (or 40 per cent of those over 65) were receiving occupational or private pensions, but the total household income they were getting from these benefits was equal to that from all forms of state pension, received by nine million old people (Silburn (ed.), 1985).

Against this background the Thatcher government's controversial reform of pensions looks less like a reversal of previous policies than yet another episode in this peculiar and unstable history. This reform involved scaling down the benefits provided by the 1975 SERPS scheme, partly on the grounds that the costs will become increasingly unsupportable, but also in an attempt to encourage a wider coverage and other improvements in private pensions, such as inflation-proofing of benefits for those changing jobs. In principle, this is by no means more inegalitarian than previous policies and indeed could provide the basis for more stable policies, provided it was accompanied by a serious effort to raise basic state retirement pensions and create the kind of universal coverage of occupational schemes found in France. In practice, however, the Fowler reforms showed few signs of this being their real intention, and seemed most likely to lead to even more divisiveness in this field. High unemployment, together with government attempts to reduce job security were, by the mid-1980s, making the prospects of gaining decent occupational benefits even more remote for many workers. Moreover, given the present organisation and funding of occupational welfare, the more pressures are placed on employers to improve existing pension rights and introduce early retirement schemes, the less likely they are to extend coverage and reduce the two nations divide in old age. Instead, new dimensions are being added to this as improved occupational pensions and savings schemes are switching resources to the more affluent groups, particularly men, entering retirement just at a time when social policy needs to pay more attention to growing numbers of the very old, including many elderly women who have been the most severely disadvantaged by post-war policies.

This unequal competition between the private and public sectors has affected all aspects of social security. It reflects, as has been implied, peculiarities of British capitalism and its state structures, where powerful vested interests and pressure groups have tended to work beyond the reaches of government, rather than, as in a number of European countries, being drawn by government into a more cooperative and corporatist framework. The fact that these groups include trade unions has in turn weakened the role of the labour movement as a countervailing force to these developments. When in office in the 1960s and 1970s, Labour has generally been forced onto the defensive in social security, and has sought consolation by focusing on improvements in 'social minimum' benefits for the poor rather than formulating imaginative, longer-term strategies. More generally, however, the public/private imbalance in social security reflects the cleavages in much of British social life referred to in Chapter 1, especially between the more comfortable and well-organised sections in the community and those 'below' with low status and skills and poor bargaining power. In social security divisions like this have been further refined by the close links in the private sector not only between stable employment and welfare, but also between benefits and rewards and occupational status and esteem. In addition, the private sector is essentially 'male territory', while women have been significantly over-represented amongst those reliant on state benefits. It is thus not surprising that women's interests, especially in child and family benefits, have fared particularly badly from the unequal social division of welfare.

RESPONSES TO POVERTY AND UNEMPLOYMENT

These divisions are thus crucially important if we are to understand Britain's failure, after the promise of the Beveridge reforms, to develop a coherent and comprehensive plan to overcome poverty. As the experience of countries like Sweden shows, the most effective strategies in eradicating poverty have been premised on notions of national solidarity and hence have sought to unite society rather than divide it. In social security this has involved genuinely universal programmes from which most households can expect real benefits and where the poor are not singled out for special treatment. The Swedes have also elaborated further the logic of Beveridge by linking social security closely with policies designed to guarantee the 'right to work' and with 'solidaristic' taxation policies and wage agreements benefiting lower paid workers (Esping-Andersen and Korpi, 1984). In Britain, by contrast, post-war policies have developed in a very different environment, in which the problem of 'poverty' has been separated increasingly from these broader issues. Thus Britain's ability to develop the kind of universal benefits envisaged by Beveridge has been limited by the growth of occupational and fiscal welfare and consequent separation of the better-off majority of the population from those relying on state benefits. The elaborate medley of tax concessions supporting this development has both drawn resources away from the state sector and led to an erosion of the tax base, hence enhancing resistance to improving state benefits. The result has been a peculiar blend of universal benefits offering only minimal protection supplemented to an ever-increasing extent by special means-tested programmes for the poor. Thus, whereas in 1948 around 1.3 million persons were living in households dependent on national assistance (renamed supplementary benefits in 1966), by the early 1970s the number had already reached more than four million (Deacon and Bradshaw, 1984). The range and scope of means-testing was also considerably extended in the late 1960s and early 1970s with the introduction of the family income supplement and national rent and rate allowances. Most of these new benefits were aimed at the 'working poor', as a means of providing some basic compensation for the failure to develop adequate minimum wages or redistributive tax measures.

A closer look at these developments would reveal other more significant limitations and constraints. It is clear, for example, that successive British governments have held back from more controversial actions, partly because of economic difficulties but also out of fear of alienating more influential supporters. These include some trade union leaders who in the past have been prominent in resisting increases in universal benefits, especially child allowances, and also in decrying some sections of the unemployed as 'work-shy' or types who 'give the respectable working man a bad name' (Sinfield, 1968). At the same time, as J.C. Brown (1984) has argued, 'older theories which attributed poverty to individual deficiencies, and newer theories which emphasised group deficiencies (the so-called culture of poverty) have continued to have a substantial influence on the policies of all governments'. While this has produced some policies which are benevolent in intent, it has led to actions 'which are based on the assumption that the sting of poverty may be necessary to deter certain kinds of economic or moral behaviour'. Comparative studies of public perceptions of poverty have also revealed less appreciation in Britain than in other European countries of the wider social causes of poverty. In an EEC (European Communities, 1977) survey conducted in 1976 twice as many British respondents attributed poverty to individual deficiencies, such as laziness or lack of willpower, as the Germans, French or Italians interviewed; and almost four times as many as the Danes and Dutch. There are plenty of indications that the pattern of welfare helps shape and sustain such attitudes. As Sinfield (1978) has observed:

People see the poor services of the public system with their limited rewards, their social controls and their maintenance of incentives and may come to think that the programmes are as they are because the poor are as they are. And so they come to accept as 'reality' the social division of welfare as seen through the eyes of the better off, the elites, the experts, and the 'rule enforcers' of the public welfare system.

To a certain extent these influences have been offset in the past by other factors, such as the very active poverty lobby, consisting of various pressure groups seeking to influence government policies on behalf of the poor. This again is a distinctive feature of Britain's policy environment, where trade unions and employers have generally been less involved with state benefits than their Continental counterparts and 'middle-class' activists have been left to fill the gap by campaigning for the poor. In the 1960s and 1970s the poverty lobby played an important role in securing improvements in many benefits, most notably for the disabled. However, studies of these groups have shown how they have had much less success in changing the direction of government policy and indeed have helped to divert attention away from broader issues of strategy by, for example, fragmenting policy into different 'issue com-munities' (Whiteley and Winyard, 1983). Unlike the powerful pension funds, they have also had less and less impact on policy as the economic climate has worsened.

All this is not to say, however, that Britain's post-war policies have been particularly ungenerous towards the poorest sections of society. In some respects the emphasis on means-testing and poverty relief has proved quite effective in the past in reducing the severity of poverty. According to an EEC report (European Communities, 1981), based on research in the mid-1970s, Britain's supplementary benefit system appeared more successful than the equivalent provisions in countries like Germany, France and Italy in minimising the numbers with very low incomes as distinct from low incomes. Studies within Britain have also shown how the benefit system became markedly more efficient in alleviating severe poverty between the 1950s and 1970s, although full employment (especially the growth of two-earner families among the low paid) also greatly contributed to this. Against this, however, British post-war policies have also differed from those in most European countries by the way the dependency status, and social control and regulation, of a large section of the poor has been increased by a greater emphasis on means-tested relief. Also accompanying this has been a growing differentiation between categories of the poor, which would appear to reflect certain judgements about their 'moral worth'. Thus the un-employed, one parent families and the homeless have generally been singled out for more grudging and inferior assistance, and subject to more official controls over their credentials and honesty.

The full implications of these policies have become evident with the economic crisis of the past decade. In Britain the deteriorating economic climate and the first dramatic rise in unemployment in the 1970s gave a significant boost to individual theories of poverty and fears about the widespread and gross abuse of benefits (Brown, J.C., 1984). This was manifested above all in the way sections of the press, and increasingly government spokesmen and certain academic economists, sought to shift the blame for unemployment onto the unemployed themselves. Deacon (1981) has shown how in the late 1970s 'the post-bags of MPs were filled with letters complaining, not about the high level of unemployment, but about the incomes and activities of the unemployed'. More generally, anti-welfare and anti-tax backlash has been most evident over the past decade, not where social spending is highest, but in countries such as Britain and the USA with a sharp 'us/them' divide and a large private sector in social security. As Korpi (1980) explains, this is because this approach to social security 'in effect splits the working class and tends to generate coalitions between the better-off workers and the middle class thus creating a large constituency for welfare-backlash. In fact the "welfare backlash" becomes rational political activity for the majority of citizens.'

THE CHALLENGES OF THE 1980s

In Britain the events of the 1980s have certainly added significant new dimensions to the divisions of welfare, and indeed also to the paradox embodied in British policies discussed earlier. The importance of state benefits has again appeared to increase: expenditures rose in real terms by 70 per cent between 1975 and 1985, and under the first Thatcher administration grew at a rate three times faster than had been planned by the Labour government in 1979. However, much of this is due to unemployment and the failure of the economy; and in reality recent policies, culminating in the Fowler reviews and reform of social security, have further marginalised state support by associating it even more than before with residual care for the poorer groups in society. Moreover, much more than in the past, the conquest of poverty was relegated under the Thatcher governments to a secondary aim of policy. As J.C. Brown (1984) has aptly put it:

The goals were the conquest of inflation, the maximum operation of market forces, the reduction of public expenditure, and the pulling back of the boundaries of the Welfare State. If in the pursuit of these new goals there were programmes which might benefit the poor, well and good; but if the goals required an increase in inequality or actions which produced a growth in the numbers of the poor, that must be accepted as the price of economic recovery and of the process of the changeover to a reduced government intervention in business and community affairs.

The government's own estimates reveal how in reality this has meant a substantial increase in the poor population of Britain. By the mid-1980s the number of people dependent on supplementary benefits had reached a record eight million, a doubling since 1975. The numbers in families with incomes below 140 per cent of the basic supplementary benefit levels rose from 11.5 million in 1979 to 16.3 million, or nearly one in three of the total population, in 1983. The 1983 figures included more than four million people living in households with a full-time wage-earner, almost double the number in 1979. Moreover, a large and increasing number of people appeared to be eligible for but not claiming benefits. In 1983 nearly three million people had incomes below the basic supplementary benefit 'poverty line': they included one million over pensionable age, 680,000 full-time wage-earners and their dependants and over 500,000 of the unemployed and their families. Another striking aspect of the change in the poor population in recent years has been the considerable increase in the number of families with children.

A closer analysis of these figures would also show how they reflect a broader process of marginalisation which is deepening divisions in the labour market and enlarging the underclass in society, whether in work or out of it. As well as the unemployed at any given time, there are now increasing numbers of workers in the 'secondary labour market', with a high risk of unemployment, low skills, poor working conditions and weak trade union protection. Many are on temporary or part-time contracts, or in the grey areas of the labour market where employers can avoid social or labour laws. These trends are evident in many other countries (see e.g. Goldthorpe (ed.), 1984; Therborn, 1986), but have become more acute in Britain recently with the more deliberate attempts to 'deregulate' the economy by reducing job security and the impact of minimum wage legislation (Winyard, 1985). These processes also affect the spreading of poverty in other ways, for example amongst single women bringing up children on their own, amongst the disabled and those in poor health who have less chance of getting back to regular work after illness, and amongst the elderly who are less able to depend on their children for support and assistance (Sinfield, 1984).

Despite evidence like this, the Fowler reviews and reforms of the mid-1980s represented a further step in the process of fragmenting poverty relief, by separating the 'needs' of one section of the poor from another. Indeed, perhaps the most striking feature of the reviews was the way they appeared to be organised, as Donnison (1985) has put it,

to carve up the issues in a way that prohibited anyone from talking about them in broader terms. As different teams examined the needs of pensioners, children, the unemployed, and so on, one deprived group was set against another. Shared concern for the hard pressed and the vulnerable was eroded.

The reforms which followed promised some improvements in benefits, particularly with the new Family Credit scheme for low wage-earners, though for many families these seem likely to be offset by reductions in housing support. However, their principal effect was to reduce the entitlements of many of the poorest claimants, especially amongst the unemployed and many women claimants, and to subject them to even more detailed official controls and discretionary aid.

It is important, however, not to see these developments as stemming merely from a change in government in 1979. As this chapter has argued, they are in a more fundamental sense the outcome of policies pursued since the 1950s, which in turn reflect deeper cleavages in British society. Moreover, by the second half of the 1980s there are growing indications that the more comfortable sections of society are no longer so willing to congratulate themselves on maintaining their distance from the 'other Britain'. Recent public opinion surveys suggest that high unemployment itself—reported as a problem experienced by more than 40% of families in one study—may be changing attitudes towards taxation and social benefits (Taylor-Gooby, 1985). Less than a quarter of respondents in the ITV *Breadline Britain* survey in 1984 saw poverty as due to laziness or lack of willpower, a sharp reduction on the number reported by the 1976 EEC survey. Likewise, there are signs that both Labour and the Alliance Parties are prepared to give priority in social policy to a major overhaul of the tax and benefit system, which would mark the first step in undermining the post-war division of welfare. Trade unions also appear more conscious in the 1980s of their potential to influence occupational welfare, especially through controls over pension fund investments. Such policies are unlikely to succeed, however, unless social security reform is closely coordinated with broader strategies designed to foster social unity and show how 'a good welfare state, far from being a burden on the productive economy, provides the essential political basis for sound economic policies' (Donnison, 1985).

6 Housing

A. M. Rees

INTRODUCTION: RECONSTRUCTION UNDER THATCHER?

In the 1980s housing seemed to be an area of public policy in retreat. Although the attitudes and actions of the Thatcher government are not the only, nor perhaps the most important, aspect of the subject which requires note in the context of a changing and relatively declining Britain, they provide a good starting point for a discussion, since housing has played a special role in the 'crisis of the welfare state'. Whereas one can argue about the reality of 'cuts' in the health service or education, the picture so far as housing expenditures are concerned seems to be clear-cut. In volume terms, total programme expenditure fell by more than 50 per cent between 1979/80 and 1984/85, while real expenditure on new local authority dwellings declined by nearly 60 per cent, and on current subsidies to council housing by not far short of 80 per cent, over the same period (Robinson, 1986). At the same time, there has been a pronounced shift in the mix of the mixed economy of housing, signalled most clearly in policies favouring council house sales. Owner-occupation, it is frequently maintained, is now not merely the leading tenure, but also the 'normal' one. Local authority housing, on the other hand, has been 'residualised' and is being fashioned increasingly into a tenure accommodating an unidentified total of the least well-off, unable to cope with the repayments on a mortgage. Better-off council tenants are faced with a choice between accepting the privileges and risks of owner-occupation, or acquiescing in the withdrawal of government subsidy and a continuing increase in rent payments. Finally, there appears to have been an almost total transformation of the political debate concerning housing—away from issues of production, the staple of controversy from before the First World War until the late 1970s, and towards issues of distribution, especially access to the various tenures.

The various elements in this by now quite familiar picture need to be reappraised before we can arrive at an assessment of the nature and extent of the 'restructuring' which has taken place. Most require at least some modification.

PUBLIC EXPENDITURE ON HOUSING

The first point to be made here is that the decline can be dated back to 1975–76 and can be seen as a lagged response to the shock of the oil price rise in 1973. Housing is bound to be especially vulnerable in periods of enforced economic stringency. Much of the expenditure is on capital account, and reduced spending on the new production and the maintenance of buildings affects established interests, especially public sector ones, less immediately and directly than cutbacks in current spending. Thus the number of homes demolished in slum clearance in Great Britain fell from 77,000 in 1973 to 51,000 in 1976, and the number of improvement grants for private owners declined from 260,000 to 80,000. Public sector starts, however, displayed some evidence of an ideological divide: they grew from 87,000 in 1973 to 124,000 in 1976, but this latter figure was still relatively small compared with the levels achieved during the previous period of Labour government.

In certain respects, the 1974–79 Labour government was more successful in its avowed aim of reining in housing spending than its Conservative successor. Grants for private sector improvement and renewal flowed more freely under the Conservative government. The number of grants paid to private owners and others was practically back to 1973 levels in 1983/84, the total of more than 250,000 representing a four fold increased since 1978/79 (Robinson, 1986). Furthermore, funds for local authority lending on mortgage were also relatively freely forthcoming, primarily to finance the sale of council housing. It is also worth pointing out that both the current subsidy system and the arrangements for regulating bids from local authorites for public funds are legacies of the Callaghan administration.

The story concerning subsidies to council tenants is also not quite what it seems from the figures quoted in the first paragraph. The reduction in Exchequer subsidies has been matched by the sharp growth in income-related rent rebates, since 1982 known as housing benefit. So there has been a major shift between headings in the public accounts, since these subsidies are now counted as social security expenditure. Robinson calculates that 'the nearly £1 million reduction in central government grants to local authorities was offset by a similar increase in rent rebates' (ibid., p. 6). So there has been a much less dramatic real reduction in total housing-related expenditures than the often-quoted figure of a 50 per cent decline would suggest, and subsidies to council tenants have remained about steady, albeit through a major reinforcement of means-tested benefits. Indeed, if certificated housing benefit (paid to those receiving supplementary benefit and to those in receipt of national insurance benefits who would previously have obtained SB payments) is included, total government subsidies to council tenants for help with housing costs have clearly grown with the increase in the numbers without full-time employment. This must, however, be seen in the context of the great increase in tax expenditures—mortgage interest tax relief cost the Exchequer, in 1985 prices, £2.27 billion in 1979 and £3.5 billion in 1985.

RESIDUALISATION

Two points can be made here. The first is that it is arguable that council provision has always been regarded as residual, except in the aftermath of the Second World War. The 1945–51 Labour administrations certainly rested their plans for post-war construction and reconstruction largely on the shoulders of the local authorities, and a similar emphasis on the local authority as a 'plannable instrument' informed the next period, that of Harold Macmillan's dash for 300,000 houses a year. However, between 1954 and 1956 the subsidy system was recast to eliminate the 'general needs' subsidy for new council housing. The number of completions for private housebuilders in Great Britain grew sharply from about 1952 onwards, although it did not surpass the total of local authority completions until 1959. Both before and after this period, however, there have always been more private houses built than public sector ones, and Merrett with Gray trace the residualist philosophy in relation to council housing right back to the Housing and Town Planning Act 1919, which required local authorities to survey the housing needs of their areas, and to derive their estimates of need by 'deducting houses likely to be built by other agencies' (Merrett with Gray, 1982, p. 5).

Secondly, if we take 'residualism' to relate to the characteristics of occupiers, it is clear that there has been a major recasting of the role of council housing so that it has become the tenure occupied by the majority of the poor; this has however been a gradual process over the past 25 years. In the 1960s there was criticism, much of it from the Left, that local authority housing retained the flavour of its post-First World War origins as a sector housing primarily the steadier members of the employed working classes, rather than those least able to compete in private housing markets. During the 1970s the proportion of supplementary benefit claimants in council accommodation grew from 49 to 59 per cent, while the percentage of both unskilled manual workers and of the economically inactive who were owner-occupiers actually *fell* (Ball, 1983, p. 277). Twice as many single-parent heads of households are council tenants as are in the owner-occupied sector; reverse proportions are found among intact families with dependent children. Local authority housing has indeed increasingly become a welfare net, but this is arguably a tribute to the success of public policies rather than a criticism of them.

Government policies on council house rents have softened with time. In 1981/82 and 1982/83 the Department of the Environment imposed rent increases in England and Wales at an assumed average weekly amount of £2.95 and £2.50 respectively. They combined these increases with a progressive withdrawal of subsidy. Since 1983, however, ministerial determinations of increases in rent have been approximately in line with inflation: 85p in 1983/84, 75p in 1984/85, 60p in 1985/86; and at the same time some local authorities found themselves requalifying for subsidy. The arrangements in force had some curious consequences. Three-quarters of the local housing authorities receiving subsidy were south of a line between Gloucester and the Wash: 'It seems', wrote Malpass (1986), 'that Bournemouth and Lewes are deemed to need subsidy, while Birmingham and Leeds are not.' The system being based on notional rather than actual rent increases, some authorities in receipt of subsidy raised rents more steeply than the government had indicated they should, with the surely unintended effect that government housing subsidy went into the general rate fund, to the benefit of all ratepayers except the 'better-off' council tenants. However, the usual beneficiaries of this softening in approach have been those tenants whose incomes are too high for them to qualify for housing benefit (or who failed to apply for benefit to which they are entitled) and this takes a little of the sting out of the accusations that the government singled out this category of householder for especially ungenerous treatment in order to bounce them into house purchase.

THE SPREAD OF OWNER OCCUPATION

Here political attitudes have also been bipartisan over many years, and largely remain so. There has, however, been significant change in Conservative policy since the early 1970s—namely a retreat from the 'hands off' stance of the 1971 White Paper, *Fair Deal for Housing* with its (rather unconvincing) promise to establish 'a fairer choice between owning a house and renting one'. Writing as late as the mid-1970s, Roger Duclaud-Williams could reflect that 'one might have thought that the clear and sincere preference of Conservatives for home ownership would have produced, at least from time to time, legislation designed to favour this form of tenure. This, with the minor exception of the House Purchase and Housing Act of 1959, has not proved to be the case' (Duclaud-Williams, 1978, p. 249). Very soon thereafter, this statement was rather falsified by the 1979 election commitment to aid existing and would-be owner-occupiers, especially those concerning the sale of council houses, and by the legislation which followed. Even here, however, a measure of bipartisanship seems to have been re-established, through the Labour Party's fear of the electoral consequences which might follow from a flat rejection of policies which seem widely popular among council tenants.

The consequences of the 'right to buy' legislation for the composition of the total housing stock are not easy to assess. To date (1986) about 10 per cent of council dwellings have been sold, mostly the more desirable single-family houses with gardens. Sales, however, peaked in 1982/83, and in most regions fell off quite markedly in 1983/84. It may be, therefore, that the market had been saturated, leading the government to attempt to step up the pace of sales again by further increasing the discounts available to purchasers. Council house sales apart, however, the Thatcher administration's policies to encourage owner-occupation were marked by caution. Doubts about the economic and financial effects of mortgage interest tax relief must explain much of this, although the concern seemed to be less about the highly regressive nature of these tax allowances than with the open-ended commitment to subsidy; it is of some interest that the upper limit of the amount of loan qualifying for tax relief was held at £25,000 for the first four years of the government's term of office. The current system of tax reliefs has also come under attack by other Establishment figures—in 1985, for instance, the Duke of Edinburgh's study commission recommended that it should be phased out over twelve years.

HOUSING PRODUCTION

The move away from concern with housing production requires extended treatment. It is certainly remarkable that political parties ceased, in the 1970s, to vie with each other in their promises to deliver a given total of new dwelling units each year. The Conservative government of the 1980s saw only a small continuing role for public sector house building, mainly in the provision of accommodation for special groups, especially the elderly.

Disillusionment with large-scale development and redevelopment certainly contributed to the feeling that the country had got poor value for money from the already rotting difficult-to-let estates of the 1950s and 1960s. The existence of such problem housing has undoubtedly played a part in the steep decline in confidence in council house construction and management—usually unfairly, for most local authority development of those years was not, and is not, like that. However, there seems no evidence that similar adverse feelings have been engendered in relation to large-scale private development. Indeed, a common response to problem estates on the part of local authorities has been to call in a major private housebuilder to sort out the mess. Yet is is not merely the sharp fall in building for local authorities which needs to be explained: there has also been a collapse in private house construction, especially in 1981 and 1982. In the latter year a total of only 170,000 dwellings were completed in Great Britain, the lowest number (except for the war years) since 1925.

A more plausible explanation for the shift concerns the belief, which grew steadily during the 1970s, that Britain could not go on adding to stock, year after year, as it had been doing between 1950 and 1975. The fear of a growing surplus of housing became endemic during the decade, and remains powerful even though the best estimate of the total annual output of new units required is still that produced by the *Housing Policy Review*, which assessed it at around 300,000 a year in the 1980s (*Housing Policy Review*, 1977, vol. 1, p. 144). Furthermore, these projections failed to take into account the impact of changes in the location of economic activity, so the shortfall, when actual experience is compared with the estimates, is considerable.

This apparently dismal record has been greeted with much more insouciance than might have been expected, so perhaps a further explanation should be sought. Debates over housing expenditures stand at the intersection of two areas of controversy—one (already discussed) concerned with public spending in general, the other concerned with the role of housing in the economy. Governments and pundits have become alarmed at the proportion of total available resources tied up in, or swallowed up by, housing. International comparisons suggest that the British housing stock is of relatively high quality. It scores especially—when compared with housing in other advanced capitalist democracies—in terms of floor area per person, the possession of standard amenities and the supply of private external space (i.e. gardens). However, might not these relatively good standards have been bought at the expense of the 'productive' economy? The Japanese may live in paper houses, but look at the increase in their Gross National Product! This fear perhaps applies to private sector expenditure in particular. Kilroy probably puts the case most cogently: he is especially concerned at the amount of 'transfer capital' tied up in housing. (In 1970 first-time buyers made up 61 per cent of those in receipt of fresh building society mortgage advances, but this proportion had fallen to 47 per cent by the end of the decade—Kilroy, 1979). Martin Pawley is more graphic:

Not many thinkers today are unaware that owner-occupation has become a juggernaut...It has...become a macro-economic phenomenon, diverting industrial and infrastructural investment, sucking in import and drying up exports. The sums that spiral away into the endless sale and resale of owner-occupied homes beggar the imagination. Housing debt, otherwise known as home ownership, will destroy the British economy if it is not brought under control. (Pawley, 1986)

However, this view is open to question. Investment in housing and in manufacturing industry may go hand in hand. In any case, many commentators would argue that the relatively poor performance of British industry has not been so much due to shortage of funds for investment—although absolute levels *have* been relatively low (see Chapter 2)—as to what has been done with this investment: the problems are ones of unit costs, labour productivity, quality of product, marketing and the rate of return upon capital.

TENURE

The upgrading of questions of distribution needs to be considered separately from the downgrading of questions of production. Tenure now is everything; most analyses of the current housing situation revolve around it. The resulting emphases fit in well with, and are sometimes explicitly derived from, a Weberian sociology, which sees relationships to the means of consumption as having largely or partly replaced in social significance relationships to the means of production. Such theories proffer a variety of 'housing classes' based on the market situation of different groups of householders. Unlike the traditional socio-economic conceptions of class, which, revolving around workplace relations, essentially split the population into two (though often with sophisticated qualifications), there can be as many 'housing classes' as there are separately distinguishable market situations. Thus owner-occupiers will be divided between those repaying a mortgage and outright owners; the latter are nearly as numerous as the former, and are older and poorer than them. And mortgage repayers can be categorised in a number of ways: there is obviously a big difference between the young couple in stable employment in their starter-home, and the immigrant purchasing a rotting house in an inner-city area with a loan at a very high rate of interest from a fringe finance house.

Housing class theories tend to direct attention towards the part played by the various groups within the political system. Peter Saunders (1980), for instance, was struck by the 'strong collective class awareness' of the owner-occupiers he studied in Croydon, as shown in their efforts to defend and enhance the value of the asset they held. Students of elections differ about the extent to which tenure exerts an independent influence on voting behaviour. Is the well-documented propensity of owner-occupiers to vote rightwards simply a reflection of their generally greater wealth, income and status, or is there something more which accounts for their patterns of party choice? Whatever the answer to that it can be said with some confidence that the belief that tenure is an independent factor has influenced the strategies of the political parties and hence the housing policies which are likely to be placed on offer.

We can now sum up the argument of the first half of this chapter. There has been change under the Thatcher administrations, but in many respects it has been less dramatic than appears at first sight. However, the dominance of tenure as the focus for discussion and argument has been considerably strengthened in recent years. Politicians keep their housing policies in separate boxes; there is one set of measures to aid owner-occupiers, another set concerned with council tenants, yet a third to deal with the problems of the private rented sector. Policy so fragmented is likely to be both incoherent and inequitable; and few would deny that housing finance, in particular, has long been, and bids fair to remain, an unjust mess. But there are powerful interests involved, and the numerical preponderance of owner-occupiers may well mean that radical restructuring is not politically feasible. It is time, however, to return to the drawing-board or at least to some first principles.

RATIONALES FOR PUBLIC INTERVENTION IN HOUSING

The aim of this section is to consider the involvement of public authorities in housing more systematically. On the face of it, housing is not an obvious candidate for public provision—it is a private consumption good which at any rate in the mid-1970s was broadly in good supply, and which reflects wide differences in tastes. Within all major tenure sectors there is a bewildering variety of products. It is easy to argue that much government intervention in housing markets has been distorting, perhaps even paradoxical and mischievous in its effects. Subsidies to aid owner-occupiers, for instance, may have had as their principal effect the raising of house prices above the level of inflation, thus increasing the entering price for those outside the charmed circle of home-ownership. It is salutory to remember that the first two great surges in owner-occupation were brought about with very little in the way of net assistance from public funds. The interwar boom took place in a period of *falling* prices and, since at the time the average earner was outside the income tax bracket, tax reliefs only benefited a minority of the new owner-occupiers. The boom of the 1950s came when the total paid out in tax expenditures was largely balanced by the amount taken in by Schedule A tax—an impost, much disliked by everybody except economists and housing experts, on the notional annual rental value of domestic property, which lasted until its abolition in the early 1960s.

There are a number of policy instruments which may be employed by central government. Four may be distinguished: direct provision (construction), direct provision (management), subsidy and regulation. There are also several different grounds on which public intervention can be justified. Three traditional rationales would be accepted in principle by even the most free market-oriented of economists: externalities and spillover effects; economies of scale; and maldistributions of income. Two further grounds for intervention concern the treatment of housing as a merit good (i.e. it is so important that steps should be taken to see that it is consumed at a quality level higher than the market alone would provide); and the need for public intervention if governments are to attain their other, more broadly-based, economic aims. None of these rationales presupposes any of the policy instruments listed above.

Externalities and spillover effects

These concern the extent to which the costs (or benefits) of economic activities are borne by (or accrue to) these who generate them, or whether they fall to others. Negative externalities were the original rationale for intervention in Victorian Britain. Disease and fire could not be contained in the single units occupied by households but could spread through the rotting timbers of whole tenements. Disease, in particular, could travel a long way from its original locus through polluted water supplies or unhygienic methods of waste disposal—even into the bosoms of the middle classes. So it was that slum clearance started as an activity blessed by statute in the 1870s, followed shortly afterwards by the imposition of a national system of building regulations under the consolidating Public Health Act 1875.

These traditional concerns of policy-makers are by no

means irrelevant today: indeed, there are several areas where public regulation remains strangely weak. For example, 27,000 households were accepted as homeless by London boroughs in 1985. Around 3500 of these were placed in bed and breakfast accommodation, often in uninspected crumbling hotels a long way outside the boundaries of the boroughs in question. Fire risks are high, and there have been a number of lethal fires affecting such premises. What seems to be called for here is regulation by local authorities in order to correct conditions which have been aided and abetted by the authorities themselves in their attempts to fulfil other statutory responsibilities. A lack of supervisory zeal may not be surprising in such circumstances.

Local authorities are also thoroughly implicated in the kind of externality which they impose, deliberately or inadvertently, on their own tenants. There has been much interest in the social effects of the apparently unowned and unpoliced public walkways, decks, corridors and minimally landscaped recreational areas of large-scale flatted developments, since Oscar Newman (1972) published his theories of 'defensible space'. In Britain, Alice Coleman has looked at several indicators of malaise and squalor—litter, graffiti, vandal damage, the number of children in care, the presence of urine and faeces in public places—and related them to the design of estates (Coleman, 1985). This approach revives the bogey of 'architectural determinism'—a doctrine much out of fashion in the 1970s—but it would be hard to deny that arrogant planning policies, and ill-thought-out design, have played a big part in creating problems which are now generally acknowledged. The only alternative interpretation, after all, is that the environmental conditions can be blamed upon residents, and that local authorities have deliberately created 'sink estates' (although Coleman found as much evidence for the dispersal as for the concentration of 'problem families').

Economies of scale

One reason for the involvement of public authorities in large-scale housebuilding after the Second World War was the belief that the operations would be of a sufficient size to guarantee substantial cost advantages over the penny-packet developments of the typical private constructor. In the 1950s and 1960s, there was added the feeling that the public sector could help to pioneer a breakaway from the essentially eighteenth-century technologies of the building industry. However, the experience of system building, involving techniques which were sometimes imperfectly understood by the operatives charged with realising them, was not a reassuring one, and the assumption of public sector superiority has been replaced in many quarters by its opposite. Local authority direct labour departments, in particular, have come under sustained political attack.

Actually the evidence remains conflicting. The productivity of direct labour and of private contractors appears to be quite similar; and most public sector building is carried out by private contractors anyway. Moreover, all comparisons are bedevilled by differences of quality between products. Houses for the public sector have usually been built to a higher standard of finish than their private sector counterparts. Between 1967 and 1981 the former, but not the latter, had to be constructed to Parker Morris standards. One should also note that during the 1970s the twenty largest private housebuilders seized a considerably greater share of the market, and over the same period the average size of room per completed house fell markedly, even in relatively expensive four-bedroom detached properties. It seems reasonable to suggest that the search for economies of scale has not brought unmixed blessings, for tenant or purchaser.

If one turns from production to management, similar doubts arise. Indeed, local councils may be reaping substantial *diseconomies* of scale. *The Economist* argued this in a long article in its edition of 23 November 1985 ('Housing for the Poor'). The evidence presented is circumstantial; the journal notes, for example, that the typical housing authority owned 1400 properties in 1945, but by 1975 the average was 14,000, and nowadays metropolitan boroughs control on average 38,000. Glasgow, the largest municipal landlord in Europe, manages 159 blocks of 29 storeys or more, clearly a formidable undertaking. Housing managers are not on paper highly qualified; fewer than 5 per cent of the staff of housing departments possess the qualification of the Institute of

Housing. The Audit Commission (1986) has documented how the combination of large tasks and undertrained staff to perform them produces a number of deleterious results—highly centralised and often notably unresponsive systems for dealing with repairs and maintenance; a growing problem of arrears,—the *Economist* noted that nearly half of London tenants, mostly in a few inner boroughs, owed some rent—and a high and growing tally of empty council properties. The examples given in such indictments are selective, but few would wish to argue with the proposition that there is a major problem of council house management.

Maldistribution of income
Houses are expensive commodities, which few people can purchase outright, although the expansion of owner-occupation over time means that many of the present generation of the middle-aged can expect windfalls through inheritance. They are also very long-lasting artefacts. For this reason, special long-term methods of financing have been developed: subsidies for council houses spread over 60 years, mortgages to be repaid over 25 or 30 years. Even so, housing costs accounted, on average, in the United Kingdom in 1982 and 1983, for rather more than 16.5 per cent of total weekly household expenditure: this represents a sizeable slice of income, and unlike food or clothing, is largely a fixed expense. Neither mortgage lenders nor local authorities tend to approve of sub-letting, the obvious stratagem for dealing with a mismatch between income and outgoings. Moreover, such adjustments in occupied living space are in any case least open to larger families who have lower per capita income and, other things being equal, higher housing costs than smaller families. Thus there is a chronic mismatch between easily ascertainable need and income.

There are plainly difficulties in paying for housing, and public intervention, in the form of subsidy, has frequently been justified on this ground alone. However, it would be easy to argue that such considerations should be taken into account primarily in the design of income maintenance programmes. Would it not perhaps be simpler to give people the money to cover average housing costs, and expel the whole matter from a discussion of *housing* policy? We have noted that housing benefit is now treated as social security expenditure, and in many respects this makes practical sense.

However, there are substantial difficulties in the way of an extension of this principle. The first is the variation in housing expenditures both between regions and within localities. Dilnot, Kay and Morris (1984), in a much discussed plan for the reform of social security, sought to wrap up housing costs in their scheme, but most commentators think it is impossible to do this equitably. Housing costs would therefore have to continue to be dealt with separately, either through payment of the actual rent, as in the supplementary benefit system, or through some complicated formula which varies the amounts paid out in income subsidy according to the housing costs incurred, like that employed in the computation of standard housing benefit.

A second difficulty is that, even if one could devise a standardised system of allowances based on notional or average figures, the need would remain for checks on the propensity of landlords to capitalise on their market situation. This is usually seen as a problem with private landlords, and is at present mainly effected, rather erratically, through the setting of 'fair rents'. However, as noted earlier some local authorities have taken advantage of the legislation which permits them to run their housing revenue accounts at a surplus. This development renders the whole problem of the control of monopoly or near-monopoly landlordship more intractable than it used to be, since local authority rents have usually been taken to be the paradigm of reasonableness by the Department of Health and Social Security. The danger is that in any warfare between the DHSS and public or private landlords it is likely to be the tenant who receives the wounds.

The third problem is what to do about low income mortgagors. The marginal owner-occupier is now no rarity, and the number of foreclosures and repossessions by building societies and other lenders has been steadily rising during the decade, albeit from a very low base. Mortgage interest tax reliefs remain a poorly targeted subsidy, even though almost everyone, except those on long-term invalidity or supplementary benefit, currently pays at least some tax at the standard rate. No coherent economic or social justification has ever been offered for permitting interest repayments to be offset against the higher rates of tax, as well as the standard rate. This concession simply encourages high earners to 'trade up' into increasingly expensive properties.

Under the Conservative government, however, concern came increasingly to be directed to the payment by the state of the mortgage interest owed by recipients of supplementary benefit, leading to the proposal to withdraw such payments from the unemployed during the first six months on benefit. Such plans suggest an unjustified equanimity about the consequences of the deliberate diffusion, or indeed creation, of indebtedness. This anti-paternalist stance appears also in the sale of council houses. Under the right to buy legislation, existing municipal tenants can demand that their local authority furnish them with a mortgage, even though they may be middle-aged and the repayment period would stretch on well into their retirement. The rule of thumb of corporate lenders that the total amount on mortgage should not exceed three times the annual income of the borrowers, and should be paid off before the old age pension is received, still has much in its favour. Moreover, there is so far little evidence about the prices which ex-council houses will command in the market. When a large supply for resale comes on stream it may well be that the apparent bargain which their purchasers have obtained will look less impressive, even taking account of the generous discounts received.

Housing as a merit good
Should governments have a concern for the health and quality of the housing stock which is both conceptually and in terms of practical policy distinct from considerations of the ability of less privilieged citizens to pay for good accommodation? In recent years answers to this question have become uncertain. Much scorn has been directed at the notion of 'tying subsidies to bricks and mortar'. Nevertheless, the life of an administration is short and that of housing is long. It may not be a bad test for a government that it should hand on to its successors the country's housing, industrial infrastructure and stock of schools and hospitals in at least as good a condition as

it received them. For some of these things public authorities are more directly responsible than others, of course, but policy instruments already exist which are designed to tempt or to warn private sector actors to take a longer view then they otherwise might.

The area where this question arises most insistently is house repair and improvement. Both Labour and Conservative administrations have sought to devise methods of controlling the amounts disbursed to the better-off in grants for home improvement. The 1974–79 Labour government was much exercised by the phenomenon of 'gentrification', especially in London, where much nineteenth-century housing has been snapped up by the well-heeled middle class and improved with funds supplied through the local council. So in 1974 Labour ministers imposed rateable value limits above which properties ceased to qualify for grants. The Conservatives embarked upon a different tack: the 1985 Green paper *Home Improvement–A New Approach* (Cmnd. 9513) proposed a system of loans for 'discretionary' repairs and improvements, rather than grants. However it was intended that grants would still be available for bringing houses up to the statutory fitness standard. The rather Victorian rationale suggested for this is that the health and safety of those living in such property is at risk, which shows the government at least recognising a continuing obligation.

As well it might. The English House Conditions Surveys of 1971, 1976 and 1981 have shown a consistent picture: continuous improvement so far as the possession of standard amenities is concerned, and unfitness being about held steady, but a deepening problem of disrepair. In both England and Wales the number of dwellings needing major repairs (over £7000 worth apiece at 1981 prices) grew by 20 per cent between 1976 and 1981. Proportionately, the problem has shifted away from private rented housing towards the owner-occupied stock. This, however does not mean that accommodation rented from private landlords has relatively im-proved—disrepair and unfitness remain highly concentrated in this sector—but simply that there is less of it than there used to be. Many old, poor dwellings have been bought up over the last few decades, often by sitting tenants. The English mainland county with the highest proportion of owner-occupiers is not Surrey or Kent, but Lancashire, with its inheritance of nineteenth-century by-law housing. Furthermore, disrepair has begun to bite into the nation's stock of inter-war housing, often now lived in by the elderly, who are the least likely to have the funds, or see the need for, improvements in their accommodation. Doubtless the Conservative leadership would maintain that the very scale of the problem means that the limited public money available should be directed towards those who would otherwise be unable to finance the necessary works. However, a repaired house is a repaired house, whoever may happen to live in it any particular time.

The concept of a merit good may also be pressed into service in instances where it is not good quality housing as such, but some particular tenure which is being commended as specially meritorious. We shall return to this possible utilisation of the term in the conclusions to this chapter.

Housing and the economic aims of governments
There are a number of questions that could be profitably considered under this heading. This section will concentrate on one: the extent to which our current housing system acts as a bar to geographical mobility. Of course, this may not be accepted as a policy priority. On social grounds, it is not obvious why any government should wish to proliferate the numbers of those who are footloose over the country. Indeed, there are plenty of signs of policy ambivalence in this area, the most notable being the restrictions on the social security available to young people who have 'got on their bikes' and sought employment in British seaside resorts. However, there are limits to the feasibility of an economic policy of bringing jobs to people, rather than people to jobs, and most commentators assume that there has to be continuous readjustment in the location of employment—indeed, that it tends to take place whatever planners and politicians may desire and decree.

In the nineteenth century, housing caused relatively little problem in this respect. Although the supply of houses, especially at the lower end of the market, never quite kept up with the demand, the system based on private landlordship was uniquely flexible. In most towns there were many landlords owning varied portfolios of housing, so that householders could move in time with changes in the size of their families or with fluctuations in their economic circumstances. Even now, the much diminished privately rented sector discharges a role which no one else seems particularly keen to perform, providing accommodation for those whose needs are short-term and who are especially mobile, like students.

Actually, *any* system of renting (as opposed to owning) should be relatively easy in, easy out. Rigidities in public housing in Britain arise largely because accommodation is owned and managed by local authorities, who have seen their obligation to lie in provision for the natives of their localities, rather than for strangers. More centralised arrangements would doubtless be managerially impossible and unacceptably undemocratic. But they would scotch the idea that there is something intrinsic in the nature of public housing which entails it locking people in to particular localities. It is rather odd that the Thatcher administration, so sensitive about what are seen as artificial barriers to the free functioning of the economy, and usually so ready to cut back the prerogatives of local authorities, attempted so little in the area of council house allocation. There has been some pressure from Whitehall, and many housing departments have loosened their insistence on residence qualifications which outsiders find difficult to acquire. But the reduced number of both re-lets and new lets becoming available renders this rather unimportant; the tenant who wishes to exchange a four bedroom council house in West Durham for a similar one along the M4 corridor from Slough to Bristol might just as well save himself the postage.

Owner-occupation provides obstacles to relocation at least as grave as those encountered in the council rented sector. One problem is that most transactions are dependent on other transactions going ahead smoothly, but research findings indicate that such chains are, on average, quite short (Merrett with Gray, 1982). A more serious difficulty is the consistent disparity in house prices between the more prosperous regions of the country and those less favoured economically. On 13 July 1986, the *Observer*'s property correspondent featured two former artisans' cottages thrown into one in West Sussex and 'ideal for further modernisation'. The asking price was £175,000. Probably the antique shops and small industries of Midhurst and Petworth would not be the first choice of the unemployed of Teesside for a job search, but such examples indicate the near impossibility of making a move to areas of high employment.

CONCLUSION

A rough parallel can be drawn between developments in housing policy and politics over the past twenty years and what has been happening to employment during the same period. The emerging patterns of class relationships seem not dissimilar, even though the fit between the two is far from exact. A substantial majority of the population is well-housed, increasingly in the owner-occupied sector, and well-placed to defend and perhaps extend its privileges. A majority, too—usually the same people—are in well-paid and generally secure employment, and, with the connivance of both employers and certain trade unions, are equally well-placed to enhance their position, through, for example, securing regular increases in real wages above the levels suggested by the per capita growth in output. A minority experiences some combination of job insecurity and low pay (sometimes the one, sometimes the other, frequently both), or has fallen out of the labour market altogether. A minority also experience some mixture of housing insecurity and state hand-outs to help with the costs of accommodation in the form of housing benefit, although with the difference that the latter has so far been set at generous enough levels to minimise the insecurity. Thus, although the total absence of accommodation—homelessness by any reasonably strict connotation—is a growing problem, it is still a much lesser one quantitatively than the total absence of employment.

Those who have been unable to secure a firm footing on the first rung of either the employment or the housing ladder are the most disadvantaged. Equity between generations has become singularly difficult to achieve, and is indeed too sensitive a subject to be spoken about very often. Of course, we are dealing here with trends and tendencies; prospects for the highly qualified young remain quite good, and some of these working in the City of London are even able to afford the house prices prevailing in the more desirable parts of inner London. In general, however, it seems that we are faced with a new set of class divisions, in employment and housing alike, between the comfortable and the established of the middle and skilled working classes, and various groups of outsiders, mostly weakly supplied with market capabilities. Included in the latter would be many of the young, a lot of unskilled and semi-skilled older workers, and a disproportionate number of black and brown Britons.

Impetus was given to the great expansion of municipal housing, especially immediately following the Second World War, by the belief that the link between the provision of good quality accommodation and the ability to pay for it could be broken. On the whole it *has* been broken: when public housing has failed, it is largely because the types of accommodation provided have been regarded as alien, which means especially unlike like those being made available by private house-builders.

Measures of satisfaction, with housing or anything else, are notoriously tricky to interpret. The British tend to be very pleased with their accommodation—more so perhaps than is objectively warranted. In the special enquiry reported in the 1978 *General Household Survey*, only 16 per cent of respondents renting from local authorities or New Town Corporations expressed themselves as 'a little dissatisfied' or 'very dissatisfied' with their housing, compared with 7 per cent of those purchasing on mortgage (*General Household Survey*, 1978, Table 4.1). However, out of nearly 60 sub-categories distinguished, the highest level of general dissatisfaction (at 30 per cent) was recorded by those living on the third floor of blocks of flats, with those on the fourth floor or above coming (at 23 per cent) some way behind. For many (half of all those taking part in the survey) the preferred housing type was a bungalow, and, although many more would rather be buying than renting, (72 per cent compared with 19 per cent) it seemed that desire for physical kinds or quality of housing took precedence over desires for particular tenures. If there is a tendency to 'fetishise' tenure, usually in the form of owner-occupation, it appears more concentrated among politicians and propagandists than among the general population.

This chapter has looked at a number of justifications proffered for public intervention in housing. Some of these are persuasive, others wanting. A main lesson, however, is surely that those who buy houses should expect to pay more for a given quality of accommodation over a stated period of time than those who rent them, since they are obtaining a disposable asset. There is reason for argument about the extent of the excess they should pay, but not about the principle. If, because of the effects of inflation, or because of special tax and other privileges, this does not happen, then intervention is surely justified to ensure that the system works fairly and with market efficiency. The discounts offered on the sale of council houses indicated a recognition that the system is currently out of gear, but the sale of council houses is a very *partial* way of recognising the problem, since the benefits cannot prudently be universalised to all council tenants (and cannot, apparently, be extended at all to even the long-term tenants of private landlords). In housing, as in other areas of public policy, the case for even-handedness needs to be forcefully restated.

7 The Family

Graham Allan

INTRODUCTION

In *The Country and the City* (1975) Raymond Williams shows how over the last 300 or so years popular imagery has consistently portrayed community solidarity as breaking down. A rosy past is conjured up to highlight contemporary problems of social integration. In much the same way family life seems in each age to be undergoing a radical transformation that appears to threaten the basis of domestic stability. Beliefs that the family as a domestic, economic and emotional unit has undergone major shifts since the Second World War need to be viewed in this light. None the less there does appear to be plenty of evidence to support the view that family life is changing quite dramatically. The most obvious changes concern the marital relationship. First, marriage is seen by many as becoming a more equal relationship as wives' economic and social dependence on their husbands is reduced through women's greater participation in the public, non-domestic realm, particularly that of employment. Secondly, there is the escalating incidence of marital breakdown and divorce, leading in turn to apparently new and more problematic family forms emerging, specifically one-parent families and step-families. Other factors, like the greater geographical mobility of families, the plight of the elderly, increased levels of cohabitation, and our heightened awareness of all forms of domestic violence are also taken to be indicative of the changes the family is currently undergoing.

Later on in this chapter three issues that have had major

repercussions for the experiences of some families in recent years and which will continue to do so in the late 1980s and beyond—divorce and its consequences; the care of the handicapped and infirm; and the impact of unemployment on family life—will be discussed. First, though, an attempt will be made to portray the extent to which family life is currently altering, concentrating on the diversity that there now is in domestic organisation; the division of labour within marriage; and the nature of parent–child relationships. The argument will be that while changes are occurring the underlying structure of family relationships has altered rather less over the last two or three generations than is often supposed.

DIVERSITY

On many counts there seems to be a great deal more variation and diversity in people's familial and domestic circumstances than there was for much of the first half of this century. Then it was quite sensible to talk of the 'family cycle' as a series of patterned and more or less predictable stages—marriage, child-bearing, child-rearing, the post-parental phase, retirement and widowhood—through which most families passed. Each stage brought its own problems and difficulties, opportunities and constraints that were to some extent shared in common, though clearly experienced differently by males and females and shaped by class position. Now with divorce, cohabitation, re-marriage and step-families there is far greater variety and less predictability about the way in which individuals experience family life. The very notion of a family cycle as a regular set of stages is far less adequate as a descriptive framework for interpreting domestic existence.

To express this slightly differently, while our cultural image of the 'normal' family is, like much social policy, based on the classic nuclear model of a husband and wife living together with their dependent children, this is becoming less and less appropriate. Currently only some 28 per cent of households consist of such families, though of course most couples do experience this form of family life for some period of time, the majority until their children become independent (*Social*

Trends, 1986). The greater diversity now found in household demography compared to the turn of this century—though not earlier in our history when many households contained lodgers, servants or step-kin, (see Anderson, 1971; Laslett and Wall, 1974)—is added to by the greater number of non-European immigrants and their descendants in the population who have somewhat different domestic conventions. Aside from the historical legitimacy of single parenthood in West Indian culture, a proportion of Asian households contain a far more extended range of kin than is common in white households. The various stages routinely delineated in conventional models of the family cycle are certainly inappropriate for analysing the domestic organisation of these families (Saifullah-Kahn, 1979; Rapoport *et al.*, 1982).

A second element of diversity found in current family patterns concerns the level of wives' involvement in paid employment. The period around the turn of the century saw the development of the specialised, full-time housewife role as increased industrial productivity required a small proportion of the population to be economically active (Oakley, 1974). Though many wives continued to supplement household income in ways that were not officially recognised or recorded, the dominant pattern became one in which wives' principal economic contribution lay in servicing the needs of other household members and transforming male wages into the family's living standards. As will be discussed later, this remains the primary responsibility of the great majority of wives, but now far more are also directly involved in some form of wage labour. Still most women are, for shorter or longer periods, full-time housewives—for example, 75 per cent of all mothers with children under the age of five are 'economically inactive' (*General Household Survey*, 1982)—but few now remain as such throughout their married life.

The changes in this have been quite dramatic. In 1951 only one in five wives was employed. Thirty years later three in five of those under retirement age were. However the extent of wives' involvement in employment varies a good deal within the population and over the life-cycle, being shaped now more by child-rearing patterns than by marriage itself. The greatest growth has been in part-time employment which increased from 784,000 in 1951, approximately 10 per cent of the female labour force, to over 3.5 million, or a third of all female employees by 1981 (Wainwright, 1984). However, this itself reflects a good deal of variation as employment is classified as part-time if it involves anything under 30 hours per week. In their national survey of women's employment patterns, Martin and Roberts (1984) found that over half of all wives were employed part-time, the majority for between 16 and 30 hours per week, but a third for less than this.

These patterns of wives' employment point to the increased diversity there now is in families' work strategies compared to the inter-war period. They have also helped generate somewhat new social and economic divisions between families. In the past the main divisions between families were determined to quite a large extent by the class position of the husband, the main income-earner. Despite its crudity, the simple dichotomy between manual and non-manual employment was a reasonable predictor of the family's circumstances and experiences. While the class position of the household clearly remains of central importance, this is no longer so accurately reflected by the occupation of the husband alone. In particular, as Pahl (1984) argues on the basis of his recent study of the Isle of Sheppey, the number of income-earners there are in households is becoming a better indicator of that household's social and economic standing than traditional measures of class.

At the bottom, forming something of an underclass, are those households without earnings who are dependent on state benefits—many of the elderly, the unemployed and one-parent families. The problems that inadequate benefit levels pose for these individuals and families have been exacerbated recently by cuts in other forms of social provision. In particular, the rapid transformation of some council housing into the slums of the 1980s, as funds for structural and material repairs are restricted by central government, gives rise to as much concern as the lack of new council house provision which has escalated the numbers of families on benefit 'housed' in bed and breakfast accommodation. Next come those households with only one earner. Some of these, especially though not only those headed by females, will be receiving little more than they could obtain in benefit. Others are better off than this but are none the less faced with an uphill struggle to make ends meet. Finally there are those households with two, and in some cases more, members in employment. These are the ones with most resources and consequently the fullest levels of social participation. As Pahl (1984) points out, they are also the ones most able to improve their domestic conditions through what he terms 'self-provisioning'. They can take advantage of the opportunities that new technologies of work within the home offer for increased living standards as they are able to afford the necessary machinery and materials.

The clear implication of all this is that with current wage levels, 'normal' standards of living are increasingly coming to depend on wives' as well as husbands' earnings. Despite the common belief that a wife's earnings are often not crucial to the domestic economy, the reality is that a family's living standards are more and more built around and dependent upon two incomes. Wives' earnings, even when they are significantly less than husbands', are needed to maintain an adequate life-style and avoid hardship. Consequently their 'choice' about whether to be employed is being whittled away as the normality of women's double burden of paid and unpaid work is built into our social expectations. As we shall see, this will not lead to a radical redistribution of household work so long as gender inequalities in the labour market remain. However, it may have some impact on the kinds of argument being made about the responsibilities and contribution wives make to family life. In particular, it may become that much harder for men to avoid domestic contribution by asserting in a straightforward fashion that a women's place is solely in the home.

MARRIAGE AND THE DIVISION OF LABOUR

However, as yet there is really very little evidence that the division of labour within marriage is altering significantly. While factors like the increased rights of citizenship obtained by women, wives' increased participation in employment and the emphasis placed within marriage on ideologies of love and self-fulfilment have been taken by some as signalling a renegotiation of traditional marital roles, the various studies undertaken have clearly shown this renegotiation to be more mythical than real (Edgell, 1980; Hunt, 1980; Porter, 1983). While husbands may participate more in various domestic activities, especially those to do with some aspects of child-care, the primary responsibilities of husbands and wives continue to be defined along conventional lines. Husbands have principal responsibility for income provision while wives retain that of managing the household and servicing the needs of its members.

One reason why the division of labour within marriage has altered rather little lies in the differential gender socialisation evident in all stages of a child's development. At nearly every turn, boys and girls are subject to relationships and images which emphasise the difference between them and the distinct paths their lives will follow (Lees, 1986). Girls continue to be fashioned into the world of caring and servicing in a way quite foreign to boys' experience. Most importantly, adult reality, both inside and outside the family, matches these earlier gender portrayals and renders their continuation sensible. The different employment experiences of men and women form a major part of this adult reality, and are particularly significant in maintaining conventional family roles. We have seen how an increasing proportion of wives are employed, but the way their labour market is structured marks it off as quite different from that of men. First, even full-time female employees earn on average only some 70 per cent of the amount earned by men in the same occupational categories but in addition about half of all employed wives are employed only part-time. The result is that most wives earn significantly less than their husbands. Secondly the range of occupations open to women is in practice much smaller than that open to men. Indeed, three-quarters of all female employees are found in just four sectors of employment—clerical work (31%), cleaning and catering (22%), junior and ancillary professions (12%) and sales (9%)—each of which to some degree represents a continuation of women's domestic servicing role (Wainwright, 1984).

The fact that a wife's earning power is normally less than her husband's does not make her earnings inconsequential either in terms of her own perceived freedom of choice and independence or for the household's economy. However, it does result in her earnings typically being seen as secondary to her husband's and consequently as not providing the rationale for any radical revision of domestic responsibilities. In the main what happens is that the husband's income is regarded as essential to the household's well-being in a way that hers is not. If it came to the crunch the household is usually thought capable of managing without her earnings but not without his. His tend to be seen as paying for the essentials of domestic life; hers provide more of what the family are likely to define as luxuries (Hunt, 1978).

But if this is so and a wife's employment is, rightly or wrongly, defined as secondary, it is not of itself seen as an alternative to her major responsibility—that of housekeeping and domestic servicing. To some degree others in the household may be required to assist more in some of the associated tasks, but primary responsibility for organising them remains hers. Consequently, in a circular fashion, any employment she has needs to be fitted around them. Hence the attraction of part-time employment, and in turn the continuation of the structural conditions that locate wives very much in the housewife/mother role irrespective of their paid work. An interesting point here is that these images of women's responsibilities and of the value of their contribution to the domestic economy are maintained with relatively little need for active reinforcement. The irony is that despite the double burden which wives' participation in employment has generated for them, in practice for many neither their work in the home nor their part-time employment is seen as 'real work' in the way men's employment is. In consequence, notwithstanding the changes there have been in their paid and unpaid work, wives continue to be socially and economically more dependent on their husbands than the latter are on them.

PARENTS AND CHILDREN

While pundits frequently assert that relationships between the generations within families are not what they were—the elderly being ignored by their families; children either being over-indulged or, somewhat contradictorily, uncared for—there is really little evidence to support such claims. The care the elderly in need receive from their children will be discussed in a later section; the focus here is on dependent children in the family. A point to emphasise initially is that as a society we have over the last two centuries transformed the nature of childhood by creating greater dependence through bestowing on children greater protective rights. While legislation limiting children's employment in the middle part of the nineteenth century was an important element, the social redefinition of childhood was symbolised most clearly by the introduction of compulsory education for all children between the ages of five and eleven in 1871. Legislative Acts and the growth of bureaucracies concerned with children's welfare continue to express ideologies of childhood which emphasise the social and emotional dependency of children. In the process the possessive character of parents' relationships with their children has been undermined and replaced by a more creative orientation. Children are now seen as needing special attention and understanding for longer periods if they are to become adequate adults. The development of child-oriented markets reflects this concern as does the heightened recognition of adolescence as a stage of personal development.

These changes in our cultural conception of childhood could not have emerged independently of equivalent shifts in parental and familial orientation. Certainly throughout the second half of this century, there has been an increasing awareness by parents of the careful treatment that children need if they are to prosper undamaged. We may not have very definite ideas of what good parenting specifically involves, but we do believe that parents have the capacity to shape, and therefore harm, children's development. As a result a good deal of effort is made by parents to provide an appropriate developmental environment for their children within the limits of their material circumstances. In this sense family life at the child-rearing phase is rather more child-oriented than in previous eras. To put this another way, both parents, though to differing degrees, have come to expect a level of personal satisfaction and reward from their parenting and from seeing the social development of their children. Though there are some class variations in this, the pattern that has emerged since the Second World War is one in which children are seen as quite central to family life, which in turn is, during this phase, oriented to the sharing with them of experiences that shape their growth. Being a part of this social creation is taken to be what family life is about rather more than was the case 50 or more years ago.

Contemporary claims that children are either undisciplined through being over-indulged or, alternatively, that there is a noticeable increase in child abuse need to be interpreted against this background. To take the latter issue first, the media have heightened public awareness of the horrific damage that some children suffer at the hands of their parents. While the patternings of events leading to such occurrences are not established, what can be recognised is that the incidence of child abuse is much less than in previous historical periods when children were seen as parents'—especially fathers'—property, and the state (or anyone else) had few powers to intervene. Even a cursory knowledge of the history of childhood indicates the far greater and more systematic use of physical force—cruelty and abuse from today's quite different perspective—that children were exposed to in previous times (Pinchbeck and Hewitt, 1973). In this respect, the moral concern expressed in the media about child abuse represents changed boundaries of parental responsibility and children's rights rather than an increasing indifference to children's welfare. Indeed many of the stories that currently make headlines would simply not have warranted such attention in previous eras.

Similarly, commonly made claims about the lack of discipline of contemporary youth need to be viewed with a little historical scepticism. While it follows from the above that children are less harshly treated than in the past and so from this perspective may be regarded as 'spoilt', there is in fact nothing new about older generations complaining about the breakdown of social order amongst younger ones. Pearson (1983) demonstrates particularly clearly how the anti-social behaviour of young people has in each generation over the last

200 years been seen as both novel and threatening to the social fabric, just as mugging, football hooliganism and urban riots are today. Given this historical perspective, it is certainly questionable whether the apparent increase in adolescent delinquency is due to some form of family breakdown or lack of parental discipline, as is often asserted. Rather, much delinquent behaviour is better explained by reference to the structural location of adolescence within our social and economic system, especially in areas of urban and industrial decline where youths' already limited opportunities for legitimate achievement and expression of self are being further undermined by the recession.

CHALLENGES FOR THE FAMILY

The impact of the economic crisis on family life is necessarily of a different form from that of many of the institutions discussed in other chapters of this book. These institutions are often directly related to the state, depend at least in part on it economically and are recognised as being within the general ambit of state control and influence. The family is in a rather different position, partly because the state has never really specified on overt policy on the family, despite the many facets of governmental action which impinge directly or indirectly on family life, and partly because the effect of the recession is experienced differently by the 20 million households/families there are in the country. None the less there are various matters to do with family life that will certainly raise important issues for large numbers of families and for social policy over the next two decades. Three in particular will be discussed here: divorce, the care of those in need and unemployment. Each has been the subject of much public debate and political rhetoric, though the causes of the first two, if not the political reaction, lie well outside the current recession.

Divorce
As is well known, the divorce rate increased very dramatically in the 1970s. The current position is that twelve marriages out

of every thousand are terminated by divorce each year. At these levels, some 30 per cent of all marriages entered into this year will end in divorce, but of course there is no real reason to assume that divorce levels will not continue to rise as this trend has been evident through this century. The tendency in recent years has also been for divorce to occur earlier within a marriage. This, together with increasing levels of cohabitation, has led some to argue that marriage itself has become weakened and less significant than it once was. People nowadays, it is said, enter marriage without sufficient thought or preparation and without the commitment to make it a life-long venture. Certainly the existence of such high levels of divorce will inevitably be reflected in people's attitudes towards marriage. While couples still appear to believe it will not happen to them, it would be strange indeed if the knowledge that one marriage in three ends in divorce did not play some part in defining the nature of the relationship for them. However, it does not necessarily follow that the marriage bond is weakened or that the union is entered into with less thought. The reality is more complex, for what is altering is the 'weight' placed on the relationship and the support it receives from elsewhere.

Marriage is increasingly expected to be a relationship in which both individuals can expect to find satisfaction and meaning to their lives. Rather than being recognised as predominantly about economic and domestic cooperation, ideologically its major rationale has shifted to one of personal happiness and emotional fulfilment, as is somewhat paradoxically most evident in divorce legislation, which now emphasises compatibility rather than contractual rights and obligations. In this sense, the expectations people have of the relationship have intensified so that they are no longer prepared to tolerate unhappy unions to the extent they were in generations past. At the same time, as divorce becomes more accepted as a legitimate solution to marital conflict, the less effort others outside the marriage will give to it. While for some this represents a weakening of the tie, to others it demonstrates the higher value now demanded of it. Similarly, increased levels of cohabitation may represent a more adequate 'apprenticeship' for marriage rather more than a rejection of the institution.

To quite a large degree, divorce is now perceived as a misfortune rather than a tragedy, especially when there are no children involved. However something like 60 per cent of all divorces do involve dependent children, a pattern that is likely to continue into the future. The circumstances of these children and the consequences of divorce for them will certainly be an issue of public concern in the coming decades. A good deal is known about the material situation of children in one-parent families, whether they arise as a consequence of marital breakdown or the increasing numbers of unmarried mothers. In particular, the extent to which marital separation results in poverty is widely acknowledged. Nine out of ten one-parent families are headed by a female, and at any time half of these are dependent primarily on supplementary benefit for their income. A further quarter have incomes which are on or close to supplementary benefit level. Similarly many one-parent families are inadequately housed, largely as a consequence of their poverty. Despite these facts being widely known, not least because of the Finer Committee on One-Parent Families which reported in 1974, very little has been done by government to alleviate their situation.

Rather less is known about the emotional and psychological consequences of marital separation and divorce on children. Relatively little research has been carried out in Britain, though what there is is supported by American data. In essence, current theorising emphasises the importance for the child of continuing contact with both parents in as stable a form as is possible. The divorce, in other words, is the end of the marriage but should not be the end of parenting, though in the majority of cases it actually is (Eekelaar and Clive, 1977). Linked directly to this is the important conceptual issue that divorce itself is a legal phenomenon behind which lies a more important social process. It is what Richards (1982) calls the 'natural history' of divorce in terms of the way conflict and tension are handled both prior to and after the separation which matters. To talk in terms of the 'effect' of divorce is consequently far too much of an over-simplification to be useful. It is the dynamics of the pre- and post-divorce situation that are important, a fact that is only beginning to be recognised officially with the gradual development of divorce—as distinct from marital—conciliation services.

A related issue that is likely to become increasingly prominent over the next few decades concerns the growing number of step-families. Increasing levels of divorce have led to there now being far more children living in step-families—currently about one in fifteen children (Burgoyne and Clark, 1982)—than at any time in recent history. As a society we have taken very little interest in such families, assuming, like many of the families themselves, that they can for all intents and purposes be treated as equivalent to natural families. Only slowly is it being recognised that the structural basis of step-families is different, as are the problems they face.

All step-families bring with them a history missing in natural families. The step-family is never fully the 'creation' of the couple in the way natural families are perceived to be. The 'unity' of the family cannot be assumed, its boundaries are not so clear-cut, because of the non-custodial natural parent who has a legitimate claim on the child(ren). Moreover there is uncertainty about the rights step-parents should have over their step-children. In an important sense, there is no approved or institutionalised role for step-parents. Instead they are caught, along with the step-children, in a web of ambiguous and contradictory pressures over the extent to which the step-parent should be like a natural parent. Step-parents are expected to take over much of the routine parenting work of natural parents, yet the barrier between child and step-parent is always likely to be greater because the necessary trust and love seen as inherent in natural parent bonds are unlikely to have developed. Often the divisions within the step-family may also be unintentionally exacerbated by the efforts of the natural parent to 'protect' the child(ren) and step-parent from each other and maintain the image of a happy family. In particular, rather than being expressed and dissipated, the minor problems and difficulties of everyday parenting may be heightened by the natural parent's attempts to act as a sort of 'buffer' between them. Ultimately such routine intervention by the natural parent is likely to be self-defeating because it limits the possibility of the step-parent and child(ren) developing satisfactory ways of confronting and solving any tensions that arise in their relationship (Allan, 1985).

Care for those in need
While step-families have as yet not really been placed on the 'public agenda', the same is not true of the second issue to be discussed here: familial care for those in need. There is a long history of public debate about the responsibilities that family members have towards one another. Much of this takes the form of a critique of current family practices which seem irresponsible in comparison to some mythical past when families 'really' cared. In reality, not only have the numbers in need of care increased dramatically in recent decades—for instance, the population aged 85 or more increased from 200,000 in 1951 to more than half a million in 1981—but, as importantly, the great majority of those in need of care, be they the elderly, the physically or mentally handicapped or the mentally ill, receive it within the context of their family, a pattern encouraged by the increased emphasis given recently to community, as distinct from institutional, care (Rossiter and Wicks, 1982; Walker, 1982; Finch and Groves, 1983; Parker, 1985).

When community care policies first came into vogue in the late 1950s, the thrust was towards the creation of small-scale homes located in residential areas which would replace the much larger, geographically isolated mental institutions that then predominated. While a small paid staff would run these homes, they offered the possibility of greater flexibility of life-style and reduced levels of 'institutionalisation' through the use of existing community, social and medical services. More recently, encouraged by the increasing number of elderly in the population, community care has come to have a rather different focus. Instead of being care *in* the community, it is increasingly taken to mean care *by* the community. This entails a shift to domiciliary care in which theoretically those in need are kept out of residential homes by a network of informal carers—kin, friends, neighbours, volunteers—backed up as necessary by the available professional social and medical services.

Despite the rhetoric of community care there is very little

evidence that networks of carers ever really do develop. In the vast majority of cases the caring is provided by a single individual who is usually a close relative. Indeed it can be argued that informal relationships like those of friendship and neighbouring are not normally premised in a fashion that makes them particularly suitable for the systematic provision of extensive caring or, in Parker's (1981) phrase, 'tending'. They may provide a good deal of help at times of crisis or more limited assistance over the long run, especially if there is no one else giving support. However where there is, friends, neighbours and other informal relationships tend not to play a very large part.

In practice, community care usually boils down to little more than family care, with relatively little help being given by those outside the household. Indeed within households there is a marked division of labour in tending, as in other domestic matters, with the primary carer normally being a close female relative: mothers, wives and daughters. Men are usually involved to a much lesser degree, except in cases where husbands are looking after their handicapped wives. One of the most telling illustrations of this was provided by Nissel and Bonnerjea (1982) who found that in their study of the care given to elderly dependent relatives, wives spent some two to three hours per day on average in caring tasks compared to their husbands' eight minutes. Broadly similar findings are reported in studies of the care given to handicapped children (Wilkin, 1979; Glendinning, 1984).

There are two issues worth emphasising here. First, if 'community care' in practice normally means 'family care', 'family care' in turn normally entails care by a close female relative. Secondly, so long as primary carers appear to be coping with the demands their caring makes of them, relatively little help is provided by others. This is so not just with respect to the informal relationships discussed above, but is also true of formal, professional help. To quite a large degree, social and medical services are attuned to 'crisis intervention'. They act when a carer is no longer able to manage and the caring situation breaks down. In other words, contrary to the community care model, those who seem to be coping, even if they are only just, as it were, keeping their heads above water, often receive rather little assistance from the formal sector.

As a consequence, the burden of caring can undoubtedly become a very heavy one. This is likely to be especially true with respect to the care of the dependent elderly—the group in need which is expanding most rapidly—as support services for this group seem least well-developed. The primary carer, normally a spouse, daughter or daughter-in-law, is herself likely to be of retirement age when the elderly person in question needs most support. The tiredness and strain of being constantly on call, of having to lift the elderly person regularly, of having sleep continually broken, etc., not only limits opportunities for leisure and social involvement, leaving the carer quite isolated, but can often also result in high degrees of friction within the household. Gradually as the tending required becomes more extensive, it comes to dominate the carer's social identity. Somewhat paradoxically given policy ideals, the support that others are able to give the primary carer may actually be reduced as the need for it increases, partly because of the organisational difficulties of shared care and partly because piecemeal intervention can cause greater disruption to the primary carer's routines than makes it worthwhile.

In the end, what is required is the continuing development of imaginative schemes of domicillary and out-care services, provided on a systematic and therefore probably professional basis, that allow carers not simply to recuperate from the burden of their work but, as importantly, to maintain a life of their own that would make the caring more tolerable. Such schemes of course require extensive funding and are thus unlikely to be developed very fully under present economic policies. With current provision, informal family care is cheap for the state but the cost can be very heavy for those doing the caring.

Unemployment

The third issue to be considered here—the effects of unemployment on the family—is clearly linked closely with the recession. As everyone knows, the numbers of unemployed have increased very dramatically over the last decade and, despite political rhetoric, there is little evidence to suggest they will decrease significantly over the next decade. In the mid-1980s well over three million people were officially registered as unemployed, though the real level is significantly higher than this. The figure excludes a good number of married women who for one reason or another have no right to claim state benefit; many older workers who have been classified as retired before reaching the standard age of retirement; and school-leavers who are involved in YTS schemes. Although all regions in the country have official unemployment rates in excess of 10 per cent, unemployment is still experienced most heavily in the traditional urban-industrial regions, and disproportionately by the old and the young. The figures for male and female unemployment are harder to compare, principally because of the more limited availability of benefits to married women. However, broadly speaking, the proportional increase in male and female unemployment has been in tandem over the last decade. Increasingly though, for many the experience of unemployment is a longer- rather than shorter-term phenomenon. Not only have 40 per cent of those currently registered as unemployed been so for more than a year, but many of those who have not, have had their unemployment broken only by relatively short periods of employment (*Employment Gazette*, 1986).

The consequences of unemployment for the individual, though to a lesser extent his or her family, are now well known. Despite golden handshakes and large redundancy payments for a small minority, the reality of unemployment for the great majority is undoubted poverty. In the early 1980s, nearly 60 per cent of the unemployed were in receipt of supplementary benefit, a figure which rose to 80 per cent for those unemployed for over a year (Social Security Advisory Committee, Second Report, 1982/83). Recent changes in both supplementary and unemployment benefit regulations, together with the increasing propensity for long-term and cyclical unemployment, have ensured that the majority of the unemployed and their families continue to suffer financial hardship. Unemployment has also been shown to affect the physical and mental well-being of the unemployed and their families, though the linkages between unemployment, poverty and health are complex (Sinfield, 1982; Warr, 1983; Fagin and

Little, 1984). The longer-term consequences for health may prove to be of particular concern. Winter (1983), for example, has argued that perinatal mortalities were significantly higher for women who experienced deprivation as children in the 1930s than for their better-off contemporaries.

It has sometimes been argued that the growth of unemployment would lead to a flourishing informal economy based on reciprocated exchange rather than monetary payment. Add to this the possibility that in some areas the only form of employment available would be defined as female and the scene is set for major modification to occur to the dominant domestic division of labour in areas of high unemployment. Recent empirical studies have shown this to be anything but the case. Pahl's research in Sheppey, for example, demonstrated that most work outside employment was 'self-provisioning', i.e. work done by household members for that household (Pahl, 1984). There was relatively little evidence of the existence of a locality-wide network in which services were exchanged in kind, as the informal economy model suggests. Moreover those most involved in self-provisioning were households whose members were employed rather than unemployed as they were the ones with sufficient resources to afford the technologies and materials required for such forms of household work. The unemployed were largely excluded by their poverty.

Equally, studies have shown that unemployment does not cause the conventional division of labour within marriage to be renegotiated. To begin with, wives of unemployed men are themselves twice as likely as other wives to be without employment, in part because of the geographical patterning of unemployment but mainly because of the way the benefits systems operate (Land, 1978). Furthermore, many wives feel that their unemployed husband's pride has suffered enough without their being asked to undertake what continue to be seen as essentially female tasks within the home, a feeling which is not undermined by the extra work a husband's clumsy efforts in these tasks can create (Morris, 1985). Another factor limiting the likelihood of any role-swapping within the home is incapsulated by Norman Tebbit's famous claim that the unemployed should be 'on their bikes' looking for work.

Whatever means of transport is used, unemployed men ideally should not be at home available for domestic tasks but should instead be active in the public domain—out looking for work, visiting Job Centres, applying to potential employers, and the like, as well of course as signing on. The need for such activities can provide a rationale for not accepting a wide range of domestic responsibilities.

In practice, however, the unemployed—and especially those who have been without a job for some period—spend a good deal of time at home. Many studies have shown how unemployment isolates individuals and their families from the wider community, even in areas of high unemployment, because of their poverty. They usually lack the resources for a more integrated social life. Consequently, where a husband is unemployed, the couple are likely to spend more time together than previously, but their worlds in the process become smaller leaving them with little to talk about apart from the manifold difficulties they face. The tensions and conflict such 'closeness' can generate was brilliantly portrayed in 'Chrissie's Story' in Alan Bleasdale's *Boys from the Black Stuff* (1983). Amongst other issues, this highlights very clearly McKee and Bell's (1984) arguments that a husband's unemployment quickly becomes his wife's 'problem' because it is she who somehow has to keep the household going with insufficient resources.

Clearly it is not just traditional male unemployment that affects family life. Unemployment of wives and post-school age children in the household can also disrupt family relationships and the domestic economy. Until very recently female unemployment attracted remarkably little research effort, with unemployment continually being treated as almost an exclusively male problem. Yet the inadequacy of this perspective is evident not simply from the number of female-headed households but also because of what is now known about the impact of wives' economic contribution to household finances.

As Martin and Roberts (1984) point out, the route into unemployment for married women is much more varied than for men, with domestic obligations sometimes making the boundaries between economic inactivity and unemployment unclear. None the less, it is evident that where family patterns of consumption have been built around two incomes, as is now the case in most marriages, wives' unemployment has significant economic consequences. To reiterate what was said earlier, avoiding poverty and meeting current expectations of 'normal' family life increasingly depends on having two, albeit unequal, incomes. The loss of the second income undoubtedly results in a drop in living standards and for many households can cause substantial hardship. Importantly, too, unemployment can alter the nature of the marital relationship by effectively trapping wives into full-time domestic work. As is now well-documented, the economic dependence and social isolation of this work facilitates greater control by husbands, however benevolently they exercise it.

Like female unemployment, youth employment has only recently begun to receive much attention from researchers. The evidence that there is certainly suggests that the presence of unemployed adolescents in a household can cause a good deal of friction. While parents may be well aware of the structural basis of unemployment, the traditional conflicts between parents and their adolescent children are frequently exacerbated, arguably more for boys than girls, by the limited contribution they make to the household's functioning. Being around with little to do, often organising their life around what may seem to their parents to be a deviant timetable; no longer being socially dependent, yet without the resources to be independent; these and other factors like them often result in tension and antagonism within the household. This is likely to be increased where unemployment crosses the generations. Where parent and child(ren) are both unemployed not only is the financial stress likely to be higher but the 'escapes' from each other's presence and from the pressing reality of unemployment that much fewer (Campbell, 1984).

One further issue of some consequence is whether long-run high levels of youth unemployment will have an impact on patterns of family formation. Traditionally economic insecurity and hardship have resulted in marriage and child-rearing being delayed. This may well be what is happening in Britain now in areas of high unemployment, though conclusive data are as yet not available. However, counter to this, it is also possible that for some unemployed females marriage and/or child-care offer the only possibility there is for what appears to be a creative and satisfying 'career'. While the supplementary benefit system would seem to discourage this, as benefit for a couple is less than for two single people, much may depend on the local housing situation, for child-bearing may offer the opportunity to leave the parental home and gain some level of independence by setting up one's own. From previous research, it is quite certain that marriages formed under these circumstances will be particularly prone to breakdown and divorce with its attendant problems.

8 The National Health Service

Joan Higgins

INTRODUCTION

Since the very inception of the National Health Service in 1948 it has faced a series of challenges and crisis. They are different in the 1980s only in their nature and intensity. The central problem has always been one of resources and because demand for health services is almost infinite and supply finite the key political dilemma has been a question of where to fix the balance between the two. This was as true in the more expansive days of the 1960s before public expenditure faced real constraints, as it is in the 1980s when a Conservative government stands accused of trying to 'dismantle' the National Health Service. Enoch Powell who was Minister of Health in 1960, and Richard Crossman who became Secretary of State for Social Services in 1968, represented different ends of the political spectrum but they were agreed upon the profound difficulties facing the Service. As Enoch Powell put it, 'The unnerving discovery every Minister of Health makes at or near the outset of his term of office is that the only subject he is ever destined to discuss with the medical profession is money' (quoted in Klein, 1983, p. 54).

Both Powell and Crossman reached the same conclusions about the inherent conflicts involved in satisfying the need for medical care in an advanced industrial society. Powell argued that:

There is virtually no limit to the amount of medical care an individual is capable of absorbing. (Further) not only is the range of treatable conditions

141

huge and rapidly growing...There is a vast range of quality in the treatment of these conditions...There is hardly a type of condition from the most trivial to the gravest which is not susceptible of alternative treatments under conditions affording a wide range of skill, care, comfort, privacy, efficiency and so on. (Finally) there is the multiple effect of successful medical treatment. Improvement in expectation of survival results in lives that demand further medical care. The poorer (medically speaking) the quality of lives preserved by advancing medical science, the more intense are the demands they continue to make. In short, the appetite for medical treatment *vient en mangeant.* (in Klein, 1983, pp. 67–8)

Thus, the more effective the Health Service becomes, the more expensive it becomes and the more demand it will generate. The availability of new and different treatments increases and public expectations grow accordingly. The National Health Service becomes a victim of its own success. Richard Crossman made a similar observation; 'The pressure of demography, the pressure of technology, the pressure of democratic equalisation, will always together be sufficient to make the standard of social services regarded as essential to a civilised society more expensive than that community can afford' (ibid., pp. 71–2).

The politician, the doctor, the administrator and many others involved in health service provision, therefore, face the constant and insoluble dilemmas of matching supply to demand and of rationing scarce resources in a way which is seen to be equitable, fair and just. This central theme runs through all public policies on health and is as alive in the 1980s as it was in the 1940s. What changes over the years is the nature of the demands placed upon those scarce resources, the needs they are expected to satisfy and the machinery for achieving that satisfaction. It is important to recognise, however, that while the problems of the NHS are special, and especially acute because of the type of service which is being provided and its end product (sometimes a matter of life and death), the problems of rationing which occur take place within a broader context. While the question of who gets what and when will always remain—regardless of the size of the cake—the domestic problems of public expenditure must be seen in terms of international dilemmas in the provision of state welfare common to most industrialised countries in varying degrees.

CONTINUITY OR CRISIS?

In the 1970s it became fashionable to talk of these contradictions and challenges in terms of a 'crisis in the welfare state' James O'Connor, for example, in 1973 was the first writer to identify what he called the 'fiscal crisis of the state' or the 'structural gap' between state expenditure and state revenues which highlighted a 'tendency for state expenditures to increase more rapidly than the means of financing them' (p. 9). Gough too, in his book *The Political Economy of the Welfare State* (1979), wrote of a 'world crisis' in welfare, stemming from a breakdown of the post-war consensus on welfare values, the inherent problems of social expenditure in industrial capitalism and changing class relationships. However, as a number of writers have subsequently argued, this talk of crisis may be both exaggerated and misleading. Peter Taylor-Gooby claims that the notion of crisis implies 'a sudden reversal or calamity' (1985, p. 5) when in his view, it is the 'continuities rather than cleavages and conflicts that provide the dominant theme' (ibid., p. 2) in the history of state welfare.

While it was anticipated that the apparent attempts to dismantle the infrastructure of welfare services in different countries would lead to popular opposition it is clear that sections of public opinion have, in fact, been mobilised behind the anti-welfare stance of right-wing parties. The late 1970s saw, not the election of socialist governments in the industrialised West, but the growth of neo-Conservatism under Ronald Reagan, Margaret Thatcher and the leaders of many European and English-speaking countries. As Taylor-Gooby observes, 'the resilience of human society outpaces that of classical crisis theory' (ibid., p. 13). Although social and economic pressures have changed the shape of contemporary social policy this does not amount to a 'sea change' in government policy and it is not 'an abrupt reversal shattering a previous order' (p. 19). Some of the changes, have, of necessity, been rather marginal and others, while challenging fundamental post-war principles, have yet to have a major impact.

George and Wilding (1984) generally share this view and

argue that 'welfare capitalist societies are experiencing severe difficulties but these have not reached crisis dimensions' (p. 229). Their detailed and thoughtful analysis of the so-called 'crisis of the welfare state' underlines the importance of political and economical changes in the 1970s and their impact on social policy. Two factors were of particular importance: first, the decline of economic growth and second, the absence of a strong positive philosophy about state welfare. The onset of severe economic difficulties, in particular, threw into sharp relief the issue of choice in social policy. As long as the economy continued to expand, unpalatable choices between competing priorities were concealed or deferred and public policy had become 'almost costless in political terms' (p. 221). The end of growth, however, demonstrated that expansion could only be financed by 'the painful forgoing of other desirable purchases' (p. 222). While this was true for all areas of public expenditure it was especially true in health where it became clear that the choice was not between frivolous or serious demands upon resources but between medical needs of varying degrees of severity. In a sense, therefore, the challenges facing the National Health Service in the 1980s are both universal and particular. At the macro-level the problem of resources for welfare is common to all societies. Similarly, the allocation of these resources (however great or small they may be) in the field of health and medicine presents special problems everywhere. The response to this dilemma in Britain, however, throws up a particular configuration of financial and administrative arrangements which are peculiar to that country and which require separate analysis. The rest of this chapter will be devoted to that task.

SIX CHALLENGES TO THE NATIONAL HEALTH SERVICE

Six main challenges face the National Health Service in Britain today:
    the demographic challenge;
    the problem of resources;
    new health problems and new needs;

reducing inequalities in access to care and in morbidity; the challenge of consumerism; the crisis of confidence in government policy.

The demographic challenge

The impact of demographic change upon the demand for health services is highly complex and only one of a series of factors which must be taken into account. Nevertheless, there is one single demographic variable which is almost certain to have striking effects upon the service and this is the growing number of over 75 year olds now living in the United Kingdom. Although the numbers of elderly people (i.e. over 65 years) generally have been increasing in the last decade—from 6.5 million in 1971 to 7.2 million in 1980—the proportion of the very elderly has gone up disproportionately from 40 per cent of the total to 43 per cent. It is estimated that this trend will continue and that the number of over 75 year olds will rise sharply up to 1991, while the overall number of elderly people levels off (Harrison and Gretton, 1984, pp. 15–16). The ageing of the population has meant a higher incidence of chronic illness and disability and the greater prevalence of degenerative diseases. As a result there have been increasing pressures on the health service which are, in part, the outcome of its successes in earlier generations. Evidence suggests that the elderly have more consultations with their general practitioner than those in their middle years (4.8 per cent consultations per year against an average per person of 3.8 per cent) and that the care of the elderly consumes a larger than average amount of the health care budget. The DHSS, for example, allows a 'dependency weighting' of 1.0 for everyone between the ages of 16–64 years, 1.5 for 65–74 year olds and 2.0 for those over 75 years of age (Harrison and Gretton, 1986, p. 88). It was estimated that in 1982/83 health care expenditure of £965 per annum for each over-75 year old was seven times higher than that spent on an individual of working age (Robinson, 1986, p. 13).

The other group who consume a large share of health services are the very young and the declining birth rate in the recent past can, to a large degree, be set against the costs of treating the very old. Between 1970–82 the birth rate dropped dramatically by 30 per cent from 16.3 per thousand to 12.8 but began to increase again by the early 1980s and is likely to rise steadily through the remainder of the decade (Harrison and Gretton, 1984, p. 16). The *General Household Survey* indicates that the under-4 year olds have 6.2 consultations each with their general practitioner, which is almost twice the average for all age groups and that their DHSS dependency rating is 2.0 (Harrison and Gretton, 1984, p. 15; Harrison and Gretton, 1986, p. 88).

Various pieces of evidence suggest that demographic changes other than those in the age structure of the population may have as great, if not greater, impact upon the demand for health services. Alistair Gray, for example, argues that single and separated people, the widowed and divorced, make greater use of the health service than do couples. This was especially marked in the use of in-patient psychiatric facilities where single men were three times as likely and single women almost four times as likely to be patients as the population as a whole. There was also a higher rate than average for the widowed and divorced and much lower rates for married couples. This pattern was replicated in the case of non-psychiatric in-patient treatment, though to varying degrees. As far as over-75 year olds were concerned, single men were six times more likely to be in psychiatric hospitals than other over-75 year olds, whereas married, widowed or divorced elderly men were unlikely to be in-patients. Elderly single men and women were twice as likely to be in general hospitals as others of the same age. If the numbers of single people continue to grow at the same rate (by 16 per cent between 1971 and 1981) the effects upon the NHS could well be significant. Other demographic changes, such as the increase in the numbers of children in single-parent families, appear to have effects upon the health of those involved. Research suggests that the children of divorced parents may, for example, be more likely to suffer from colitis and psychiatric illness (Harrison and Gretton, 1986, p. 89).

The demographic challenge facing the National Health Service in the 1980s then is, as ever, one of uncertainty and complexity. Increasing numbers in those age groups which are heaviest users of the service (the very young and the very old) and the increase in marital breakdown and both single-parent and single-person households creates new and different pressures from those of the recent past. The demographic challenge itself, however, is not new but it evolves and changes in its composition.

The problem of resources

The continuing debate about resources in the NHS has grown more acute since the 1970s when public expenditure cuts first began to bite. The dispute grew increasingly bitter under the Conservative administration which came to power in 1979 with, on the one hand, its claims to have increased spending by 24 per cent since then and, on the other, the closure of hospitals, the 'privatisation' of support services, and the loss of ancillary workers' jobs. Identifying the real extent of increases and cuts is far from easy but the picture seems to be neither as rosy as that painted by the government nor as black as that painted by its critics. The National Health Service presented the government with particular problems in its overall plans for public expenditure. When it first came to power in 1979 it was committed to public expenditure cuts and to 'rolling back the state' for two reasons, one of which was economic and the other ideological (Robinson, 1986). While it anticipated political support for public expenditure cuts in many areas of welfare it became clear that the National Health Service remained a highly popular social institution and there were less votes to be gained by weakening it than there were in extending it. Robinson (1986), O'Higgins (1983) and others have demonstrated that in most areas of social policy the rhetoric on cuts has outstripped the reality in a number of ways. Robinson shows that the government between 1979 and 1985 had been less successful than it claimed in reducing public expenditure overall but it had also spent far less on the NHS than its public statements implied. Total public expenditure appears to have risen, in real terms, by nearly 10 per cent between 1979/80 and 1984/85. A good deal of the increase was taken up by higher social security spending and some growth in health and personal social services, while the education budget remained static and public expenditure in housing declined rapidly (Robinson, 1986, p. 3). At the same time public expenditure increased from 39.5 per cent of Gross Domestic Product in 1979/80 to 42.5 per cent in 1984/85 (ibid., p. 4).

However, the individual components of public expenditure require separate analysis and here it becomes clear that the real increase in expenditure on health was much less than the 24 per cent which government figures suggested. Estimates differ on how great the increase (if any) actually was. Robinson, for example, suggests that the growth in 'health service inputs' was 8.3 per cent and not 24 per cent after 1979, while the National Association of Health Authorities put the figure at 0.59 per cent 'in real terms' (Radical Statistics Health Group, 1985, p. 50). The Parliamentary Select Committee on the Social Services in 1984 concluded that the figure was somewhere in between at 7.2 per cent (quoted in Harrison and Gretton, 1986, p. 85). These wide discrepancies clearly illustrate the fact that there is no agreement at all on how 'expenditure', 'growth' and 'cuts' should be measured in the National Health Service. Nevertheless, most observers concurred that there was indeed some growth (however modest) in public expenditure on health care.

There was also an increase in nursing and medical manpower. Robinson (1986, pp. 12–13) shows that the number of hospital, medical and dental staff increased from 37,000 to 41,000 between 1979 and 1984, and the number of nursing and midwifery staff went up from 358,000 in 1979 to 397,000 in 1982, remaining at that level into 1984. However, in 1980 the length of the working week was reduced and 15 per cent of this increase was taken up with compensating for this reduction. Between 1981 and 1984 the numbers of ancillary workers went down from 172,000 to 150,000 and the onset of their decline preceded the job losses which occurred later through competitive tendering, when all the laundry, catering and cleaning services in the NHS were put out to tender.

The really important point in analysing these figures is that the demands upon health care resources grow and change and an apparent expansion one year can be under-resourcing the next. Three particular pressures were brought to bear upon the NHS budget after 1979 and it was these which reduced the apparent 24 per cent growth to much more modest levels.

First, there was medical inflation (the cost of drugs, medical supplies, etc.) which ran well ahead of general inflation. Second, there were costly technological innovations and advances (such as joint replacements and transplant surgery) and, third, the growing numbers of the very old. In addition, health authorities were required to finance nurses' and doctors' pay awards in 1985/86 and 1986/87 from their own budgets and from 'efficiency savings'. By 1986 it had become clear that many of them could only do so by reducing services to patients, by closing down facilities and by curtailing developments. For many people on the 'front line', therefore, there was poverty in the midst of government reports of plenty.

New health problems and needs
When the National Health Service came into existence in 1948 it was broadly assumed that the demand for health services was finite and that once the outstanding backlog of health problems from the pre-war years had been cleared the costs of the service would steadily decline. It was barely a matter of months before this confident expectation was called into question. Since the 1940s we have seen the steady growth of unforeseen and unforseeable needs coupled with an increasing technical ability to treat both them and more long-standing medical problems. The net effect of these changes has been not a reduction but a rapid increase in health service expenditure.

One of the major achievements of health services (coupled with better hygiene and nutrition, better housing and higher incomes) has been the reduction of infectious diseases, especially amongst the young. In 1950 they accounted for one in four deaths amongst the under-fives and one in five or six deaths amongst children aged 5–14. Although a certain proportion of young children still die from infectious diseases the risks for other age groups are very small. In the 1980s, the major killers at most ages were cancer, heart disease and strokes, each of which had become increasingly significant. Only deaths from chest disease appeared to be decreasing steadily. Perhaps the most striking change, however, has been the increase in accidents as a cause of death amongst 15–24 year olds, 70 per cent of whose deaths now occur in this way

(Harrison and Gretton, 1984, pp. 17–19). The real dangers for this age group lie not at work or on the roads (where fatal accidents have been decreasing) but in the home. As Harrison and Gretton put it, 'for many people, this is now a far more dangerous place to be than it once was' (1984, p. 19).

With these developments as a general backdrop there have been a number of specific changes in the 1980s which have placed increased pressures upon the National Health Service, many of which relate to personal habits and lifestyles. Three major areas of concern—smoking, alcohol consumption and use of addictive substances—have recently been joined by a fourth, with the identification of AIDS (Acquired Immune Deficiency Syndrome) as a new and fatal disease. With the first of these areas, smoking, the picture in the 1980s has been mixed, with a reduction in the number of young men but an increase in the number of young women taking up the habit. For the first time in 1982, the number of non-smokers outnumbered the smokers in every socio-economic group and the trend in consumption appears to be moving gently downwards (ibid., p. 22). In 1984 total sales had fallen to 100,000 million from 137,000 million in 1973 and the proportion of smokers declined from 52 to 36 per cent amongst men and from 41 to 32 per cent amongst women (Open University, 1985, pp. 137–8). However, it appears to be the light smokers who are giving up and the heavier smokers (who place more demands upon the Health Service) who are persisting, so that overall costs may not be reduced. A report in December 1985 from the Health Education Council and the British Medical Association, entitled *The Big Kill* claimed that, despite these improvements, 55,107 men and 22,667 women die from smoking-related diseases every year—in other words, one person every six minutes. It claimed that hospital admissions in England and Wales cost the NHS £111,325,000 per annum (Anderson, 1985, p. 1525).

While these statistics are gloomy enough, the figures for alcohol consumption are even less encouraging with a significant increase in consumption dating from 1960. The heaviest drinkers in the 1980s were men under the age of 24, 13 per cent of whom were drinking more than the so-called 'safe' level of 50 units (the equivalent of 25 pints of beer, 50 glasses of whisky or 50 glasses of wine) each week. Thus Harrison and Gretton anticipate that 'as today's young people become middle-aged, we can therefore expect more alcohol-related illness. That being so, again the implication is one of increasing pressure on health resources' (Harrison and Gretton, 1984, p. 23). However, we need not wait a generation to see the effects of excessive alcohol consumption upon heavy drinkers and those around them. As another publication comments, 'alcohol can kill and injure in a variety of ways—directly through conditions such as cirrhosis of the liver and indirectly through road traffic accidents, domestic violence and, when heavy drinkers lose their jobs, through a deterioration in living standards' (Open University, 1985, p. 134). The same source attributes 5000 to 10,000 premature deaths in the UK every year to alcohol and alcoholism and quotes McDonnel and Maynard's estimate that the minimum social cost of alcohol abuse in 1983, from absenteeism from work and demands on health services, the police and the judiciary was in excess of £1500 million (ibid., p. 134).

If smoking and alcohol consumption are the measurable 'addictions', a much greater problem lies in identifying and measuring the extent of drug abuse and the use of other addictive substances (such as glue). However, the number of registered drug addicts went up from 7155 in 1981 to 10,993 in 1983, and it was estimated that the figures for 1984 would show a further 28 per cent increase (Alleway, 1985, p. 831). Most commentators are aware that this is only the tip of the iceberg and the Secretary of State, Norman Fowler put the real figure for drug dependence at around 40,000 (Strang, 1984, p. 1203), while others claim that it is more like 100,000 (Alleway, 1985). Strang refers to two recent studies which conclude that, for every identified problem drug-taker, there are another five unidentified in the community.

The 1980s in Britain saw the spread of a new and fatal disease—Acquired Immune Deficiency Syndrome (AIDS). It originated in Africa, became prevalent in America in the late 1970s and was discovered in Britain some time later. In October 1985 there were 241 known cases but many more were carrying the AIDS antibody (HTLV-111). At this stage the disease was concentrated geographically and in one particular social group. Nearly 80 per cent of the cases occurred in London and 87.5 per cent of those affected were homosexuals. It has been estimated that, by 1988, there will be 6000 recorded cases of AIDS and for each one of them there may be another 50–1000 people who are infected by the virus. Because the AIDS virus is transmitted through blood, the treatment of patients involves special skills and facilities which can be very costly. Health economists suggest that each patient will require care costing between £10,000 and £20,000, which means a minimum increase in resources of £60 million by 1988, if estimates of its incidence are correct (*Health and Social Service Journal*, 28 November 1985, p. 1507).

Aside from these new needs and new problems there have been a number of social changes which have created further demands upon the health service. The most obvious of these is unemployment, but there is very considerable controversy about the ways in which unemployment may affect individual and family health and about the precise relationship between the two. Fagin and Little, in a detailed review of the impact of unemployment, 'strongly suggest' that there is an association between ill health and unemployment but the link is 'far from straightforward' (1984, p. 205). Although cigarette consumption, for example, and all its related consequences appear to increase during periods of unemployment, alcohol consumption goes down. Similarly, many of the unemployed and their families suffer psychological stress not only through the loss of work but also through the loss of income, while others benefit from the reduction of pressures imposed by their jobs. Most studies concur that the unemployed make greater use of the health services when they are out of work.

Reducing inequalities
The fourth challenge to the NHS has a long-running history dating back decades (if not centuries)—the elimination of inequality. There are many aspects to this problem including inequalities in access to care and in the use of the service, inequalities in morbidity and mortality, and geographical inequality in the distribution of resources. There is no space here to discuss these issues in any depth and there is, in any case, little to add to the conclusions of The Black Report on

Inequalities in Health published in 1980. It found that:

despite more than thirty years of a National Health Service expressly committed to offering equal care for all, there remains a marked class gradient in standards of health. Indeed, that gradient seems to be more marked than in comparable countries...and in certain respects has been becoming more marked. (Townsend and Davidson, 1982, p. 15)

However, it also found that the causes of (and hence the solutions to) inequalities in health went beyond the scope of the National Health Service. Essentially they lay in environmental factors—housing standards, levels of income, working conditions and unemployment, standards of nutrition, education, cultural norms—in behavioural factors and in wider societal influences. The Black Report, therefore, underlined what had been argued for some time—that health services and medicine have only a limited impact upon the nation's health and are ill-equipped to eradicate inequalities and mortality on any substantial scale. As McKeown put it, in his controversial book *The Role of Medicine*:

The appraisal of influences on health in the past three centuries suggested that we owe the improvement, not to what happens when we are ill, but to the fact that we do not so often become ill; and we remain well, not because of specific measures such as vaccination and immunization, but because we enjoy a higher standard of nutrition and live in a healthier environment. (McKeown, 1979, p. 79)

This is not to argue that clinical medicine has no role to play in treating illness and in keeping people healthier longer but there is now a recognition that medicine, on its own, cannot create a healthy population.

Perhaps the greatest change in the 1980s, in this respect, has been in the response of groups and organisations both inside and outside the health service to questions of diet, exercise and smoking where beneficial behavioural changes have occurred relatively rapidly. Although many observers have been rightly critical of government's ambivalent attitude towards preventive care, the 1980s have seen important advances. There is now stricter control of cigarette advertising and there has been a significant extension of no-smoking areas in public places. The consumption of saturated fats is going down, as is the consumption of white bread and sugar. However, there is a direct relationship between household income and the purchase of different foods. Households with incomes of less than £67 per week eat high proportions of white bread, sugar and preserves while households with incomes of more than £180 per week eat increasing amounts of wholemeal bread and fresh fruit (Harrison and Gretton, 1984, p. 66). The health education messages on nutrition, therefore, are taken up differently by different socio-economic groups and may result in a widening rather than a narrowing of inequalities in morbidity. It is also the case that powerful vested interests (the tobacco, brewing and drugs industries and the farming lobby) have consistently constrained government activities designed to encourage healthier lifestyles and the real challenge in the 1980s lies in weakening their stranglehold.

The challenge of consumerism
The fifth challenge to the National Health Service in the 1980s has been the challenge of consumerism, reflected in the growth of pressure groups and self-help groups (especially women's health groups) and the increasing recognition in official documents of patients as 'customers' or 'consumers'. The resort to litigation when things go wrong is also a measure of consumer awareness.

The 1984 Griffiths Report on management in the NHS, written by the Managing Director of Sainsburys, was critical of the National Health Service's treatment of patients. It was open to question, Roy Griffiths argued, whether the NHS was meeting the needs of the patient and whether it could be demonstrated that it was doing so. While this is generally true, the patient surveys which have been undertaken reflect high levels of satisfaction, though almost all contain the same complaints about waiting times for treatment and lack of information. The management arrangements introduced as a result of the Griffiths Report place a new emphasis upon 'quality assurance' and upon service to patients. The challenge of consumerism may grow difficult to ignore not only for reasons of managerial efficiency but as a result of the politically sensitive choices now embodied in health policy. As Harrison and Gretton put it, 'More probably than at any time in its 40-year history, the NHS needs its customers. It needs them to use the service but more than anything else, it needs their active and vocal support' (1984, p. 115). This leads to the sixth and most important challenge facing the NHS in the 1980s which is one of political legitimacy.

Confidence in government policy
Although the notion of a 'crisis' in the welfare state was earlier rejected as an inaccurate description of the changes which have been taking place in social policy since the late 1970s there is one sense in which the concept of crisis is appropriate. If the reality of public expenditure cuts does not match the rhetoric there was, nevertheless, a radical change in ideology and thinking about the National Health Service under the Conservative government in the 1980s. The assumption that the NHS should be financed out of general taxation and free to all at the point of need was challenged both intellectually and in practice. The expectation that the public sector would have a monopoly of health care provision was also questioned and meant that government policy encouraged the growth of alternative suppliers especially in the private acute sector and the long-term care of the elderly and in the provision of ancillary services.

George and Wilding have argued that although the arguments about a 'legitimation crisis' in the welfare state cannot be fully sustained there appears to have been a decline in the sense of common purpose in society and 'an increasing distrust of government morals and competence' (1984, p. 228). Since the 1940s the NHS in Britain has acquired a significance which goes beyond the routine delivery of health services. Aside from the mystique of medicine itself, the service has proved a cohesive force in a fragmented and changing society. In Klein's words it has performed 'a general social role as a symbol of social reassurance' (1983, p. 147). It is this role which seemed most under threat in the 1980s. The Conservative Party's claim during the election campaign of 1983, for example, that 'the NHS is safe in our hands' was regarded with widespread cynicism by many observers. This distrust was exacerbated by the doubts about the accuracy of the Conservative government's published 'growth' figures (not least from the All-Party Parliamentary Select Committee on Social Services) and by regular media 'leaks' about policy options (especially 'free market' options) which the government was said to be considering. In 1982, for example, the unpublished report of the Central Policy Review Staff to the Cabinet was alleged to have recommended a radical restructuring of the financing of medical care both through compulsory private health insurance and by introducing charges for visits to GPs and to hospital. Such was the controversy over the report that the furious debate which ensued in Cabinet on 9 September was said to have been expunged from the records (*Guardian*, 21 September 1982).

If government in the 1980s had doubts about the NHS in its present form those doubts did not seem to be shared by the public at large. The *British Social Attitudes Survey* 1984 showed high levels of satisfaction with the service, with only 25 per cent of the sample describing themselves as either 'dissatisfied' or 'very dissatisfied'. The majority (64 per cent) felt that the NHS should continue to offer a 'universal' service and respondents put health well above all other policy areas (such as education, housing, defence and the police) when asked to identify public spending priorities. The results of this survey are consistent with virtually all other surveys of public attitudes to the health service, though there are variations in detail. They confirm the view that the NHS continued to be the most popular social institution or public service in Britain (Bosanquet, 1984, pp. 83–7).

The popularity of the service combined with government reservations about its costs and performance to create a crisis of confidence in governmental willingness and ability to continue to expand the service on post-war principles. The challenge here then was not only to the future of the NHS but also to the political popularity of the government.

RESPONDING TO THE CHALLENGE

The response to these challenges has come not just from government but from other interest groups—not least the private suppliers of health care. The outcome, as writers like

Laing (1985) have illustrated, has been a highly complex pattern of suppliers and financiers of health services and products. In looking at the long-term institutional care of the elderly, for example, he shows that in 1984 55 per cent of total care was publicly supplied and publicly financed, 11 per cent was publicly supplied and privately financed, 10 per cent was privately supplied and publicly financed and 24 per cent was privately supplied and privately financed (Laing, 1985, p. 30).

Similar patterns are evident in the provision for other care groups and other needs. Over a relatively short period there has been a rapid expansion in the number of private rest homes and nursing homes and in the number of private hospital beds. During a period when public sector expansion has drawn to a halt or declined, the number of places in private residential homes has increased from 31,998 in 1979 to 76,300 in 1984 and the number of nursing home places has gone up by around 8000 (Laing, 1985, p. 32). Similarly, as the number of pay beds in NHS hospitals has steadily declined, the numbers of private acute beds outside the NHS have gone up from 6578 in 1979 to 10,155 (ibid., p.14). Although the stability of the private sector is uncertain there is likely to be continued growth throughout the 1980s. Private sector institutions have demonstrated that they have both the capacity and the inclination to rise to the demographic challenge, to the challenge of new needs and to consumer demands in an entrepreneurial, flexible and swift manner.

The more equivocal response of central government had two key elements—the first managerial and the second ideological. It used to be argued that politicians, especially socialist politicians, have a tendency to wish to 'throw money at problems'. The Conservative reaction in the 1980s in many areas of domestic policy, has been to throw managers at problems. This has been especially true in the NHS where, after the second reorganisation in eight years which took place in 1982, Roy Griffiths of Sainsburys was commissioned to undertake a management inquiry. His recommendation was that management should be restructured centrally and locally, that decision-making should be quick and more direct, and that greater attention should be given to consumer service. 'Consensus' team management at district level was to be superseded by the appointment of general managers who would have both the personal responsibility and the authority to make ultimate policy decisions. These recommendations were accepted by government and by 1986 were being implemented in all health authorities. The effects of these changes are unlikely to be seen fully during the 1980s. In the short term, the disruption which the new arrangements have caused in the localities and the opposition of certain professional groups, especially nurses, has led to considerable anxiety about the future of the service. The more beneficial effects of these managerial changes are likely to be seen (if at all) over a longer time-scale. The key themes of public health policy in the 1980s have been 'effectiveness' and 'efficiency' in the use of resources and most of the energy of central government has gone into ensuring that these objectives are met.

The second response of government to the challenge facing the NHS has been ideological. Although the Conservative government's desire to encourage the growth of the private sector in health may have been exaggerated a number of decisions have been taken since 1979 which have had this effect. The most significant decision, taken early in the 1980s was to change consultants' contracts in a way which would allow them to undertake a greater volume of private practice while retaining the benefits of a contract with the NHS. This apparently modest change may well have given a boost to private health care which exceeds anything accomplished by the efforts of private insurance and private hospital companies. A second development which occurred more by default than by design was the rapid expansion in the numbers of elderly people in private residential care funded through social security payments. Their numbers went up from 11,000 in 1979 to 42,500 in 1984, and after particularly generous benefit limits were set in 1983 the annual increase in places was 65 per cent. There is no suggestion that these changes were intended as a direct subsidy or encouragement to private sector expansion but they did generate a boom in rest homes and nursing homes which had significant effects. However, the boom may have been short-lived and revised social security regulations in 1985 setting lower benefit limits, have introduced a new volatility in the private sector whose outcome is uncertain.

These indirect incentives to private sector growth have been accompanied by much more explicit measures to 'privatise' the ancillary services in the NHS. In this case very firm central directives have been issued to health authorities to test the cost-effectiveness of their services through competitive tendering. It has been this element of government policy which has particularly attracted the condemnation of health service unions and there is little doubt that the debate has been about ideologies as well as jobs.

Despite these individual skirmishes, however, the real ideological battles have not been fought 'up front'. There have been strong rumours to indicate that certain members of the Conservative Cabinet (including the Prime Minister) favoured a radical restructuring of the NHS which involved insurance funding as well as an increase in income through charges. More cautious members of the Cabinet—sustained, no doubt, by popular support for the status quo and fears of electoral defeat—resisted these arguments.

These unresolved debates at the micro-level may be relatively insignificant in themselves but they represent the first major challenge to the principles of health policy laid down in the post-war years. The Butskellite consensus which began to break down in most areas of domestic policy in the 1960s lasted rather longer in the field of health care, though it received a real battering in the 1970s as health service unions began to sharpen their claws in the political arena. The 1980s saw the short spectrum of ideological views on health care become increasingly stretched—not so much to the political Left where the 1948 position was regarded as a more or less satisfactory end point, but towards the political Right where new options based on free market principles began to open up. More than in any other area of domestic policy the values of individualism had come hard up against the values of collectivism.

INTO THE FUTURE

In looking into the future three propositions seem safe bets, if not cast-iron certainties:

(i)   demands upon the health service will continue to increase and the ability to meet these demands will remain static or will decrease;

(ii)   there will be growing complexity in payer/provider relationships;

(iii)   the ideological battles have only just begun.

Each of these conclusions emerges from the earlier debate and is more or less self-explanatory. The shape of the future lies essentially in domestic political decision-making and in the capacity of the economy to generate more ingredients for a larger cake. Even so, as the Black Report and international comparisons have demonstrated, more expenditure on health services does not necessarily mean better health. Indeed, if good health is the agreed goal, it may be more cost-effective to put any growth money into the housing and social security budgets rather than into the National Health Service. However large the budget for health (both public and private) the question of priorities and objectives will not go away. Nor will the debate about how best to meet those objectives. The Conservative government in the 1980s not only thought the unthinkable about the NHS but was bold enough to say it. The protected status of the NHS, unchallenged since the 1940s, is now open to question.

In looking into the future it is important to recognise that Britain is unique in the arrangements it makes for the health care of its population. All other industrialised societies contain much larger elements of fee-for-service, direct payment, insurance funding and private provision. If Britain moves down this road it joins the majority. The ideological and economic pressures to do so may become increasingly irresistible. They may, however, be outweighed by the social and political pressures to maintain the status quo. As Rudolf Klein observes: 'Whatever its strengths and weaknesses as an instrument for delivering health care, the NHS has...been a successful instrument for delivering support to the political system' (1983, p. 146). This being so, it will be a rash and single-minded government which attempts to reshape it beyond recognition. The resolution of key issues facing the future of health care in Britain will be a barometer of wider changes in the social and political system.

9 The Police

J. P. Martin

INTRODUCTION

The period since the end of the Second World War has been one of dramatic change for the police service of England and Wales. It increased in size, its organisation has altered in many ways, technological change has had a major impact, and fashions in methods of policing have come and gone. At the same time, however, the enduring values of the police sub-culture have tempered, and sometimes frustrated, the efforts of senior officers and police authorities to develop new methods to cope with the problems of social change. Moreover, certain themes of police history have recurred, albeit in somewhat modified forms. This is not surprising, for the fundamental tasks of policing derive from well-established human traits, and from longstanding problems of regulating the interests of different groups in society.

DEVELOPMENTS IN THE STRUCTURE OF THE POLICE SERVICE

It is convenient to summarise the major changes in the size and composition of the police service in England and Wales in a single table, based on data extracted from the Appendices to the Reports of HM Inspectors of Constabulary. The years chosen are 1984 (the latest for which figures are available) and 1949; this covers a 35-year period starting fairly soon after the

Table 9.1: *Composition of the Police Service in England and Wales, 1949–1984*

	1949 No.	1949 %	1984 No.	1984 %	1984 as % of 1949
No. of separate police forces in England and Wales (including Metropolitan Police District and City of London)	127		43		
Police officers – male	58,865	98.1	109,490	90.8	186
– female	1,125	1.9	11,983	9.2	985
Total	59,990	(100.0)	120,573	(100.0)	(201)
Civilians* – clerical	–		20,622		
– technical	–		9,903		
– domestic	–		8,373		
– traffic wardens	–		4,860		
Total	3,881	(100.0)	43,258	(100.0)	(1,115)
Total strength of police service	63,871	(100.0)	164,331	(100.0)	(257)
Ratio of Police officers to population	1:713		1:411		

* Excluding Cadets, Special Constables and First Police Reserve, but including part-time staff, each of whom is counted as 0.5.

Sources: Report of HM Inspectors of Constabulary 1949; Report of HM Chief Inspector of Constabulary 1984.

end of the Second World War before the major changes in the service began.

Historical comparisons are bound to be imprecise, but the principal structural changes have been as follows:

1. The police service as a whole now involves a significantly larger number of people, and consequently resources, than it did at the end of the Second World War. The number of police officers has doubled and, with civilians, the service as a whole absorbs at least two and a half times the resources it did in 1949.

2. Although on the face of it we are much more heavily policed than before—a 75 per cent increase in police officers in relation to the population—on normal occasions much of this increase is illusory. As Martin and Wilson (1969) have shown the improvements in police terms of employment—shorter hours, more leave and less systematic overtime—have sharply reduced the number of hours of policing actually undertaken per officer. When allowance is also made for greatly increased training it can be concluded that about 50 per cent of the increased strength has been used up simply in offsetting improved conditions and better training.

3. Greatly increased specialisation has also been a feature of post-war changes, and this has led to increased efficiency in performing certain tasks, but it has correspondingly decreased the flexibility of the organisation. In effect it has removed significant numbers of officers from availability for ordinary patrolling duties. Considering all these changes together it seems that, on ordinary occasions, the number of patrol officers actually out and about, potentially meeting the public, probably does not much exceed those available in the less specialised forces of the past. Indeed, in a recent article Davies (1986) has shown that in London a 'relief' (or shift) of 40 officers is unlikely to deploy more than six on foot patrol, plus some of the three 'home beat' officers.

4. The table also shows a large absolute and proportional increase in the number of women police officers. They now comprise about 10 per cent of the uniformed force; relatively few are in the CID. The recruitment figures for 1984 showed that they formed an even higher proportion of recruits, averaging nearly 20 per cent outside London. The

Metropolitan police was found by the PSI survey to have operated an unofficial 10 per cent quota among recruits but, according to the Commissioner's Report for 1983 (p.20), this has since been abolished.

The consequences of the increase in the proportion of women remain to be seen. As with other occupations which have been resistant to the entry of women the general educational level of women recruits has been higher than that of male entrants. No doubt there will be wastage due to marriage and child-bearing, but in the longer term it would be surprising if the influx of women officers did not have some effect on styles of policing.

5. A particularly important change has been the increase in the size of individual police forces and the reduction in their number. Smallness has not been regarded as beautiful. Larger size has made specialisation and heavy capital investment in transport and communications easier, and it has enabled forces to police their new larger areas with little outside assistance. At the same time, however, it has made that assistance easier to organise when necessary. Finally, and perhaps most significant, it has given much greater status to Chief Constables and a new political potency to them and their Association.

CHANGES IN TECHNOLOGY

Martin and Wilson (1969) demonstrated how slowly the police service adapted to technological change before the 1960s. The first phase of major development began with motor vehicles. Investment in vehicles had been pretty static throughout the 1950s, and the prevailing concept of the police car was of a large vehicle equipped with radio and used for patrol duties, particularly with traffic. The change came about 1960 with the realisation that the heavy vehicles needed for traffic patrols were neither necessary nor appropriate for town work. Thus was born what came to be called the 'panda car', so named because of the striped paintwork adopted in some forces. There was a heavy investment in panda cars, partly as a result of the introduction of the scheme of patrolling known as Unit

Beat Policing which was devised in the 1960s.

Panda cars were cheap compared with traditional patrol vehicles, and in addition they did not need to be fitted with expensive radio equipment. This was because of the first real technological breakthrough to affect police work, the invention of the personal radio. Experiments were undertaken in a number of areas in the 1960s, but credit for the lead should probably be given to the Lancashire force whose Chief Constable, Sir Eric St Johnston, became HM Chief Inspector of Constabulary in 1967.

It took some time for the teething troubles of the personal radio to be overcome, but its implications were immense. For the first time the individual patrol officer could communicate with, and be contacted by, his supervisors and colleagues. He might be alone, but he was not out of touch. Supervisors were at last able to call on officers, and if necessary assemble them rapidly; officers needing help could summon it urgently. Some, such as Reiss and Bordua (1967, p. 49), have argued that this has tipped the balance of control within the police back from patrol officers to the management, that it has strengthened the bureaucracy, but the balance of opinion (Reiner, 1985), while recognising this, maintains that the handling of face-to-face encounters is still unavoidably at the discretion of the officer on the spot.

The gain to officers has been great—they can call for help and, perhaps most significant, anyone on the radio net is aware of what is going on, and can respond, thus making the job notably more exciting. The advantages to senior officers and to the public in such situations are less certain—reactions to calls for help are very difficult to control and over-reaction is common, while the ability to get rapid support may reduce the need for officers to develop their social skills to handle situations without recourse to the threat of overwhelming force. It is notable that policewomen, who are not able to handle situations in a 'macho' way, seem to develop higher levels of skill on such occasions.

The application of computers to police work came slightly later. However the possibilities were far-reaching, particularly in managerial terms and in access to records. Broadly speaking the combination of computers and radio communication has meant that the deployment of officers and vehicles can be monitored comprehensively, and more or less continuously, and the use made of resources can be reviewed as never before. The checking of the identities of suspected persons and vehicles has been revolutionised, with immediate reference to lists of wanted people and stolen vehicles. Provided such lists and facilities are used legitimately the advantages are great and obvious.

The consequences of the move to a more technologically sophisticated police have been mixed. On the one hand improved transport and communications have made it possible to deploy many more officers more rapidly than ever before if needed to maintain public order. Indeed it is probably only in major crises that the increased nominal strength of the service will be reflected in the numbers actually on duty. At a lower level of activity officers on routine patrol can be directed where needed, improving response times, while the ability to run computer checks on individuals and vehicles has probably enhanced the likelihood that 'stops' will identify those 'wanted' for one reason or another. On the other hand, police officers in cars are inevitably in less close contact with the public, and their detailed knowledge of local people is likely to suffer. If public confidence in the police depends on local contact, then having fewer officers on foot may affect how the public feel about the service though, as research has shown, it is unlikely to make much difference to the volume of crime (Clarke and Hough, 1984).

THE POLICE SUB-CULTURE

The fact that so much police work involves officers using their individual discretion makes it vital to understand what may influence the exercise of that discretion. In theory, discretion is limited by the law and the orders of the senior management of the service, but it is abundantly clear that patrol officers prize their autonomy and go to considerable lengths to maintain it. The law is not enforced by police officers acting as automata, but by men and women with their own values who are also deeply conscious of the need to fit in with, and be accepted by, their working colleagues. Indeed solutions to the problems of the service can only be discussed adequately on the basis of a thorough understanding of the police sub-culture. Police officers themselves are very well aware of this, and the author vividly recalls how, when doing research on the police in the 1960s, he kept being asked: 'Is it possible for an outsider to understand the police mind?' Fortunately, thanks to many sociologists, including in this country Banton (1964), Cain (1973), Chatterton (1979), Holdaway (1977 and 1983), the Policy Studies Institute (1983) and Reiner (1978 and 1985), to name only some, it is possible to get a very good idea of what tends to preoccupy 'the police mind'. Reiner's latest book provides a neat summary, though much of the best evidence is contained in his earlier study, *The Blue-Coated Worker*. The description that follows is an amalgam drawn from all these sources flavoured with a little of the author's own observations.

Much of the police officer's working life touches on authority and deference. The patrolling officer is at the lowest level of a clearly-defined hierarchy, yet in dealings with the public the authority of the office of constable must be maintained at all times. The officer has to be something of a chameleon, always aware that relationships with superiors or the public may erupt unpredictably into 'trouble'. The service is characterised by meticulously thorough administration and by a discipline which at best is firm and at worst, as Mark has described, little short of petty tyranny. All too often it has been shown to be rule-bound in an insensitive and unimaginative way. The officer, therefore, must, as far as possible, avoid any report or other information going to his superiors in a form which might in some way 'bounce'—hence the tendency to report events prosaically and to play contentious issues with a dead bat. The flow of information upwards must be filtered and rationed.

It follows from this that the only really easy relationships are with those of the same rank, and the confidences of such colleagues have to be strictly respected. Above all nothing must be done to land a colleague in trouble; the uncertainties of the job are such that you never know when their support might be vital. Reciprocal obligations are fundamental, hence the golden rule, solidarity at all times.

Solidarity is enhanced by the sense of being a group apart. More than most occupations the police are cut off from their contemporaries by their hours of work and the need to avoid close social involvement with people they may come up against in the job. Officers have to move with the job, young officers tend to live in police housing, and it quickly becomes easier to relax in police company where the strains of the job can be eased and there is less need to be careful about what one says.

People working in a tight-knit group naturally develop a shared view of the world, and this is particularly true of the police; handling people and situations is crucial to their craft. The police view tends to be pessimistic, if not cynical. This is not surprising, for the police so often see people behaving at their worst that they are constantly aware of human failure and folly. Along with this goes a highly developed sense of suspicion. The officer always has to avoid being caught out, to be alert for signs of trouble or danger, and to be aware that people may have something to hide. It becomes very difficult to switch off this attitude and, indeed, to behave like a civilian at anytime, as most police families will testify (Young, 1984; Reiner, 1985).

The police sub-culture tends to encourage a very 'macho' attitude to life. Officers hold strongly that 'real police work' is about 'thief-taking' and 'fighting crime', an attitude encouraged by TV, fiction and the rhetoric of politicians. They have mostly joined to be part of a 'man's world', so that it is not surprising to find much heavy drinking, not to mention a rather crude and denigrating attitude towards women. The PSI report (admittedly based on what may be the extreme case of the Metropolitan Police), describes both particularly vividly and exposes the effects of the drinking culture among CID officers, and the general unwillingness of male officers to accept that women could do the job adequately. However, this was clearly because they saw the use of force as a major part of the job, sometimes by their aggressive style provoking 'the violent behaviour which, they said, only they as men could deal with' (PSI, 1985, p. 377). Irrespective of the actual behaviour of officers, in the Met. the norm was 'to talk about violence as something interesting and exciting, to exaggerate the extent and frequency of violent incidents in police work and to tell tall stories about one's own violent exploits' (ibid., p. 371).

The reality of the job does not often live up to these myths. Patrol work is usually dull and devoid of incident, so officers are always ready to respond where there is any prospect of action; hence the over-response to calls for assistance and the keeness to join in any chases that might take place. Whatever the ideals of senior officers it should never be forgotten that the majority of officers are young men attracted by the action involved in the job, and not at all averse to getting into a scrap from time to time. Indeed, Cain illustrated this with a story of how a 'patch' was made peaceful by careful patrolling—a result which some officers described as having 'spoiled' it by removing the opportunities for action (Cain, 1973, p. 65). Reiner, too, found that police officers tended to take a narrow view of the job, attributing low value to the service activities which constitute much of their contact with the public and which, paradoxically, have such an influence on public support for the police.

Despite the deviations from respectability allowed in the macho elements of the sub-culture, the police service and police officers tend to conservatism—certainly in the non-political sense and possibly politically too. The police service ensures its members at very least an upper working-class status and offers considerable scope for social mobility. Increases in pay have now put constables into the same bracket as many school teachers, while superintendents and above are in the top 2 per cent of the population in terms of earnings. The society whose order the police are meant to maintain gives them every incentive to support the status quo.

Perhaps a by-product of its conservatism is the generally pragmatic attitude of police officers and of the service. The technical innovations of the last 20 years have been exceptional. The more established tradition has been one of rather slavish efficiency in carrying out established procedures; senior officers such as Sir Kenneth Newman who produce elaborate statements of policy are exceptional. Even Sir Robert Mark's impact on the Metropolitan Police was mainly to make it rather more like a provincial force than to introduce a new philosophy. The one major attempt to develop a new method of policing—Unit Beat Policing—was to a large extent sabotaged by the rank and file, who seized upon the opportunity it gave for riding around in cars while downgrading its emphasis on getting to know the area and its people and fostering good relations with them.

It also follows from the identification of the police with the existing social order that they are not particularly sympathetic to, and indeed often do not understand, people or groups who appear to reject its values. Their working philosophy allows for a certain amount of peaceful dissent, but questions of civil liberties and the position of deviant groups are treated primarily in terms of whether they threaten police control. When this concern for order is linked with the incredulity, contempt and even detestation felt for the deliberately deviant, they can react with what to dispassionate observers seems totally disproportionate force. A recent example was the series of attempts to prevent a 'hippie convoy' from holding a midsummer festival at Stonehenge in 1985 and 1986. The vehemence of the reactions to this bizarre group of nonconformists betrayed officers of all ranks into behaviour or comments greatly at variance with the official image of a calm and disciplined body concerned only with the maintenance of public order. In 1985 police discipline cracked; in 1986, under the eyes of press and television it held, but the resources used were immense in relation to the threat to public order. It was as if the hippies struck at a raw nerve in the police psyche.

The extreme case of the difficulties of dealing with minorities is that provided by non-white groups. It is not easy to discuss in a short space because there are grounds for believing that attitudes differ between parts of the country. However from the police literature as a whole an early conclusion, quoted by Reiner, sums up the position as follows: 'Are policemen prejudiced? The answer is yes, but only slightly more so than the community as a whole. Policemen reflect the dominant attitudes of the majority people towards minorities' (Bayley and Mendelsohn, 1968, quoted in Reiner, 1985, p. 100).

It seems clear from the literature that police in England and Wales tend to express racist attitudes in private, but this does not necessarily show itself in actual encounters with the public.

Tuck and Southgate's research in Manchester (1981) showed levels of satisfaction with the police among black people as quite high, though slightly lower than the level for white people. Their main complaint was of being treated with less respect than they should have been—a finding which, though regrettable, was not so damaging as actual misbehaviour would have been. The position in London, however, may well be worse. It seems clear that, even if officers behaved correctly in the presence of researchers (which was perhaps to be expected) racist attitudes can erupt in ways that make one fear for the future. There is now an increasing series of reported incidents where officers' prejudices seem to have overflowed in quite indefensible behaviour.

At the time of writing the most recent example was of an occasion in 1983 when some officers in the crews of three police vans in North London jumped out and assaulted a racially mixed group of five youths, two of whom subsequently needed hospital treatment. They later received substantial sums in compensation from the police. Naturally there was a complaint but in February 1986, two and a half years later, the Police Complaints Authority had to issue a statement admitting that it had been unable to identify the officers involved (and hence institute proceedings) because, as the chairman later said in a letter to *The Guardian*, (7 February 1986): 'eight out of the twenty-four officers who were in the vicinity of the incident were lying'. The sinister, unlawful side of group loyalty was thus showing itself. In the event Scotland Yard was so galvanised by the public outcry at this ineffective inquiry that it set up a further investigation, with a secret telephone line, and obtained sufficient evidence to enable prosecutions to be brought.

In conclusion, the police sub-culture may be summarised as being a potent influence on the policing we experience. It is a sub-culture which dominates the lives of the lower ranks, though curiously, more senior officers seem to be able to discuss policy almost as if it didn't exist. It is suffused with a view of the police task which is so much at variance with what most patrol officers actually do, and indeed with the main tasks of the service, as to justify being called a myth. Unfortunately this myth is not oriented towards relations with the public or towards many of the matters which cause concern to the public. The focal concerns of most male officers centre on maintaining control in all encounters with the public, particularly those in certain 'inferior' categories who tend to be viewed as police 'property'. Work that does not fit the police myth of law enforcement and crime fighting is frequently described as 'rubbish'. Much of the job is boring, hence the enthusiasm for any sort of action and, indeed, for violent confrontions from time to time. A prime craft skill is to distinguish between people and to handle them accordingly in order to maintain the officer's authority. This, coupled with a degree of racial prejudice, is liable to lead to conflict in encounters with minority or deviant groups who appear to challenge the police view of the world.

KEY PROBLEMS OF POLICING

Crime

Although much of the rhetoric of policing is about crime, particularly its detection, this emphasis is a distortion both of history and current facts. The modern police forces of England and Wales were set up to maintain public order and to *prevent* crime in a general way by patrolling. The contemporary emphasis on detection is an aspect of the general myth about policing already referred to. The historic aim was crystallised in the famous instructions to the Metropolitan Police formulated in 1829: 'It should be understood at the outset, that the object to be attained is the prevention of crime' (Critchley, 1967, p. 52). Indeed it is clear from subsequent research that the fundamental task actually undertaken by the police is the maintenance of public order rather than law enforcement, leave alone the detection of crime (Reiner, 1985, pp. 111–22).

The evidence is that the police find it difficult to face two of the most important facts about their work. The first is that a high proportion of their time is spent on what they do not define as 'real' police work, particularly on those calls for service which are so much appreciated by the public. The second is that the vast majority of crimes that are cleared up are solved because of information given by the public. The detection rate for crimes where there is no such lead is typically very low.

Clear-up rates for some very serious crimes against the person (including homicide) can be high, but this is usually so because either the offender's identity is easy to establish or police effort has been on an astronomical scale. Even immense effort may be unproductive—the celebrated 'Yorkshire Ripper' whose identity was sought in a massive inquiry (during which he was interviewed by police more than once) was finally caught thanks to an alert patrol officer not involved in the inquiry. Normally, therefore, the police can do little to prevent crime by detection, though specially directed efforts may have some effect (Clark and Hough 1984, p. 9). It is notable that Sir Kenneth Newman in his Report for 1983 produced a lengthy analysis of the police task and the problems of dealing with crime which was essentially based on similar reasoning (Commissioner of Police for the Metropolis, 1984, Ch. 1).

Corruption
Britain has, on the whole, been fortunate in that the tradition of incorruptibility in public life has applied in large measure to the police. The obvious exception has been the criminal investigation departments, particularly in large cities where major crimes are attempted. Here the profits of crime are such that the bribing of police officers can become a source of immunity from effective law enforcement. Sir Robert Mark (1978) has graphically described the nature of the problem which he made major attempts to solve, but which may well be endemic in large, in-bred detective forces. With eternal vigilance, it may be kept in check, but it seems unlikely that it can be eliminated completely. Sir Robert and his successors deserve great credit for trying, but until detective work is microscopically supervised by incorruptible senior officers the problem seems unlikely to be completely solved.

Terrorism
The prevention of terrorism and the detection of terrorists has for police in Britain the great advantage of being warmly approved by the great majority of the public. Provided the

political process ensures the proper representation of minorities there is no mandate for political violence in this country. The protection of public figures on ceremonial occasions seems to be successful, but with no knowledge of the seriousness of the threat success is difficult to measure. Detection is more difficult than in most homicides because of the lack of obvious suspects and the planned nature of the operations. Its effectiveness depends on a blend of luck and the use of vast resources, with the principal danger being that the pressure to achieve results may lead to the use of illegal methods and dubious prosecutions. Likewise preventive measures may restrict public freedom to an unacceptable degree. Terrorism is as much a challenge to the police sense of proportion as to their technical efficiency. However, in an increasingly dangerous world it is a form of 'real policing' which is preferable to some of the other manifestations of the more macho side of police activity.

Patrolling and public relations
Despite the actual increases in police numbers, at almost all times in the last 35 years the police have complained of shortages of manpower, particularly for beat patrols. This has partly been due to the fact that although the officer 'on the beat' is an important part of the police image, and of police mythology, in practice it is unpopular as a job, and managers of the service usually fill all other posts first. Often it has the lowest priority. Various attempts have been made to overcome the shortage of beat patrol officers, usually by putting them in cars and requiring them to cover larger areas, helped by better mobility and communications. This process was encouraged by a phase in police thinking, influenced by operational research, which emphasised rapid responses to calls for assistance. Response times are easily measured, so paying attention to them was one way of demonstrating a type of effectiveness. In the late 1960s this was codified into the system of Unit Beat Policing which has, however, theoretically gone out of fashion. Nevertheless Unit Beat Policing tried to solve certain problems, and the outcome was instructive.

It tried to solve three problems: boredom, lack of mobility and the need for local knowledge and contacts. The panda car's contribution to mobility was obvious and successful. The scheme also recognised that much patrolling is uneventful and boring, and it tried to deal with this by stressing the opportunities for gathering 'criminal intelligence', i.e. information about the location and way of life of known or suspected criminals, and about suspicious events. Such information was to be gathered informally by all officers, but particularly by the 'neighbourhood beat' officer who had the task of getting to know his area and its inhabitants by patrolling almost as he felt best. The criminal intelligence in a subdivision would be assembled in a repository of local knowledge by an officer known as the 'collator'.

The scheme has been officially disavowed because it led to so few officers being on foot. Cars were popular with officers because of the protection from the weather and the mobility which greatly increased the chances of excitement by joining in chases and responding to calls for assistance. However they inevitably reduced face-to-face contact with the public, and they also gave far more scope for a 'macho' attitude which was apt to alienate the public and, at its worst, led to some deplorable instances of insensitive and bullying behaviour. The attitudes to which it could give rise have been well depicted by Holdaway (1977 and 1983) and by the Policy Studies Institute (1983).

The problems of public relations which were aggravated by macho motorised policing have been tackled by Chief Officers by attempting to reassert the traditional values associated with patrolling on foot or bicycle. The phrase 'Community Policing' has been much used in this context and its importance was endorsed by Lord Scarman (1981, p. 88), when he referred to it as meaning 'policing with the active consent and support of the community ... too important a concept to be treated as a slogan'. Perhaps the most celebrated recent exponent of this emphasis was John Alderson (1979) then Chief Constable of Devon and Cornwall. His interpretation involved a greater degree of police initiative in fostering police–public relations than many of his colleagues would have favoured, but since Scarman the general case has been accepted even if local applications have varied in their methods and, above all, in their enthusiasm. It is noteworthy that the Commissioner of the Metropolitan Police devoted a major section of his *Report* for 1983 to stressing the need to adopt a community policing model in contrast to the 'crime control model' of aggressive policing (of which his own force had provided some of the more notable and least happy examples in previous years).

It remains to be seen how these attempts to reinforce what is, after all, the central principle of British policing, work in practice. What is required is not merely good public relations at relatively senior levels, but better supervision at lower levels. In a curious way the capacity to assemble a number of officers quickly to deal with one or two individuals has effects rather similar to those described by Alderson in relation to arming the police which:

changes personality by inducing a feeling of dominance and power in the minds of those concerned. In such conditions ... it is likely that the police will become more assertive, even aggressive, as they rely less and less on public respect for their safety and more and more on their own potential for the solution by force. (Alderson, 1979, p. 25)

Public order

The most severe tests faced by the police service in England and Wales have concerned the maintenance of public order. They developed in two main types of situation—large-scale industrial conflicts, and anti-police riots with a strong racial element involved. Given the right predisposing context the mishandling of minor patrol incidents, or searches of property, can erupt into large scale disorder. It is an unhappy fact that the 1980s have seen more riots, mainly racial, than at any time in the last 50 years. It has been particularly shocking because of the contrast with the generally peaceful nature of post-war life and the impact of seeing riot and destruction on national television. (In fact, Britain has a history of social disturbances going back hundreds of years, but they were never televised and politicians have conveniently tended to forget them.)

The key document on the subject, and the one which most directly attempted to influence policy was Lord Scarman's Report on *The Brixton Disorders 10–12 April 1981* (Scarman, 1981). It was the immediate governmental response, carried out rapidly and almost single-handed. It invites comparison with the classic Kerner Report (*Report of the National Advisory Commission on Civil Disorders*, 1968), ordered by President Lyndon B. Johnson following widespread rioting in the United States in 1967. However the Kerner inquiry was on a vast scale involving not only the Commissioners but a staff of nearly a hundred, not to mention consultants, contractors and advisers of whom an incomplete list ran to over 170 including many distinguished academics in law and the social sciences. As a result the Report made a major contribution to understanding the history, politics and sociology of the disorders in a way which Scarman could not possibly attempt. It is clear that Scarman had it very much in mind during his inquiry, and it is notable how relevant the Kerner analysis is to the British situation, albeit with appropriate qualifications due to the different history of immigration in Britain and the smaller proportion of the population constituted by non-whites.

The essence of the inner city riots in England has been that minor incidents have occurred in the policing of communities smouldering with resentment at the discriminatory treatment of young people, mostly but not entirely black. Often this resentment had been fuelled by what was called 'hard policing' involving the stopping and searching of many young people in what was felt to be a racist and harassing way. The incidents, whatever they were, suddenly triggered outbursts of hostility and riots began which often spread over several days, leading to major destruction and some loss of life (fortunately small).

Explanations varied. The government emphasised the looting and destruction involved and claimed the riots were simply large-scale criminal acts. Others stressed their roots of anger and frustration about unemployment and social conditions, aggravated by 'unimaginative and inflexible policing' to use Lord Scarman's shorthand description. Subsequent events have run fairly true to the pattern discerned by Kerner. The police, encouraged by a government elected on a law and order ticket, have sought the comfort of more and more technology—special clothing, shields, CS gas and, as yet unused, water cannon and what are euphemistically termed 'baton rounds' (plastic, but potentially lethal, bullets).

In the US this increase in the police armoury was also accompanied by major social programmes which did much to reduce social tension. This was not so much a matter of improving physical conditions as of improving social mobility for blacks and, above all, integrating them into the mainstream of political life. Blacks duly became mayors of several major American cities, and their entry to the political scene gave hope and protection to the disadvantaged. Britain lags far behind, with its black population limited by its small size and educational disadvantages, and with only minimal political weight. A wise government will surely do all it can to break down the sense of alienation and encourage the integration of ethnic groups so that they can feel they have a political voice.

The policing of such riots is a major problem for senior officers. They have to assemble men, appraise the situation and control whatever action is taken. Tempers are high, people are scared, rumour is rife and all the resentments and prejudices of both sides are on the boil—no wonder that in Brixton there were actions described by Lord Scarman as 'unworthy of a disciplined force'. 'Such behaviour', as he said, 'despite extenuating circumstances, must be stopped' (p. 70). Unfortunately the history of riots shows that it is very difficult, if not impossible, for senior officers to avoid losing control and to prevent the trading of violence and insults which makes things worse.

By comparison with the spontaneity of inner-city riots the policing of major industrial disputes, such as the miners' strike of 1984–85, tends to be a ritual confrontation which erupts into violence only occasionally. Most strikes are policed relatively peacefully, particularly when they concern local issues (Kahn *et al.*, 1983, Ch. 5), though if disputes are protracted there is a danger that the long build-up of tension can lead to pitched battles which some police and strikers seem to enjoy. There is, however, a second type of strike where the stakes are wider, and as much political as industrial, and in these the impartiality of the police is compromised by the overt political support which they receive—the miners' strike of 1984–85 being the extreme example.

The policing of both industrial and racial disputes in the 1980s has undergone a radical change from the relatively peaceful methods of the previous 40 years. The riot gear developed after 1981 seems to have been used in conjunction with colonial style policing methods in the later miners' strike and the Wapping picketing of Times Newspapers. When combined with what appear to be charges by mounted police the action has become essentially military, designed to show who has the greater force and thus intimidate protesters.

Such paramilitary policing may be successful in dispersing crowds, but as law enforcement its achievements have at best been limited and at worst counterproductive. A celebrated incident at Orgreave led to the prosecution of a large number of miners which failed ignominiously when it came to court. It was notable that during the miners' strike the most abrasive incidents were with police brought in from outside forces, and that local officers often tried to calm situations, being mindful of the need to resume normal policing after the strike.

However the greatest danger to the police is that their paramilitary operations come to be seen not as the traditional neutral 'holding of the ring' between the parties to the dispute, but active intervention on one side. This is particularly so in strikes where the government has clearly taken sides and the police have to support them. If the ensuing incidents allow officers to indulge their personal prejudices—political or racial—then police impartiality may be compromised for years to come.

Accountability and serving the community

Underlying all the problems discussed so far in this chapter is the fundamental issue of accountability and how the community is best to be served. The years of the Thatcher government have both strengthened and weakened the police. There are more of them, paid more than ever before, and formed into more mobile, better equipped forces. Yet corruption, technological change and political identification have weakened their moral standing. The conviction, dismissal or premature resignation of nearly a thousand Metropolitan officers in ten years has confirmed beyond all possible doubt that the police, particularly detectives, can be corrupt. Overforceful behaviour in riots, demonstrations and in street encounters has shown how close to the surface lie passions and prejudices shared with many in the community but totally unbecoming an officer of the law.

High-technology, too, has created a distance between the police who have it, and citizens who do not. Riot gear may protect policemen, but it also sharply differentiates them from the rest of the community. It is less easy to see them as fellow citizens in uniform. The enthusiasm of the Home Office and Chief Constables for military weapons and techniques is surely mistaken, for the use of weapons known to be lethal will rapidly undo the work of their predecessors who, since 1829, strove to achieve public order by the minimal use of force.

The machinery of accountability—to Police Authorities in the provinces and to the Home Office in the metropolis—is less important than it should be, for the Police Act 1964 was ambiguous about their powers. At present (1986) the Home Office is tending to side with Chief Constables against the attempts of Police Authorities to curb some of their enthusiasm for high-tech policing. This is understandable with a 'law and order' government, but the precedent could easily turn sour with a change of government. Sir Robert Mark's skilful use of publicity, with its mainly well-chosen and popular targets—police corruption and the IRA—has been a misleading example to other Chief Officers without his touch and, sometimes, with views less in the mainstream of public opinion. It is not easy for those at the top of large hierarchical organisations to get frank advice, particularly if they take a strongly moralising attitude to the job. Their sensitivity to social and political situations may therefore be impaired, thus increasing the risk of blunders in delicate situations. Perhaps the most prudent principle for those with power over other citizens is to be cautious in exercising it.

Policing—the use of public power to settle disputes between citizens—can never be a completely uncontroversial subject, but if the balance between police and citizen is to be restored and maintained the modern officer must still heed the instructions so forcefully expressed in 1829:

He [the constable] will be civil and obliging to all people of every rank and class.

He must be particularly cautious not to interfere idly or unnecessarily in order to make a display of his authority ... particular care is to be taken that the constables of the police do not form false notions of their duties and powers. (Critchley, 1967, p. 53)

10 Education

Eric Briggs

INTRODUCTION

The spirit of universalism that dominated social policy formulation after the Second World War was relevant, for most of the population, in the provision of free medical treatment and education. In education, the academically gifted were to be offered the opportunity to fulfill their potential within the state system, regardless of family income. The result of this was a rapid expansion in government provision of resources to this sector; an increase which had to accommodate not only the 'bulge' in the birth rate immediately after the Second World War, but also the heightened expectations of parents and pupils who, faced with a rapidly expanding economy in the 1950s, saw new rewards from educational achievement. Both major parties managed to meet this new demand, and there developed a situation of political 'consensus' regarding education: both parties accepted the expansion of education provision as a major part of their domestic policies. Certainly the education system, outwardly at least, gave the appearance of being flexible in relation to increased demand. In the 1950s more schools were built, more teachers trained; in the 1960s more universities and polytechnics were created as the demand worked through the system.

However, the goals of the policy-makers of 1944 began, as the 1950s progressed, to produce results different from those they intended. Initially, the changes of 1944 had been aimed at reducing class differentials in education: academic ability was to be the sole criterion for success, and all children were to have an equal chance to gain this success. However, the failure to provide sufficient resources for secondary modern and technical schools to enable them to compete with grammar schools, resulted in the latter's pre-war eminence remaining unchallenged. While the 11+ examination efficiently channelled the apparently most able pupils to them, research began to show that the most able tended to come from middle and upper middle-class homes. With places in higher education becoming more in demand, grammar schools became increasingly efficient at processing pupils through the rationing mechanisms of O and A level examinations. The system became increasingly geared to the production of an intellectual elite. Little thought was given to what this elite might contribute to the economy; it was simply assumed that a more educated workforce would result in greater efficiency and increased production. The rapidly expanding economy of the 1950s seemed to prove this connection, while low levels of unemployment suggested that even those with no formal educational qualifications were being absorbed into the labour market.

By 1964 academic research had made the defects of this highly selective system apparent—in particular the loss of able pupils through premature selection procedures and the self-fulfilling prophecy effect thought to occur in secondary modern schools. In Labour's election manifesto for 1964 a radical change in education policy was promised. Comprehensive secondary schooling was introduced by means of a DES circular in 1966. While Labour's intention was undoubtedly to reduce class inequalities, a broadening of the curriculum in these schools was seen as a first step to improving the supply of manpower to industry.

Criticism of the educational system came from various sources, and grew with the increasing economic troubles of the 1970s. High inflation, and a greater awareness that British industry was falling behind its competitors, led to a growing uncertainty about the role of the education system, especially in relation to economic recovery, and to the vast sums being spent on education by central government. In politics, this uncertainty surfaced in 1976 when the then Prime Minister,

James Callaghan, launched the 'great debate' about education. Callaghan argued that the educational system was failing to meet the needs of an economy which increasingly demanded a more flexible and technical workforce. While the great debate never really got off the ground, Labour began a searching examination of government spending on education and managed to reduce the percentage of the GNP allocated to this from 6.9 in 1975 to 4.8 in 1979. The university sector, in particular, was thought to be too expensive, and in some respects irrelevant to the demands of an increasingly technological economy.

The election of a Conservative government in 1979, on a manifesto of a reduction in public spending, was unlikely to increase the share of public expenditure allocated to education: indeed, the fall in the birth rate that had taken place in the late 1960s, and early 1970s, indicated to the Conservatives that education was an area where expenditure could be reduced with obvious legitimacy. Empty places in classrooms were seen quite simply in terms of wasted expenditure. However, the educational system had a number of characteristics that made contraction more difficult to achieve than the expansion of the 1950s and 1960s or the trimming of the mid-1970s.

When compared with other centrally funded services education is manpower intensive. The main component of the service—teachers—have contracts of employment with local authorities that virtually ensure employment for life. Thus while expansion was easy to achieve, contraction—especially where it might result in reductions of manpower—is a far more difficult problem. Manning also to an extent reflects the statutory commitments imposed on local authorities by central government through legislation. Again, reduction here would be difficult to achieve.

A further hindrance to change in the system was the development of a system of decision-making at various levels which gave central and local government limited scope for manoeuvre in relation to policy changes. Curriculum development and the control of teaching are vital factors in the allocation of resources in schools. Yet the inputs to change come from various levels—local authorities, governors, heads of department, teachers and parents—all of whom can have different values and some authority to pursue policies based on these values. A similar situation exists in some sectors of higher education, such as polytechnics and colleges of further education, where diverse sources of funding, and academic control, have made policy changes from central government difficult to achieve. As a partial recognition of this situation, it has been a characteristic of policy-making in this area that changes on education grounds have by and large, been brought about by a process of consultation between interested parties.

In the first budget of the new government the Rate Support Grant (RSG) to local authorities was cut by £300 million, and since one half of the RSG is allocated for expenditure on education, the implications for local policies were clear. Coping with reduced funding was going to present local authorities with a fundamental challenge in terms of re-tailoring their provisions. Some relief was offered in the 1980 Education Act which removed some statutory requirements such as the provision of school meals and milk, and indeed the then Secretary of State for Education believed that 80 per cent of economies could be found in these areas. Thus there was a reduction of £127 million on spending in 1981–82 in these two areas. A further practical problem faced by some authorities was the fact that the birth rate had not shrunk evenly throughout their area. Some inner city areas suffered a greater fall than other parts of local areas, posing problems of redeployment of staff and the closing of some schools. Reductions in staff levels have been achieved—26,400 between 1979 and 1983—but only with difficulty and any further shrinkage can only be ensured by new powers being given to authorities, especially in relation to compulsory redundancies. But this financial challenge to local authorities should not mask the fact that the educational system has been faced with other more general problems for a number of years, some of which will now be outlined.

EDUCATIONAL STANDARDS

It has been widely argued that academic standards in schools have been falling in recent years. For many, the rot began to set in with the introduction of comprehensive schools in 1966; it has been argued that this resulted in a levelling down of academic standards for the majority of school children rather than raising standards for those who were offered least by the previous system. But schools have been faced with an increasingly complex task. Rising levels of juvenile unemployment in the 1970s and 1980s have led many pupils to doubt the value of formal educational qualifications. In some areas of the country even school-leavers with qualifications are faced with the prospect of indefinite unemployment. Nevertheless, over the 20-year period 1963/83 the standards attained by pupils who actually achieved examination success have improved, albeit only slightly. The percentage achieving two or more A levels, for example, has increased from 11 to 15 per cent, while the number achieving five or more O level grades of C or better (or the equivalent at CSE) has risen from 21 to 27 per cent (DES, 1985a).

Of more importance however, is the reverse of the coin: 38 per cent of school-leavers in 1983 achieved less than five O levels and just over 10 per cent left school with no qualifications whatsoever. Reductions in resources for teaching have resulted in increasing practical difficulties for teachers. The sharing of books and other resources has undoubtedly complicated the situation of many schools and teachers. Further, an increasing number of pupils come from broken homes, or from domestic situations where both parents have jobs and little time to control and stimulate their children. Factors such as these make effective teaching a more demanding, and difficult, goal.

That standards must be raised has been a challenge recognised by politicians of every shade. Yet, committed to a policy of reducing public expenditure, the Conservative Party's approach contained a basic contradiction—arguing on the one hand that standards in schools must be improved, and ensuring on the other that fewer resources were devoted to achieving this aim. This challenge of standards in schools was recognised by Sir Keith Joseph in a speech to the North of England Education Conference in January 1984. Arguing for a complete reappraisal of the school curriculum Sir Keith outlined four criteria that must be met by schools in the future—breadth, relevance, differentiation and balance. To achieve this the system of examination at sixteen was to be replaced with a new nationally uniform examination, the GCSE. In fact the old system had been in need of an overhaul for some time. Its critics had claimed that 'O' levels and CSEs were not a measure of ability, only a rank ordering of achievement, that they had little relevance to industry, and were wasteful through duplication. The new examination would have a strong emphasis on practical skills and the application of knowledge rather than the recall of fact. Since the candidates would be graded against a set of predetermined standards, the competitive elements of the existing system would be removed. Grades achieved would be an indication of what a candidate has achieved in terms of skills, knowledge and understanding. There would be a system of differentiation between candidates and also a greater emphasis on course work in the final assessment. The advantages could be great; a greater relevance for all pupils, stress on achievement and skill, a spur for pupil motivation and, perhaps most importantly, greater public awareness of what goes on in schools. Through this it is hoped that 80–90 per cent will be able to reach the level considered average—a CSE grade 4 pass. For brighter pupils, an AS level would be introduced in 1989 which would be at 'A' but only half a syllabus—basically intended to reduce over-specialisation at this level. At the time of writing there are serious problems concerning central government's level of funding for the new examinations, and the training of teachers for the syllabuses (*New Society*, 1986).

However, the revamping of the examination system has not been the only approach to standards in schools; parents have been given a crucial role. Since 1980 schools have had to publish annual examination results, enabling parents to have visible criteria on which to base their choice of school for their children, which in a time of falling rolls could prove a powerful impetus to improving standards. Parents were also given the chance of being elected as governors of schools by fellow parents, a move that will have a variable impact according to the social class composition of the school and surrounding area. Also, the Education Act 1986 has increased governors' powers in relation to schools, even to the point of enabling them to draw up their own curriculum policy for their school. Increased parental involvement raises another important issue: as state funding for schools has been reduced the relative importance of funds raised by parents' associations has increased. It is already clear that in some middle-class areas parents' associations, through fund-raising activities, and the organisation of covenants, are providing schools with significant sums of money. In other areas this is not the case, thus raising the spectre of a two-tier system of state provision. It should also be noted that middle-class interest in their children's schooling has also had the effect of turning many parents away from the state system. The 1986 Independent Schools Information Service Census reported that demand for private education rose by 1.2 per cent, the largest increase for over five years; however demand for non-boarding schools rose by over 4 per cent. Research by Fox (1985) has shown that nearly a third of fathers of children privately educated come from middle- and not upper middle-class homes; the appeal of private education seems to be broadening.

One other area of challenge in education relevant to educational standards requires attention—the impact of heavy concentrations of ethnic minorities in schools. Ethnic minority pupils present schools with a number of problems. A few are new to the country and speak no English, while others come from homes where the principal language spoken is not English. Their very physical concentration, often in the most deprived inner city areas, means that schools can have over 25 per cent of school entrants born to women from the New Commonwealth and Pakistan (OPCS, 1977). Financial support is available under section 11 of the Local Government Act 1966, and government has embarked on a policy of attempting to encourage potential teachers from ethnic minorities to enter the teaching profession and work in areas with a high minority population. However the scale of the problem is immense and in a situation of scarce resources is one that must have an impact on all pupils in State schools.

THE TEACHING PROFESSION

A recent report by Her Majesty's Inspectorate was led to comment that the quality of work in classrooms was being adversely affected by the quality of the teaching in roughly 30 per cent of all lessons they observed. Many factors determined teaching quality including some concerned with the individual personality of the teacher (see DES, 1986) but one element common to most serving teachers is that they have undergone a teacher training course in a recognised college/university. In 1983 a White Paper, *Teacher Quality* outlined standards that teacher training courses must meet if they are to be recognised. These begin with a far more rigorous selection procedure for potential teachers; the aim is that all teachers will have obtained a degree before starting their careers. Other criteria include the completion of successful teaching practice by students, especially in relation to teaching methods; the completion of at least two years of study of the main subject to be taught and, perhaps most importantly, evidence that those who are training student teachers have themselves undertaken a period of successful teaching. To ensure a tightening-up of standards the Inspectorate is carrying out a review of teacher training courses and the government has set up a Council for the Assessment of Teacher Education to monitor courses and advise the government on those which may, or may not, be approved. Once qualified, the training process is to be continued by an expanded in-service training programme, which the present government intends to fund through specific grants to LEAs and, if necessary, to enforce through legislation.

One further factor was discussed at some length by the HMI: the mismatching of teachers' qualifications and experience with the teaching that they were expected to perform. About 13 per cent of classes observed were adversely affected by this: but of all classes considered unsatisfactory one third suffered from mismatching. While a number of authorities have adopted staffing policies directly linked to a defined curriculum, the HMI report an increase in mismatching in one eighth of the authorities visited in the previous twelve months. The results of this in schools included subjects deleted from the curriculum, teaching taking place after school hours, classes grouped, and remedial teaching severely reduced. It was often the case that the less able pupil was affected most by this problem (DES, 1986).

A major contributory factor to this situation has been the difficulty in recruiting sufficient specialist teachers in specific areas. A comparison of unfilled vacancies from 73 authorities in September 1985 showed not only a 50 per cent increase over the previous twelve months, but also that mathematics, sciences, craft design technology and English were the main subject-areas affected. Nationally this problem is going to get worse; applications for post-graduate teacher training in mathematics in March 1985 were only two-thirds of those likely to be required—and this was one quarter down on the previous year.

Indeed teaching as a career for graduates from all disciplines has become increasingly less popular. The public perception of the status of teachers has never been consistent. While the public has always found much to praise about the teaching profession, it has also found much to blame in it as well. Part of the problem stems from teachers themselves in that they have conceived of themselves as being part of a low-status profession. Attacks on educational standards in schools have invariably been seen as attacks on teachers themselves, and their own lack of control over their 'professional qualifications' has, in comparison with other professions such as medicine, seemed to reduce them to semi-professional status. However by the 1980s other more specific factors were having an impact on recruitment. First and foremost was salaries. The last time teachers' salaries were brought into line with equivalent occupations was the Houghton award of 1974. Since then salary differentials have widened, especially for graduates in science, technology and computing for which industry has a buoyant demand. In 1986 the National Union of Teachers estimated that teachers would need a 34 per cent increase to restore salaries to the relative levels set by Houghton. Further, falling school rolls and cuts seemed to mean declining promotion prospects. Also the demands placed on teachers were increasing. The job had to be done with fewer resources, but changes in examinations, administration and curricula imposed an increasing strain on the profession.

The industrial action in the profession in 1985–86 brought a number of these issues to a head. While the dispute was mainly about salaries, two other aspects gained attention. The first was the notion that teachers were not giving the country value for money: ensuring greater teacher 'efficiency' would mean better value for the taxpayer. Connected to this was the demand for the regular appraisal of teacher performance in the classroom. The actual mechanics of this are at the time of writing somewhat vague, but the implications are clear—bad teachers would either improve or be removed.

While the challenge of increasing standards of teaching can probably be met by more vigorous training programmes, the problem of generating new recruits in some subject areas will prove more difficult to solve. The payment of an enhanced grant during training in certain prescribed subject areas, e.g. mathematics, has not aided recruitment markedly, and the option of a system of enhanced salaries for certain subject groups is unlikely to find favour with the teacher unions. The unions themselves have made the point most forcibly that the only way to attract better graduates is not only to increase salaries to a more realistic level, but also to make the whole career package more attractive—and that of necessity would mean vastly increased government expenditure. This was to a certain extent recognised by the Conservative government, but such was the rift between this government and some teacher unions that in December 1986 legislation was passed conferring unprecedented powers on the government to control teachers' salary negotiations.

EDUCATION AND THE ECONOMY

In recent years the educational system has been frequently criticised because of its seeming inability to supply industry with the skilled manpower it needs. This role of provider to the economy was the basis, as mentioned earlier, of Callaghan's 'great debate' on education in 1976. However, the issue has gained greater importance as Britain's main rivals in world trade—Japan, USA and Germany—are seen to be recovering from the world recession faster than ourselves.

However, while a great deal of blame has been laid at the door of the educational system, it is difficult to show conclusively that individual characteristics of education will affect industrial performance one way or the other. The relationship between education and industry is complex: industry's demands on education have become increasingly varied and variable and one of the major problems in this area has been the means by which these demands have been expressed. Employers tend to prefer employees with general intelligence and ability, expressed in the possession of educational certifications, rather than those with specific skills. Thus pupils tend to see what is rewarded best and the system tends to perpetuate itself through pupil choice. The very presence of a highly competitive examination structure reinforces this syndrome, as does the inability of industry at times to articulate its needs in a way comprehensible to schools and teachers. A great part of the academic activities undertaken at school are seen, quite simply, not only as irrelevant to modern industry, but basically 'pursuing aims at variance with, if not directly contrary to its own' (DES, 1980).

In 1980 the DES carried out a survey of employers to discover precisely the sources of their dissatisfaction with the educational system. Four main areas of discontent were isolated. First, pupils were felt to display an 'anti-industry' bias which schools had a crucial responsibility to combat, although it had a variety of possible sources, including the publicity given to strikes and the development of 'anti-work' attitudes by the least qualified as a response to unemployment. Secondly, while employers gave a surprisingly low priority to vocational training, they felt schools failed to nurture such general qualities as 'powers of leadership' and 'the ability to take responsibility'. The curriculum itself was held to be too narrow and academic, and to offer too little to those of less academic ability. Thirdly, there was criticism of educational standards, directed as much at basic levels of numeracy and literacy as at the possession of technical skills. Finally, the educational system was seen as failing to respond rapidly enough to changes in employers' demands for labour (DES, 1980).

The educational system is responding to some of these criticisms already, but education does not exist in a social vacuum and changes in some areas, e.g. pupil attitude, are not going to be achieved through schools alone. The family, trade unions, employers and government all have parts to play. Industry itself could go some way to remove some of the preconceived ideas that schools and pupils have of the workplace. Closer cooperation with careers officers in local authorities is obviously important but equally important must be a reappraisal by industry of its own training and educational role. In 1982, Sir Richard O'Brien, Chairman of the Manpower Services Commission, was able to comment: 'We in Britain have over the years consistently under-invested in human capital and this must be remedied to improve basic careers conceptions in industry.'

Of all the criticisms levelled by employers at school one—the lack of training in skills related to the workplace—does stand out in relation to our major economic competitors. Research undertaken by Prais (1981) on the vocational qualifications of the labour force of Britain and West Germany shows that while both countries are more or less comparable at degree level, West Germany has twice the percentage of workers with intermediate levels of technical and vocational training. Why Britain suffers such a deficiency is easy to see: in Britain just under 70 per cent of school children leave school at 16 and many of these are lost to education for ever. In West Germany on the other hand, an equivalent proportion either enter full-time vocational education or undertake apprenticeships which involve off-the-job training and lead to the acquisition of publicly-validated qualifications.

The reason Germany is so efficient at producing such a high level of trained workers is obvious: the education system is specifically geared to the production of technically qualified pupils. The system is relatively simple; after a general education up to fifteen or sixteen, 65 per cent enter either the dual system (sandwich/day release courses) or attend a full-time vocational college for specific job training. In 1983 there were 439 recognised training occupations sanctioned by the federal government. As important as this is the fact that there is a continuous flow of labour market data which makes the ability to vary supply easy to recognise (NEDC, 1984). Another striking feature of the system is that both employers and unions make a major contribution to the success of the scheme.

That schools were failing to meet the needs of the less able in relation to training and employment has been recognised by all interested parties for years. The acceptance of the need to 'do' something about it has been universal: the rise in school leaver unemployment—by 120 per cent between 1972 and 1977—made it imperative. Neither Labour nor Conservative governments saw a solution to this problem through education: central control was difficult, changes took too long to work through the system and funding too complex. The Manpower Services Commission was free of these constraints, and had a further avantage in that it was closer to the needs of industry.

The initial response of the MSC was essentially pragmatic: to devise a scheme to find unemployed school-leavers some sort of job—the Youth Opportunities Programme. In its first year 1.8 million placements were achieved and the advantages for governments obvious—reduction of official unemployment figures, low cost, obvious evidence of government concern, and the shifting of responsibility for unemployment towards the workforce and away from the economic and political system. After the YOP scheme, the MSC began increasingly to move into areas of education and training that had previously been the domain of the DES and local authorities. The decline in influence of the DES in this area has been documented elsewhere (Moos, 1985), but it is undeniably true that the MSC has been very successful in perpetuating the idea that the DES was only catering for an academic elite and ignoring the rest of school-leavers.

The YOP scheme was to a certain extent a stop-gap solution, and the MSC realised a more permanent bridge would have to be forged between school and work. Thus the Conservatives set up the Youth Training Scheme (YTS) which would follow on from leaving school and involve some off-the-job education and training. MSC funds have become increasingly important in further education to the extent that the MSC was to provide one quarter of the work-related provisions in this area by

1986/87 (DES, 1984). Thus the MSC had acquired a unique position for itself in relation to education, training and industry. Indeed it could be argued that the DES itself has strengthened the position of the MSC. As Moos argues, in the negotiations over the introduction of the new 17+ examination it became clear that the DES preferred a vocationally oriented approach and a move away from more traditional examinations. The ideas in the DES were beginning to reflect developments initiated by the MSC. But because of its unique control over its funds the MSC was favoured by the Conservatives as the ideal mechanism to bring about quick, effective changes in policy.

Thus when Margaret Thatcher announced the setting up of a new programme for technical and vocational education for 14–18 year olds in 1982—the Technical and Vocational Education Initiative (TVEI)—it was to the MSC that she looked to organise and control this experimental venture. This announcement was to come as a major shock to a number of interested parties—the DES, local authorities and teacher unions had not even been warned about it, let alone consulted beforehand. Even some members of the MSC were caught by surprise. As Dale (1985) has argued, its introduction conformed to none of the accepted routes for educational change—it was political intervention from outside the accepted system.

In terms of the challenge to education to provide more vocational training, TVEI is crucial. For the first time the MSC was to be allowed to run courses for pupils under school-leaving age in schools. Further, the courses were to be explicitly vocational, the intention being that they should be a decisive break from previous education thinking and policy.

The essence of the initiative is that pupils should complete a common core of subjects such as computing skills, sampling, industrial studies, etc. coupled with a number of options to be tailored to match local employment opportunities and where possible leading to formal qualifications. Work experience is central to the whole scheme. It was the responsibility of local authorities to promote schemes for inclusion and in the two years following its inception 48 pilot projects commenced. An interim assessment by the DES in 1984 reported that 'a climate conducive to constructive change has been established' (DES, 1984) although there had been a lack of specialist teachers in some areas and the workload in schools had increased significantly. But by July 1986 Lord Young, the Employment Secretary, was able to announce that there was to be a rapid expansion of TVEI in the coming ten years. However, it remains to be seen whether this expansion will be matched by a commensurate increase in funding. Thus the MSC's original timid steps into the education system may well herald a transformation of schools and schooling the like of which has not been seen since 1944.

HIGHER EDUCATION

Of all the educational policies pursued by governments since the Second World War none has been so outwardly successful as the provision of places in higher education. As the 'bulge' worked its way through the education system it was obvious that a bottleneck would be created in the demand for places in higher education. Hence in 1961, the Conservative government appointed the Robbins Committee to examine the problem of the development of higher education. Its recommendations are well known—places in higher education should be available to all who possess the inclination and ability to benefit from them. Few official reports have ever had such an impact on government policy—all the recommendations for expansion were carried out in all sectors, with teacher training and further education exceeding their targets. But for the present, one point needs to be noted: the rationale for the expansion of universities was response to student demand and little attention was given to the demands of industry for the products of these institutions.

The main part of university finance is provided by central government and disbursed through the University Grants Committee (UGC). In the immediate post-Robbins period the UGC was able to influence the academic developments within universities by the provision of grants for specific capital projects ('earmarking'), e.g. buildings, equipment. Non-industrially-related subjects such as social sciences, the humanities, increased dramatically, in response to demand. This period of expansion led universities to begin to look on their quinquennial grant from the government as a permanent endowment, and to a certain extent a feeling of financial complacency set in. The unconditional nature of the grant seemed to enhance the autonomy of the university system.

Two years after the Robbins Report Labour began to develop what became known as the 'binary' policy: the upgrading of a number of colleges to polytechnic status, with the emphasis on courses of a more occupational bias. While academic differences between the two systems became increasingly blurred, the financial and administrative cores were distinctly separate. There was a much greater local input in polytechnic funding, reflecting local needs and requirements, which consequently limited the control that could be exercised over policies from the centre. This problem of control of polytechnics was overcome by the setting-up of the National Advisory Board in 1982. It has become very similar in function to the UGC.

The slowdown in the growth of government expenditure on education that took place in the late 1970s affected higher education as much as other sectors. For some time there had been a number of civil servants in the Treasury who considered recent university expansion to have been excessive in relation to the country's industrial and social needs. The Labour Party's response to this was nothing more than a gradual paring of expenditure, which affected mainly academic salaries, and the freezing of vacant posts.

The Conservatives, however, saw the chance of more extensive economies in the university system. Most university funding came directly from central government and could easily be reduced when compared to other sectors of education; there was no statutory requirement to provide a given number of places; staff student ratios were generous, especially when compared with abroad. There were also other problems: the fall in the birth rate would by the late 1980s lead to a reduced demand for places in this sector, so fewer places would be needed. However playing the 'numbers game' in relation to demand can be a very speculative exercise since the birth rate for families in social classes I and II, from which a large proportion of applicants come, has in fact risen from 17 per cent of births in 1964 to 28 per cent in 1978 (Royal Society, 1983) and the demand for university places is not solely from 18 year olds—mature students are applying in increasing proportions, as are female applicants.

A reduction in overall university resources of about 8 per cent was announced by the government in 1981, to be made effective by 1984. The reductions to individual universities varied greatly, with no coherent policy apparent, other than a reduction in places—projected at 7 per cent by 1982/83. In spite of the increasing criticism of the universities' contribution to the economy some 'technological' universities—Salford, Bradford, Aston—were particularly hard hit. The speed with which the universities had to cope with this reduction was a major challenge in itself and achieved primarily through voluntary severance and early retirement. However, some small departments merged, academic, technical and secretarial staff were not replaced, and maintenance of buildings was reduced. The cuts of 1981 produced a new tenor in relations between the universities and the government. The UGC which had historically acted as a buffer between the two, increasingly adopted a more positive policy and planning role; indeed, to many it seemed to have become a mouthpiece for government policies.

The change in government attitude was made clear by Sir Keith Joseph: universities in particular, and higher education in general, were to be increasingly judged by the criteria of the market-place. They were to become efficient, economical and, above all, produce a product for which there was a demand. As one vice-chancellor was to comment, higher education was to enter 'a new era of realism, adventure and experiment, with no holds barred on what is challengable'. Part of this challenge was to be found in the future funding of universities, who were increasingly encouraged to find resources independent from central government. Some, such as Salford, have already achieved quite startling successes in this respect.

The 1985 Green Paper on *The Development of Higher Education* reinforced this attitude; while in 1979 we produced more graduate scientists and engineers than any of our major competitors (DES, 1984), the government feared our main competitors were now outstripping our production of graduates in vital areas and the economy was suffering accordingly. But as the Green Paper admitted 'the problem cannot be solved in a simple or direct way' (DES, 1985b). Indeed the problems faced by higher education are similar in many respects to the problems faced by schools in recruiting mathematics and science teachers—a lack of supply of the basic relevant commodity—undergraduates. In recent years there has been a significant reduction in the number of applications for science places in higher education and the quality of these candidates has deteriorated. The Green Paper offers no real solution to this problem other than to stress the widening of the school curriculum to include a broad science course in the last two years, and a plea for employers to adopt a more positive approach to education and training. Indeed the challenge to employers in this respect is seen as being as vital as that to higher education. The government has argued that industry could expand sponsorship schemes in universities and become more positive about the benefits in terms of employment, pay and promotion of a career in technology.

But the problem of the production of good science and technology graduates in higher education goes further than the supply factor. Universities and polytechnics have found it very difficult to attract top quality staff in these areas because levels of pay in these institutions fall far behind that currently being offered in industry. At the time of writing, a science lecturer aged 27 with six years training in higher education will start at a salary of only £8020 rising to £12280 after a further ten years. Also the career structure is limited, as it is in schools: 40 per cent of all lecturers are at the top of the lecturer scale with little chance of promotion. Such are the problems here that the 'new blood' recruitment scheme to attract new lecturers into specified areas failed to fill a number of posts.

Apart from the specific demand for more skilled graduates the Green Paper pointed out other more general challenges. It argued that higher education must foster a more positive attitude to work and industry. Part of this approach should include the development of more links with industry. Given that the government expects higher education to raise more of its funds from private sources such a movement is highly likely anyway. Consultancies, science parks and industrial professor-ships are already established features in a number of institutions. The stress on connections with industry is matched by the need to improve relations with local communities. Higher education, and in particular, the university sector has long been criticised for its detachment from its immediate environment. Universities are usually only occupied for about 30 weeks a year and most possess a high level of cultural and recreational facilities which are under-utilised in vacations. The extension of these facilities to the local community can become an important bridge in improving relations locally.

It has been argued that the real crisis in higher education will not come until the mid-1990s when, the demand for places in higher education will certainly be reduced. The number of 18 and 19 year olds will have fallen by about 30 per cent between 1984 and 1996 and it has been argued that higher education will have to adapt accordingly. More streamlining is inevitable. Mergers and even the closing down of certain institutions have been mooted as possible responses. But perhaps this situation provides higher education with its biggest challenge of all. Entrance to higher education has been dependent on success, at one level or another, in the race for academic qualifications that dominates our educational system. A lessening of the pressure on higher education gives schools, and higher education itself, a chance to reappraise the bonds that connect them and perhaps widen the social and academic bases of their operations. In 1981/82 the percentage of school-leavers entering higher education in Great Britain was 29 per cent, compared with USA 43 per cent, Germany 71 per cent, Japan 70 per cent. The system, and especially the university sector, is highly selective. Formal exposure to higher education is a scarce good that does not meet everybody's needs; the success of the Open University is testament to this. Perhaps the broadening of entrance qualifications to fill spare capacity in this sector could result in a more radical approach by institutions to their role as educators.

CONCLUSION

The challenges that have faced education in recent years have, by and large, been forced on the system by the Conservative government's reliance on monetarism as a basis for its expenditure plans in the public sector. Reducing the amount allocated to major areas of expenditure has been a major aim of policy. Indeed, given the size of the annual amounts spent on services centrally financed, it would have been surprising if there had *not* been the potential for economies and room for a more efficient, and effective, use of resources. In 1985/86 education ranked fourth in terms of government expenditure, yet in comparison to other services such as social security, it is servicing a shrinking market and will be until the mid-1990s. Thus it is not surprising that the system has come under increasing scrutiny: this would probably have taken place no matter which political party gained power.

The challenges outlined in this paper are by no means the only ones that the education system faces: there are others which have long been apparent but whose very longevity has blunted our awareness of their import. Success in the examination system still has a distinct social class bias, and as a nation we judge academic success through examination success. The increased popularity of private education may have been caused by the declining reputation of the public sector, but the connections between public schools and entrance to certain institutions, educational and otherwise, are as strong as they have always been. The value of pre-school education for the under-fives has been long recognised: yet provision for this sector has been patchy and, since there are no statutory requirements in this area, reductions in provision have been popular with local authorities faced with declining resources. At the age of 16 a significant proportion of school-leavers are lost permanently to the education system; the system has only recently tried to emphasise the fact that education is an on-going process and provide facilities for adult study. The riots in inner cities in 1980 and 1985 have placed race relations and youth unemployment firmly on the political agenda. Ethnic minority children have been an increasing proportion of our school population for years; yet the academic debate concerning their education has been increasingly concerned with 'remedial services' and 'special needs': a damning indictment of education by the system itself.

The challenges presented in this paper touch on central issues in education, in relation not only to the role of education in our society, but also to what actually happens in our schools. Education affects *future* generations and *future* resources. Yet decisions that are taken over educational issues have been increasingly dominated by political exigencies. Education has always been a political issue—the introduction of comprehensive schooling is a prime example—but by and large, educational considerations have at least played as much a part as financial constraints. In recent years finance has tended to dominate educational issues, to the extent that at the time of writing (1986) education is very much at the top of the political agenda. The teachers' industrial action of 1985 and 1986, the effects of reduced funding on school activities, the closure of schools, the problems over the introduction of GCSE in Autumn 1986, have forced education to the forefront of the issues for the next election. A new Secretary of State for Education, Kenneth Baker, may well bring a new broom with new ideas, but he will still be faced with perhaps the biggest problem facing the educational system of all: its relationship to the economy, and its contribution to the problem of unemployment. Indeed, this challenge will confront Secretaries of State for Education, from whatever party, for many years to come and their response will have a major impact on the role that education fulfills for future generations.

11 The State

John A. Hall

INTRODUCTION

I think that the English people of the twentieth century were a fine people and deserved better leaders than on the whole they got. (A.J.P. Taylor, 1977, p. 18)

Twenty years ago, a collective assessment of British society would not have contained a chapter on the state. Revival of sociological interest in the state seems to me wholly commendable, yet it remains sufficiently novel to need defence. A spin-off of the defence offered here is the establishment of criteria for 'success' and 'failure', inevitable products of exercises in social accounting such as this. The broad thrust of the paper is indicated by the legend to the chapter, but it is worth highlighting the nature of the argument. I offer an explanation for the relative failure of the British state which is rooted in social structure rather than morals. In other words, the relative failure in question seems to me historically normal.

STATES AND SOCIETIES

We can approach the state through three propositions (cf. Hall, 1986a, Introduction). These do *not* exhaust state theory, but they are sufficient to advance the argument of this chapter.

Proposition 1: Classes affect states
Neo-Marxism, to its great credit, was responsible for renewed

interest in the state, and this proposition encapsulates its concerns. Neo-Marxist theorists did not for a moment wish to abandon Marx's insistence that the state was the instrument of a dominant class, but made this general approach more sophisticated. The state was seen as having a measure of autonomy from social classes in order that it could be 'the best capitalist'; the 'capitalist state' provided a social infra-structure necessary for the long-term health of capitalist society, even though individual capitalists, blinded by short-term interests, resisted such reform. Such autonomy is limited, or relative, in two ways: by the fact of recruitment to state positions from the capitalist class and by certain courses of action being ruled out altogether because of the fundamental interests of capital.

What was noticeable about this theory was its functionalist character: the state was necessary to capitalism, and it 'did its work'. Such functionalism was politically depressing for those on the Left, and the same theory was occasionally recycled in optimistic vein. Thus Jurgen Habermas argued that capitalism needed a state which was relatively autonomous, but that it no longer had it; there was in consequence a 'rationality crisis' because insistent demands, especially from organised labour, meant that the state had insufficient room for manoeuvre to 'steer' the system (Habermas, 1976). The same argument was made by conservative authors who spoke of an 'overload' on government, and the 'ungovernability' of the advanced societies of the West (e.g. Brittan, 1977).

Proposition 2: States affect classes
Neo-Marxism is often tautologous, abstract and question-begging, yet often, too, it is suggestive. But let us consider one place where it *is* quite misleading. This second proposition highlights the fact that the state is not always passive in the face of classes, but rather that its form affects the conflict between capital and labour.

A comparison of Britain with Imperial Germany makes this clear. Serious class struggle, that is, class struggle which takes on a political, socialistic colouring, is created more by a repressive state apparatus than by capitalism *per se* (McKibbin, 1974; Lipset, 1983; Crouch, 1986; Hall, 1986b

Ch.5; Mann, 1987). If the state is liberal in allowing free trade unions, class struggle tends to be delimited to the industrial arena, as generally happened in late nineteenth-century Britain. In contrast, the repressive apparatus of Wilhelmine Germany, armed with anti-socialist laws, forced unions to 'take on' the state, not least in order that they might gain the right of industrial organisation. This is a simple but vital point, the consequence of which we shall address later.

Proposition 3: States live in societies
The first two propositions are ones which work *inside* the boundaries of a national state. We usually define society as a national society. But a moment's reflection shows that this inheritance from classical sociology can easily mislead us. All Western European nation-states are part of the larger society of international capitalism, and some of them belong to the military alliance of NATO (Hall, 1986c).

The most obvious consequence of this proposition is that any concern with the state has to take into account its geo-political role, that is, the need to protect autonomy in what Immanuel Kant termed the 'asocial' society of states. Importantly, there is very considerable autonomy for the state elite when it comes to the making of foreign policy. This matters. The fundamental force for social change in the twentieth century has not been class struggle; rather, in Trotsky's words, war has been the 'locomotive of history'.

None of this is, however, to deny the importance of international capitalism. Historically, the adoption of capitalism—as well as of its mutant, state socialism—has often been made necessary by pressure of state competition. But capitalism is more extensive than states, and there is an important asymmetry that results in class terms. Capitalist firms have the possibility of leaving a particular nation-state, a possibility which may enhance their influence inside it; in contrast, as the break-up of the Socialist Second International in 1914 showed, working classes are embedded *within* their nation-states. Workers fight for their nations rather than for their class. Many nation-states have corporatist arrangements inside their boundaries, but there is no international corporatist agreement of any sort.

STANDARDS OF JUDGEMENT

If we are to evaluate the performance of the British state we need standards of assessment. The two that follow from the previous three propositions are obvious: the success of a state is to be measured in terms of its capacity to protect its sovereignty and in terms of its ability to so rationalise its society that it can function inside capitalist society. A key modern work appreciating the importance of the latter is Mancur Olson's *The Rise and Decline of Nations* (1984). He notes that the leading edge of capitalism has rarely rested in the same place for long, as is apparent once we think of the succession from Northern Italy to Portugal, to Holland, to Britain, to the United States, to Japan and, perhaps to South East Asia. This process is explicable because leading societies institutionalise their moment of success, and are thereby unable to respond to new circumstances.

The single most important argument made in this chapter is that rationalisation is forced on societies by their states as the result of defeat in war; such defeat, in other words, is responsible for giving the state genuine autonomy, historical moments of freedom allowing for fundamental social change. To say this is to insist that the shell of the international market, whilst perhaps ruling out some options absolutely, is generally best conceived as having *constraining* rather than *controlling* powers over a state. If institutional rigidities of one sort or another are removed, there is no reason why a nation state cannot prosper in this larger surround (Goldthorpe, 1984; Katzenstein, 1985).

There is, of course, a third vantage point from which state behaviour can be evaluated, namely its capacity to provide internal order through force, fraud or bribery. This function has often been forgotten in Britain where an unwillingness to take things to extremes has long been applauded as one of the most signal virtues of 'national character'. The liberal form of the state partly accounts for this orderliness, but a further fundamental explanation for seemingly automatic social cohesion over the last century and a half must be borne in mind throughout: the first industrial nation was exceptionally rich, and was thereby able to buy off discontent to a remarkable degree.

Let us turn from these conceptual matters to concrete analysis of the British state. This chapter offers an interpretation, an explanation, of facts which are not in question. The argument begins with an historical account, as is necessary given that continuity has been the essential hallmark of British historical experience. We live in institutions that have descended from a previous era. My argument will be that these institutions are ill-adapted to present purposes, and that current discontents are so serious that problems of internal order are beginning to become troublesome.

THE PATTERN OF THE PAST: COMMERCE AND LIBERTY

Adam Smith was right to argue that the British pattern was one which, quite miraculously, combined commerce with liberty—or, to be more precise, capitalism with a liberal society based on the rule of law and the right to opposition (Hall, 1986b, Ch. 5). This pattern was firmly established by the eighteenth century. The state was one which very definitely served the interests of both aristocratic and urban components of a commercial order. State actors cooperated with other elites, as perhaps had to be the case given that the state had no standing army with which it could have freed itself from civil society. The fact that private and public power pointed, so to speak, in the same direction, contrasted with the French case where, as Tocqueville later stressed, there was a sustained power stand-off between aristocracy and state (1958).

Let us consider this institutional pattern from the points of view of labour and capital. What is most noticeable from the former perspective is that the pattern had gelled long before the emergence of an industrial working class. This situation can be contrasted to that of most European countries where the transition to the modern world went hand in hand with the creation of a working class. The difference has a great deal to do with the absence of corporatism in British life, something that will concern us later.

It is worth characterising the pattern of industrial politics in British life. The middle classes were not threatened by large-

scale suffrage, and could correspondingly afford to keep the
state liberal; and the presence of a liberal state meant that the
working class sought essentially reformist rather than
revolutionary objectives (Lipset, 1983; Geary, 1984). But that
the British working class was more than an occupational
category can be seen by comparing it to that of the United
States. There citizenship rights were widely spread in most
states at the time of Independence, and they were generalised
as the result of conscription for war in the 1860s. In this
situation, labour restricted itself *entirely* to economic grievances; no labour movement of real significance has ever dis-
rupted this liberal pattern (Crouch, 1986; Mann, 1987). In
Britain, in contrast, the working class had to fight for citizenship and, even though its victory was relatively easy, its
struggle gave it a real class presence. But it was class loyal
rather than class conscious. It tended to have its own
religion—Methodism, however, rather than Marxism!—and
conflict thereby did not take on the intensity of that in
countries like France where being on the Left meant adopting
socialism *and* anti-clericalism. The British working class had
its own culture—and a culture which was non-political at that.
It gambled, kept pigeons, grew flowers, and massively
attended a Football League which was *not*, as tended to be the
case in Imperial Germany, organised by its political organ.
Political consciousness in Europe tended to be associated with
living in crowded municipal tenement flats that drove male
workers to pubs; while such a pattern was evident in Glasgow,
the characteristic British situation was one of more privatised
existence made possible by large numbers of houses. The
British working class was an estate of the realm without an
overwhelming grievance. This class was correspondingly loyal
to the Crown whose antics Bagehot held to have 'dazzled' it.
The situation as a whole is neatly captured in a single image.
Where Lenin and Kautsky sat in cafés dreaming of revolution
and composing theoretical works of great extravagance,
Arthur Henderson, probably the key British labour leader of
the early part of this century, was otherwise engaged. He was a
leading Methodist lay preacher and an expert player of lawn
bowls (McKibbin, 1984).

Let us turn to capital. Historians have made us aware of

peculiarities of capital in Britain. Commerce came well before industry, and dominated it thereafter (Ingham, 1984). The analysis of men of wealth in the late nineteenth and early twentieth centuries has demonstrated that the rich did not come from Manchester or Birmingham but from the aristocracy and from the City of London (Rubinstein, 1981). The division between finance and industry became particularly clear at the turn of the century. Britain had been the leader in industrialisation both because of her commercial past and because of her geopolitical success, and this allowed an incredible dominance—well above 50 per cent in 1850—of world trade. It was scarcely surprising therefore that Britain passionately argued for free trade in the world system, and that she often tried to impose it by gunboat diplomacy. However, the economic development of Imperial Germany and the United States *behind* tariff walls inevitably made argument about British policy intense. In the late nineteenth century demands grew for the abandonment of free trade within the Empire. Even if this had been achieved it would not have brought real success: trading in protected markets tends to lead to economic stagnation. In any case the strategy had little chance against the opposition of the Liberal Imperialists, backed by the City of London, whose profits depended upon acting as the banker of an open world economy (Semmel, 1960).

It is often claimed that international capitalism functions most smoothly when it is dominated by a hegemonic power (Sen, 1984). With hindsight, we can see that the inability to agree on leadership of the whole capitalist system between 1880 and 1945 was a contributory factor to world crisis. Perhaps the British state could have been more intelligent in moving from primacy towards the establishment of a system of world order. But even if it had, it is doubtful whether it would have escaped the geopolitical challenges that faced it in the twentieth century; these were fundamentally political in origin. The outbreak of war in 1914 was essentially *normal*, the traditional recourse of states in a competitive system continuing their politics by other means.

Victory in the First World War counts as an historic success, but the same cannot be said of the making of the peace treaty, although it would be mistaken to blame the character of the treaty on Britain alone. The peace fell between two stools. It was neither vindictive enough to prevent the rise of Germany ever again, nor generous enough to assuage the crisis that beset German society in the face of defeat in war. A peace was made, in other words, that could not be enforced and the seeds of renewed conflict were thereby laid. It would be wholly mistaken to argue that the rise of Nazism was simply the result of external factors and to the extent that this was not so victory in the Second World War must again count as a triumphant vindication of the wisdom of the British state and the character of its people. The honour in which Britain was held in 1945 throughout the world is entirely comprehensible, and well worth bearing in mind as a counterpoint to the more negative comments which become increasingly necessary when assessing the performance of the British state in the post-war world.

HARDENING OF THE ARTERIES

In 1943 Stalin insisted that the victors of war should impose their social systems upon the areas they dominated. This was not just a statement of Stalin's own intent but a sound sociological prediction about the West as well. For the United States ruled out the activities of the far Right and the far Left in European states, and created a type of industrial politics very largely in its own image (Maier, 1981). Thus in Germany and Japan, new institutions were imposed and the commerce *with* liberty equation was cemented from without. But institutional change was *not* simply a matter of imposition (Milward, 1984). All mainland European countries had suffered a collective catastrophe, and situations of pure institutional genesis resulted. States had room to manoeuvre, not least because of widespread demands for national renewal and reconstruction.

What about the British case? Victory had brought in its tail exhaustion. The United States used its huge power to insist upon its primacy in the new institutions of international capitalism. Any hope that Britain might be able to continue to play a genuinely independent role was rudely destroyed in the wake of peace. Despite the closeness of the Alliance, in 1945 America summarily halted financial aid, and thereafter further flexed its economic muscles to show that hegemony in the world system had now definitely been transferred. This was deliberate. Roosevelt had been as suspicious of Churchill as of Stalin, believing that Britain wanted to restore its Empire—something which was anathema to the American liberal mind. The consequence of economic exhaustion was that geopolitical responsibility had to be handed over to the United States, as in the imposition of the post-war settlement in Greece.

All that has been said to this point is that there was considerable change in the attitudes and activities of the British state. Britain too was touched by demands for social reform, and it seemed as if Britain would be part of a general new dawn. Obviously the true extent of change in attitudes needs to be examined, and we can do so in turn for foreign and economic policy. It will become obvious in both cases that beneath the surface of new attitudes, these remained very considerable institutional continuity. How could it have been otherwise? Britain may have been exhausted by war, but she was unquestionably a victor. Was it not natural to presume that the institutions of the state and of society had proved their effectiveness in victory? Equally important, the fact of victory left the established pattern of power in place; there were no new social forces prepared to push for fundamental social change.

The geopolitical record of the British state has considerable achievements of which to boast. The most important success was surely that of decolonisation. This was demanded by the United States, and it was made inevitable when the Empire was deprived of the services of the Indian army; without that army the policing of imperial possessions, especially in the face of nationalism, would have been sustainable only by means of a massive drop in Britain's own standard of living. A similar situation faced other European powers, but whereas Britain ceded most of its colonies relatively peacefully, elsewhere there was sustained resistance to the end of empire. This was beneficial not only for the ex-colonies themselves but also for Britain itself: political stability and internal order remained unquestioned in the two decades after 1945.

A second strand of foreign policy deserves praise, although this whole area is one which is extremely contentious. Clement

Attlee and Ernest Bevin played a considerable part in encouraging the United States to act in a generous manner to Europe after the Second World War. The most obvious way in which this was true was in the matter of defence. Western Europe was exhausted by war, and Britain played a particularly active role in soliciting American military help; that help has provided a generally acceptable political shell—not least because of the way in which it solved 'the German problem'—for most of the post-war era. Equally important, Britain helped secure US economic aid via the Marshall Plan, and this played some part in the thirty-year period of fabulous economic growth in post-war Europe. Obviously, the external action of the United States can be interpreted in terms of its own national interest: that its interest took this form owed something to the actions of the British state.

There is, however, a negative side to be considered. Britain did *not* really abandon her pretensions to act as a major force on the world scene; indeed the creation of a special alliance with the United States is best interpreted as a Machiavellian ploy whereby a world role could be played on the coat-tails of the new hegemonic power. One important consequence of this was that Britain chose to remain a considerable military power, in terms of the size of forces maintained, the insistence on possessing nuclear weapons and in terms of the proportion of research and development—currently about 55 per cent (Kingman, 1986)—devoted to military purposes. The most recent manifestation of the militarism of the British state is, of course, the purchase of Trident missiles. This purchase was approved by the Labour Party quite as much as by the Conservatives; it is entirely correct to talk, here as elsewhere, of a consistent policy in the part of the state elite.

The attempt to continue to play a world role must be judged harshly. It seems that economic success in the post-war world is related to low expenditure on military research—a generalisation to which the United States, because of the sheer size of the military market and its demand for high technology, may possibly be exempt. More obviously, the state elite was deluded in thinking that the special relationship would encourage the United States to ignore its own national interest in order to offer special privileges to its most loyal ally. A long list of decisions—from Eisenhower's response at the time of the last imperial gamble at Suez, to Kennedy's protection of nuclear secrets, to Reagan's invasion of Grenada, have demonstrated that affection has not deterred the United States from pursuing its own interest. Although possession of nuclear weapons does bring a type of prestige, it is worth remembering that such possession does not by itself allow for real autonomy in defence matters. Trident missiles are provided by the United States, will have to be serviced there and will be targeted via American communications systems.

The difficulty in assessing the geopolitical vision of the British state results from having to consider the possibility of an alternative role. That Britain refused to join the European Economic Community at its inception is evidence of the desire to play a modified world role. The sclerosis of the political elite—again, including both Left and Right of the political spectrum—was manifested in a disastrous array of decisions that saw Britain joining the EEC only at a time when its institutional form had set in such a manner as largely to oppose it to British interests. Interestingly, that full membership of the EEC has not completely sorted out British identity problems was demonstrated in the debates over the future of the ailing Westland helicopter company that took place in 1985/86. Probably the best policy in this affair, from the British perspective, would have been the complete bankruptcy of the company since a general move towards more civilian research is needed in Britain. But there is a case—which I hint at later—for a European defence industry. One aspect of such a case is that profits from arms might be gained through being able to share research costs and as the result of access to greater markets. The British elite is now torn between these two options.

Let us turn to the better-known territory of relative economic failure to which, as we shall see, the initial decision not to enter the EEC probably contributed. Economic failure has produced a vast literature on the cause of British decline, and three principal schools of thought need to be identified.

The aristocratic embrace
The thesis that has been most discussed in recent years is that

which asserts that the culture of Britain has been subject to an aristocratic embrace. Puritanical and dissenting early Victorian culture is held to have produced entrepreneurs and scientists. This culture is held to have been destroyed in time by the anti-industrial and upper-class atmosphere of the traditional centres of elite education. The world of William Morris and Laura Ashley is held to have replaced that of Isambard Kingdom Brunel and Samuel Smiles (Wiener, 1981).

All the evidence that is available demonstrates that the political elite continues to be recruited very heavily from those who have a background in public schools and in Oxbridge—and if reform at the latter goes through it may cement the position of the old universities in the national culture. There have been variations—slightly less of the party political elite is recruited in this way, slightly more of the military and civil service, however, now is from this background (Noble, 1981)—but the broad pattern remains the same. It matters. When President Mitterrand of France announced his nationalisation programme, he immediately put civil servants into the industries concerned so that they could prevent them being run down before nationalisation was completed. It is doubtful whether the British Civil Service could boast of equivalent talent. Certainly all the attempts made to get Treasury officials to spend periods in industry have been a complete failure, something which should give considerable cause for thought for those in the Labour Party favouring state-run industries.

The Wiener thesis does not make much sense in terms of anti-industrialism *per se*. Most European intellectuals have disliked industry and technology, and something like the aristocratic embrace can clearly be seen in Thomas Mann's famous novel *Buddenbrooks*. Moreover, there is considerable continuity to elite recruitment in many European countries, perhaps most notably France. The way in which there is some truth to the thesis is simpler. European elites faced crisis and reacted to it; they were forced to appreciate the virtues of industrial society. In contrast the British state elite has not really been scared; it is massively complacement. We can see that this is so by thinking of the differential standing of sociology as between Britain and the other advanced societies.

National reconstruction in nearly all these societies led to sociology gaining genuine prominence; in Britain the low standing of sociology goes hand in hand (need we be surprised!) with an almost unquestioned dominance of historical studies.

Two versions of capital

A further problem with the anti-industrial spirit thesis is that it suggests that the aristocratic embrace is followed by fading gentility preferably enjoyed in a country cottage decorated with Laura Ashley wallpapers. We can see that this is wrong when we think how expensive is such a life. It is often enjoyed on a weekend basis by those who make money elsewhere.

The point being alluded to is the continual division of capital in Britain (Semmel, 1960; Ingham, 1984). Any graduate wanting to make a really large income in this country is, of course, better advised to enter the City of London rather than manufacturing industry. It is customary now to point to the fact that having 87 per cent in work, most of whom have had a continual rise in living standards, is sufficient to ensure social stability and, perhaps, the chances of re-election for the Conservative Party (Gelb and Bradley, 1980). But what is more striking is that for merchant bankers the years since 1973, when exchange rates were allowed to 'float', have been ones of quite exceptional profit.

The British state has been heavily influenced, through the Bank of England and the Treasury, by the well-articulated demands of the City of London. This helps explain why the British state, alone with the United States, favours free trade, and delays entry into the European Monetary System. Importantly City profits are made through short-term transactions, i.e. through money-lending operations rather than through industrial investment (Ingham, 1984).

The absence of corporatism in Britain

The third explanation concentrates on the militancy of the British working class. This view is accepted by some on the Left (Glyn and Sutcliffe, 1972), and it has in recent years been almost uniformly accepted by politicians, commentators and intellectuals on the Right. When it was discovered that British strike rates were not especially high, attention was focused instead upon two more specific targets: levels of productivity and the absence of the form of industrial politics characteristic of virtually every other economically advanced state inside capitalism, namely corporatism.

As there is so much invective, so much heat and so little understanding there is something to be said for thinking about the matter in aseptic, social structural terms. There is certainly a difference between the working class in this country and those of Germany and Sweden. Participation in the industrialisation process in Sweden, as noted, led to its labour movement thereafter being aware of the nature of industrial organisation. One example of this must suffice. In the inter-war years, and indeed thereafter, the labour movement in Britain concentrated its demands on gaining high benefits; in Sweden, in contrast, the labour movement also demanded mobility allowances so that the needs of industry could be properly serviced. The contrast with the contemporary German situation is as important. There *can* be a type of informal corporatism in Germany because the heads of the fifteen huge industrial unions can communicate and 'bind' each other. The absence of defeat in war meant that union reorganisation did not occur in Great Britain.

Whenever a set of factors is offered, it becomes vital to see how they relate to each other. In this case, three points need to be made. First, the absence of defeat in war meant that the state had no need to seek fundamental autonomy from civil society; success meant that the state did not even seek to rationalise society in any fundamental way. To speak of the autonomy of the state being limited, or of its limited room within which to steer the economy, seems to me to put the cart before the horse: the British political elite *had* unquestioned authority for at least two decades after 1945 and it did nothing with it. This first point is to stress the sleepiness of the political elite as a whole; we see this most clearly in economic matters, but we should remember that it affects the choice that is made about our role in the world as a whole. The second point is to stress the impact of the City of London. It has been more important than industrial capital, and it has affected many more decisions than has the organised working class (Strange, 1971).

If we take the first two factors together, that is, the continuity of elite institutions as a whole and the interests of finance capital, it becomes obvious why I placed A.J.P. Taylor's comment at the start of this chapter. For very much less important is the third factor, the behaviour of the organised working class. This has not helped the British economy in nearly twenty years, but it is not really responsible for the nature of the British state—that was created before it came into being. This should not surprise us very greatly: the organised working class has affected social evolution far less than Marx predicted, whereas the impact of elite behaviour is sustained and important.

This weighting of factors is dense and needs amplification, and this can be provided by briefly placing Britain in comparative perspective. Defeat in war presented a particular crisis for the Italian political elite since the form of that defeat made it possible for a powerful communist working class to aim at the seizure of power. Linda Weiss (1984) has brilliantly demonstrated how the political elite maintained power by pioneering the development of small business. This came, it must be insisted, not through the adoption of *laissez-faire* attitudes by the state, but by state guidance to the market—in particular through the provision of credit arrangements that allowed and encouraged small industry. In contrast, the French state chose to develop large-scale industry, including state multinationals which are now capable of acting inside the world economy. Interestingly, the adoption of crucial policies inside the European Community took place because the French state felt that it had to build institutions to contain the German threat (Milward, 1984). In contrast, the British state elite has not been threatened by disturbance caused by defeat in war. Its working class has historically been, as it were, *too* passive—it has accepted so much that the elite has scarcely had to pay it much attention.

Gordon Causer demonstrates in Chapter 2 that important causes of British economic decline have been the desire to maintain sterling as a top currency and trading for long periods in stagnant markets. Interestingly, European recovery after 1945 depended upon exactly the opposite mixture:

intra-European trade in high-technology combined with initial protection against the world economy. The moral of all this is clear. Britain held on to its traditional political economy even though changed circumstances made it hopelessly inappropriate. It is important to highlight what is involved in this judgement in so far as perceptions of the British state are involved.

It is clear that the British state was not limited by either industrial capital or by labour in the first two post-war decades, and it is equally clear that its policies have not been functional for British industry. But we still need to say something about finance capital. Was the British state forced into adopting particular policies because of the impact of the City? Whilst it would be silly to deny the importance of the City as a lobby group, it seems to me that the evidence does not, at least on certain crucial occasions, suggest that the state's autonomy has been limited by finance capital. It is quite clear that the attempt to regenerate British industry made in the early years of Harold Wilson's premiership was defeated by the desire to protect sterling. But Wilson was not the tool of the City in this; certainly there is no evidence that he was forced into a particular course by City pressure. Wilson's desire to protect sterling, that is, his resistance to the devaluation of sterling, derived fundamentally from the belief that Britain was and should remain a great power (Blank, 1978).

A final word now needs to be said about the British working class. Continued relative economic failure has led to increasing militancy, and the autonomy of the state has been restricted since the late 1960s by the negative resisting power of the trade unions. It is further true that wholesale institutional reform of union structures, perhaps so as to emulate the simplicity of the German situation (itself designed by British experts after the war!), would help the emergence of corporatist agreements in Britain—although it seems to me quite inconceivable that changes of this magnitude could take place without the fundamental rethink that is only ever imposed by defeat in war. But the point that needs to be stressed is that militancy on the part of British workers is not the cause of decline, but a response to it. This makes it extremely disturbing that the

British state, that is, the political elite as a whole, has come to diagnose labour militancy as *the* problem needing to be dealt with in the political economy. It *is* now a problem, but the greater difficulty remains that of the lack of dynamism and wisdom of the state elite itself.

BREAKING OUT

Does all this matter? Is it not possible for us to grow old gracefully, to live with our inefficiencies? Is it not a signal achievement of the British state that its people have consistently considered themselves the happiest in Europe? The answer to such speculations must be that decline *is* important, and for two reasons. First, from 1979 onwards the Thatcher government attempted, by means of increased state power, to change the course of Britain; it wished to treat economic decline as the equivalent of defeat in war, and to rationalise society accordingly. We cannot ignore this. Secondly, the economic decline that has taken place is dangerous, perhaps terrifying. Already Britain, with high unemployment, inner city riots, racial tensions, stalemate in Ulster, and union militancy is no longer an orderly and restrained society. There is not enough money to paper over the cracks, and no sign of sufficient will to handle these questions with political intelligence in the absence of the solvent of economic growth. Furthermore, it is possible that the demand for political devolution may yet increase if the economy collapses, and this would fundamentally alter the British state (Nairn, 1977). Each trade cycle has pushed Britain further down and one wonders if a time may come, perhaps with the exhaustion of North Sea oil, when sustained negative growth may face us. Reaction to these changes has been repressive; greater police powers, limitations on the right to strike and the basic attack on the right to demonstrate. History would lead us to expect a greater degree of illiberalism if decline continues—first from the state and then, in consequence, from society.

So it is obviously necessary to consider the question of reform and it is equally important to begin with a consideration of Thatcherism. One can but praise Mrs Thatcher's realisation that Britain exists inside international capitalist society, and that it has to survive in that arena; that this was forgotten, both by Conservatives and by national chauvinists on the Left, was perhaps *the* principal piece of evidence of the sleepiness of the British elite. One cannot be so sanguine about Thatcherite policy. The Thatcherite revolution was deeply impressed with arguments about the anti-industrial spirit and about the aristocratic embrace administered by the public school/Oxbridge cycle. But it understood the thesis very crudely, and anyway it is noticeable how pusillanimous were the conclusions drawn when they accepted the thesis: logically it might well have required the destruction of the aristocratic embrace rather than paying for a few more engineers! More importantly, it is now clear that the economy *cannot* flourish under Thatcherite principles. There is considerable variation in the running of various industrial political economies, between the extension of socialist measures in Sweden and the consolidation of micro-corporatism in Germany, but in each case the state plays a very active role in helping to compete in the world market. Monetarism may lead to a disciplined and servile workforce, but this is of no use in late industrial society, ever more dependent upon high-technology. If British wages fall so as to create a low-wage economy, we can expect a huge and savage fall in living standards, for we would then compete with Taiwan and Hong Kong. Most other economically advanced societies of the capitalist world have large social infra-structures designed to train workforces capable of responding to the modern world. The future of the advanced societies consists in establishing a high-wage, high-productivity economy. Many European societies are following that route; the direction of the Thatcherite revolution suggests that we may not be in their company.

What about the Left? Several options have been offered by the Left, and it is extremely hard to be fair in any short summary. But a process of genuine development is observable from the position advocated by Tony Benn in the 1970s. That position favoured free collective bargaining, state planning diluted by workers' cooperatives and anti-European and anti-

American sentiments in both economic and defence policy. Such a package had *no* chance of success, most obviously because it would have engendered a run on sterling within a very short period—less because of distrust of socialist measures than because the package seemed to have no economic sense. The most noticeable change in recent years is that the Left is becoming European—or at least the intellectuals of the Left are moving in that direction, in so doing probably leaving their troops well behind. The terms of capitalist society are, of course, dictated by the United States, and only joint action by a handful of states could change those terms—allowing, for instance, borrowing on non-deflationary terms. Whether strong economies of socialist hue would wish to bail out a Leftist government in Britain without insisting upon fundamental social change is a moot point. There are at least some socialists who favour greater European involvement precisely to encourage the social change they wish for, but cannot create.

As it happens, I think there are good arguments for reorienting Britain towards Europe. For the EEC itself to become a transnational force of some sort, free to create its own foreign and economic policy, a far greater measure of European defence, possibly only of a conventional variety, is almost certainly required. Some of the Left recognise this, even if more are still a little naive about the need for defence. But is a policy of this type likely to be adopted? Regrettably, I think that the answer to this question must be in the negative. In 1986, Britain joined Germany in asking the United States to reject Gorbachov's latest missile reduction offer, and less and less interest is being shown in alternative policies. More generally, is it really the case that British politics are now at some sort of turning-point, as both Mrs Thatcher and Tony Benn, each of them loathing the Butskellite years, once loved to tell us? I think the answer to these questions is probably negative. The rise of Tony Benn and Mrs Thatcher led to the emergence of the Alliance, that is, an appeal to the status quo: Neil Kinnock and John Biffen realise this, even if Tony Benn, Mrs Thatcher and David Owen do not.

My concluding comment must then be pessimistic. There is no indication that the decline of Britain is about to be arrested;

certainly there is no sign that the state will lead society on a more progressive route. Perhaps this is scarcely surprising. There are some examples of leaders who have 'turned a society around' in the middle of decline, but they are few in number. One suspects that foreigners visiting Britain are right to insist that relatively little significant change has taken place in Britain in the last decade. It is historically normal for recovery, as in the case of Spain, to take a very long time. This can give British people little consolation in itself, and less when we remember that international competition is more rapid now than it has been in the past.

Bibliography

Abrams, P. and Brown, R. (eds.) (1984), *UK Society: Work, Urbanism and Inequality*, London, Weidenfeld and Nicolson.

Alderson, J. (1979), *Policing Freedom*, Plymouth, Macdonald and Evans.

Allan, G. (1985), *Family Life*, Oxford, Basil Blackwell.

Alleway, L. (1985), 'A Better Deal for Addicts', *Health and Social Service Journal*, 4 July 1985.

Alt, J. (1979), *The Politics of Economic Decline: Economic Management and Political Behaviour in Britain since 1964*, Cambridge, Cambridge University Press.

Anderson, F. (1985), 'Associations Link-Up in Attempt to Reduce Death Through Smoking', *Health and Social Service Journal*, 5 December 1985.

Anderson, M. (1971), *Family Structure in Nineteenth-Century Lancashire*, Cambridge, Cambridge University Press.

Arthur, P. (1983), *The Government and Politics of Northern Ireland*, London, Longman.

Audit Commission (1986), *Managing the Crisis in Council Housing*, London, HMSO.

Bain, G. S. (ed.) (1983), *Industrial Relations in Britain*, Oxford, Basil Blackwell.

Bain, G. S. and Price, R. (1983), 'Union Growth: Dimensions, Determinants and Density', in G. S. Bain, (ed.), *Industrial Relations in Britain*, Oxford, Basil Blackwell.

Ball, M. (1983), *Housing Policy and Economic Power*, London, Methuen.

Bank of England Quarterly Bulletin, (1985), 'Services in the UK Economy', vol. 25 no. 3.

Banton, M. (1964), *The Policeman in the Community*, London, Tavistock.

223

Barnett, A. (1982), *Iron Brittania*, London, Allison and Busby.
Bates, I. *et al.* (1984), *Schooling for the Dole: The New Vocationalism*, London, Macmillan.
Batstone, E. (1984), *Working Order*, Oxford, Basil Blackwell.
Beechey, V. (1986), 'Women's Employment in Contemporary Britain', in V. Beechey and E. Whitelegg (eds.), *Women in Britain Today*, Milton Keynes, Open Univerity Press.
Benson, I. and Lloyd, J. (1983), *New Technology and Industrial Change*, London, Kogan Page.
Blank, S. (1978), 'Britain: The Politics of Foreign Economic Policy, the Domestic Economy, and the Problem of Pluralistic Stagnation', in P. Katzenstein (ed.), *Between Power and Plenty*, Madison, University of Wisconsin Press.
Bleasdale, A. (1983), *Boys from the Black Stuff*, St Albans, Granada.
Boddy, M., Lovering, J. and Bassett, K. (1986), *Sunbelt City—A Study of Economic Change in Britain's M4 Growth Corridor*, Oxford, Clarendon Press.
Booth, A. (1982), 'Corporatism, Capitalism and Depression in Twentieth-Century Britain', *British Journal of Sociology*, vol. 32, no. 2.
Bosanquet, N. (1984), 'Social Policy and the Welfare State', in R. Jowell and C. Airey (eds.), *British Social Attitudes: The 1984 Report*, Aldershot, Gower.
Braverman, H. (1974), *Labour and Monopoly Capital*, New York, Monthly Review Press.
Brittan, S. (1977), *The Economic Contradictions of Democracy*, London, Temple Smith.
Brown, C. J. F. and Sheriff, T. D. (1978), 'De-industrialisation: A Background Paper', in F. Blackaby (ed.), *De-industrialisation*, London, Heinemann Educational Books/National Institute of Economic and Social Research.
Brown, J. C. (1984), *Anti-Poverty Policy in the European Community*, London, Policy Studies Institute.
Buchanan, D. and Huczynski, A. (1985), *Organizational Behaviour*, London, Prentice-Hall.
Buck, N., Gordon, I. and Young, K. with Ermisch, J. and Mills, L. (1986), *The London Employment Problem*, Oxford, Clarendon Press.
Burgoyne, J. and Clark, D. (1982) 'Reconstituted Families', in R. N. Rapoport, M. P. Fogarty and R. Rapoport (eds.), *Families in Britain*, London, Routledge and Kegan Paul.
Cain, M. (1973), *Society and the Policeman's Role*, London, Routledge and Kegan Paul.

Cameron, D. R. (1984), 'Social Democracy, Corporatism, Labour Quiesecence and the Representation of Economic Interest in Advanced Capitalist Society', in J. H. Goldthorpe (ed.), *Order and Conflict in Contemporary Capitalism*, Oxford, Oxford University Press.

Campbell, B. (1984), *Wigan Pier Revisited*, London, Virago.

Carrington, J. C. and Edwards, G. T. (1981), *Reversing Economic Decline*, London, Macmillan.

Central Statistical Office (1986), *Economic Trends, Annual Supplement*, London, HMSO.

Chatterton, M. (1979), 'The Supervision of Patrol Work under the Fixed Points System', in S. Holdaway (ed.), *The British Police*, London, Edward Arnold.

Clark, J., Jacobs, A., King, R. and Rose, H. (1984), 'Industrial Relations, New Technology and Divisions Within the Workforce', *Industrial Relations Journal*, vol. 15, no. 3.

Clark, J., King, R., McLoughlin, I. and Rose, H., (1985), *TXE4 Modernisation in British Telecom*, University of Southampton, New Technology Research Group.

Clark, J. and Lord Wedderburn (1983), 'Modern Labour Law: Problems, Functions and Policies', in Lord Wedderburn, R. Lewis and J. Clark (eds.), *Labour Law and Industrial Relations*, Oxford, Oxford University Press.

Clark, J. and Lord Wedderburn (1987), 'Juridification—Universal Trend?', in G. Teubner (ed.), *The Juridification of Social Spheres*, Berlin and New York, Walter de Gruyter.

Clarke, M. (1986), *Regulating the City*, Milton Keynes, Open University Press.

Clarke, R. V. and Hough, M. (1984), *Crime and Police Effectiveness* (Home Office Research Study no. 79), London, HMSO.

Coakley, J. and Harris, L. (1983), *The City of Capital*, Oxford, Basil Blackwell.

Coates, D. and Hillard, J. (eds.) (1986), *The Economic Decline of Modern Britain*, Brighton, Wheatsheaf Books.

Coleman, A. (1985), *Utopia on Trial: Vision and Reality in Planned Housing*, London, Hilary Shipman.

Commissioner of Police for the Metropolis (1984), *Report for the Year 1983*, London, HMSO.

Confederation of British Industry (1985), *Change to Success: The Nationwide Findings*, London, CBI.

Connor, H. and Pearson, R. (1986), *Information Technology Manpower into the 1990s*, Brighton, Institute of Manpower Studies, 1986.

Cooke, P. (1986), 'The Changing Urban and Regional System in the United Kingdom', *Regional Studies*, vol. 20, no. 3.

Coombes, D. (1982), *Representative Government and Economic Power*, London, Heinemann.

Critchley, T. A. (1967), *A History of Police in England and Wales 1900–1966*, London, Constable.

Crouch, C. (1982), *The Politics of Industrial Relations*, 2nd edition, London, Fontana.

Crouch, C. (1986), 'Sharing Public Space: States and Organised Interests in Western Europe', in J. Hall (ed.), *States in History*, Oxford, Basil Blackwell.

Dale, R. (ed.) (1985), *Education, Training and Employment: Towards a New Vocationalism*, Oxford, Pergamon.

Daniel, W. W. (1968), *Racial Discrimination in England*, Harmondsworth, Penguin.

Daniel, W. W. and Millward, N. (1983), *Workplace Industrial Relations in Great Britain*, London, Heinemann.

Darby, J. (ed.) (1983), *Northern Ireland: The Background to the Conflict*, Belfast, Appletree Press.

Davies, N. (1986), 'How Police Numbers Added up to a Loss', *The Observer*, 25 May 1986.

Deacon, A. (1984), 'Was There a Welfare Consensus? Social Policy in the 1940s', in C. Jones and J. Stevenson (eds.), *The Yearbook of Social Policy in Britain 1983*, London, Routledge and Kegan Paul.

Deacon, A. and Bradshaw, J. (1983), *Reserved for the Poor: The Means Test in British Social Policy*, Oxford, Basil Blackwell and Martin Robertson.

Deakin, N. (1984), 'The State in Social Policy: Retrospect and Prospects', in C. Jones and J. Stevenson (eds.), *The Yearbook of Social Policy in Britain 1983*, London, Routledge and Kegan Paul.

Department of Education and Science (1980), *Education Policy and Industry's Needs in the 1980s*, London, DES.

Department of Education and Science (1984), 'International Statistical Comparisons in Higher Education', *Statistical Bulletin*, 9184.

Department of Education and Science (1985a), *Better Schools*, Cmnd. 9469, London, HMSO.

Department of Education and Science (1985b), *The Development of Higher Education into the 1990s*, Cmnd. 9524, London, HMSO.

Department of Education and Science (1986), *Report by Her Majesty's Inspectors on the Effects of Local Authority Expenditure Policies on Education Provision in England, 1985*, London, DES.

Department of Employment and Department of Education and

Science (1984), *Training for Jobs*, London, HMSO.

Department of the Environment (1977), *Housing Policy Review*, four volumes, London, HMSO.

Department of the Environment (1983), *English House Conditions—Survey 1981*, London, HMSO.

Dilnot, A. W., Kay, J. A. and Morris, C. N. (1984), *The Reform of Social Security*, Oxford, Clarendon Press.

Donnison, D. (1985), 'Social Security: How Should We Respond?', *Poverty*. No. 61.

Duclaud-Williams, R. H. (1978), *The Politics of Housing in Britain and France*, London, Heinemann.

Dunleavy, P. (1979), 'The Urban Bases of Political Alignment: Social Class, Domestic Property Ownership and State Intervention in Consumption Processes', *British Journal of Political Science*, vol. 9, no. 4.

Dunleavy, P. and Husbands, C. T. (1985), *British Democracy at the Crossroads: Voting and Party Competition in the 1980s*, London, Allen and Unwin.

Dunleavy, P. and Rhodes, R. A. W. (1986), 'Government Beyond Whitehall', in H. Drucker, P. Dunleavy, A. Gamble and G. Peele (eds.), *Developments in British Politics 2*, London, Macmillan.

Dyson, K. (1983), 'The Cultural, Ideological and Structural Context', in K. Dyson and S. Wilks (eds.), *Industrial Crisis*, Oxford, Basil Blackwell.

Economist (1985), 'Housing for the Poor', vol. 297, no. 7241.

Edgell, S. (1980), *Middle-Class Couples*, London, Allen and Unwin.

Edmonds, J. (1984), 'Decline of the Big Battalions', *Personnel Management*, March.

Eekelaar, J. and Clive, E. (1977), *Custody after Divorce*, Oxford, Centre for Socio-Legal Studies.

Esping-Andersen, G. and Korpi, W. (1984), 'Social Policy as Class Politics in Post-War Capitalism', in J. H. Goldthorpe (ed.), *Order and Conflict in Contemporary Capitalism*, Oxford, Oxford University Press.

European Communities (1977), *The Perception of Poverty in Europe*, Brussels, Commission of the European Communities.

European Communities (1981), *Final Report from the Commission to the Council on the First Programme of Pilot Studies and Schemes to Combat Poverty*, Brussels, Commission of the European Communities.

Fagin, L. and Little, M. (1984), *The Forsaken Families*, Harmondsworth, Penguin.

Field, F. (1980), *Inequality in Britain*, London, Fontana.

Field, F. (1983), 'Breaking the Mould: The Thatcher Government's Fiscal Policies', in F. Field (ed.), *The Wealth Report 2*, London, Routledge and Kegan Paul.

Finch, J. and Groves, D. (eds.) (1983), *A Labour of Love*, London, Routledge and Kegan Paul.

Fine B. and Harris, L. (1985), *The Peculiarities of the British Economy*, London, Lawrence and Wishart.

Flanders, A. (1975), 'What Are Trade Unions For?, in *Management and Unions*, London, Faber.

Foot, M. (1982), *Aneurin Bevan 1945–1960*, London, Granada/Paladin.

Forrester, P. G. (1985), *Post-Graduate Management Education*, London, ESRC/CUMS.

Fothergill, S. and Gudgin, G. (1983), 'Trends in Regional Manufacturing Employment: the Main Influences', in J. B. Goddard and A. B. Champion (eds.), *The Urban and Regional Transformation of Britain*, London, Methuen.

Fox, A. (1974), *Beyond Contract: Work, Power and Trust Relations*, London, Faber.

Fox, I. (1985), *Private Schools and Public Issues*, London, Macmillan.

Franklin, M. (1985), *The Decline of Class Voting in Britain*, Oxford, Oxford University Press.

Fryer, B., Manson, A. and Fairclough, A. (1978), 'Facilities for Female Shop Stewards', *British Journal of Industrial Relations*, vol. 16, no. 2.

Gamble, A. (1985), *Britain in Decline*, 2nd edition, London, Macmillan.

Gamble, A. and Walkland S. A. (1984), *The British Party System and Economic Policy, 1945–83*, Oxford, Oxford University Press.

Garnsey, E., Rubery, J. and Wilkinson, F. (1985), 'Labour Market Structure and Work-force Divisions', in R. Deem and G. Salaman (eds.), *Work, Culture and Society*, Milton Keynes, Open University Press.

Geary, D. (1984), *European Labour Protest, 1848–1945*, London, Methuen.

Gelb, A. and Bradley, K. (1980), 'The Radical Potential of Cash Nexus Breaks', *British Journal of Sociology*, vol. 31, No. 2.

George, V. and Lawson, R. (eds.) (1980), *Poverty and Inequality in Common Market Countries*, London, Routledge and Kegan Paul.

George, V. and Wilding, P. (1984), *The Impact of Social Policy*, London, Routledge and Kegan Paul.

Glendinning, C. (1984), *Unshared Care: Parents and Their Disabled Children*, London, Routledge and Kegan Paul.

Glyn, A. and Sutcliffe, R. (1972), *British Capitalism, Workers and the Profit Squeeze*, Harmondsworth, Penguin.

Goden, P. (1985), 'Education Policy, 1979–84', in D. Bell (ed.), *The Conservative Government: An Interim Report*, London, Croom Helm.

Godley, W. (1986), 'A Doomed Economy?', *New Society*, 17 January 1986.

Golding, P. and Middleton, S. (1982), *Images of Welfare*, Oxford, Martin Robertson.

Goldthorpe, J. H. (1982), 'On the Service Class, its Formation and Future', in A. Giddens and G. MacKenzie (eds.), *Social Class and the Division of Labour*, Cambridge, Cambridge University Press.

Goldthorpe, J. H. (ed.) (1984), *Order and Conflict in Contemporary Capitalism*, Oxford, Oxford University Press.

Goldthorpe, J. H. and Payne, C. (1986), 'Trends in Intergenerational Class Mobility in England and Wales 1972–1983', *Sociology*, vol. 20, no. 1.

Gough, I. (1979), *The Political Economy of the Welfare State*, London, Macmillan.

Habermas, J. (1976), *Legitimation Crisis*, London, Heinemann Educational Books.

Hall, J. A. (1986a), *States in History*, Oxford, Basil Blackwell.

Hall, J. A. (1986b), *Powers and Liberties. The Causes and Consequences of the Rise of the West*, Harmondsworth, Penguin.

Hall, J. A. (1986c), 'Theory', in M. Haralambos (ed.), *Developments in Sociology*, vol. 2, Ormskirk, Causeway Press.

Hare, P. (1985), *Planning the British Economy*, London, Macmillan.

Harris, J. (1981), 'Social Policy in Britain During the Second World War', in W. J. Mommsen (ed.), *The Emergence of the Welfare State in Britain and Germany*, London, Croom Helm.

Harrison, A. and Gretton, J. (1984), *Health Care UK, 1984*, London, Policy Journals.

Harrison, A. and Gretton, J. (1986), *Health Care UK, 1986*, London, Policy Journals.

Harrop, M. (1986), 'Voting and the Electorate', in H. Drucker, P. Dunleavy, A. Gamble and G. Peele (eds.), *Developments in British Politics 2*, London, Macmillan.

Hawkins, C. (1983), *Britain's Economic Future*, Brighton, Wheatsheaf Books.

Heath, A., Howell, R. and Curtice, J. (1985), *How Britain Votes*, Oxford, Pergamon.

Hewton, E. (1986), *Education in Recession*, London, Allen and Unwin.

Holdaway, S. (1977), 'Changes in Urban Policing', *British Journal of Sociology*, vol. 28, no. 2.

Holdaway, S. (1983), *Inside the British Police*, Oxford, Basil Blackwell.

Huhne, C. (1986), 'Share Boom Halts Equality Trend', *Guardian*, 23 September 1986.

Hunt, P. (1978), 'Cash Transactions and Household Tasks', *Sociological Review*, vol. 26, no. 3.

Hunt, P. (1980), *Gender and Class Consciousness*, London, Macmillan.

Husbands, C. (1985), 'Government Popularity and the Unemployment Issue', *Sociology*, vol. 19, no. 1.

Hutton, S. and Lawrence, P. (1981), *German Engineers*, Oxford, Clarendon Press.

Independent Schools Information Service (1986), *Annual Census*, London, ISIS.

Ingham, G. (1984), *Capitalism Divided? The City and Industry in British Social Development*, London, Macmillan.

Institute of Manpower Studies (1985), *Competence and Competition*, London, National Economic Development Office/Manpower Services Commission.

Institute of Marketing (1984), *Marketing in the UK: a Survey of Current Practice and Performance*, London, Institute of Marketing.

Jenkins, R. (1984), 'Understanding Northern Ireland', *Sociology*, vol. 18, no. 2.

Jenkins, R., Bryman, A., Ford, J., Keil, T. and Beardsworth, A. (1983), 'Information in the Labour Market: The Impact of Recession', *Sociology*, vol. 17, no. 2.

Johnson, P. (1985), *British Industry*, Oxford, Basil Blackwell.

Jones, B. (1983), 'Destruction or Redistribution of Engineering Skills? The Case of Numerical Control', in S. Wood (ed.), *The Degradation of Work*, London, Hutchinson.

Kahn, P., Lewis, N., Livock, R. and Wiles, P. (1983), *Picketing: Industrial Disputes, Tactics and the Law*, London, Routledge and Kegan Paul.

Katzenstein, P. (1985), *Small States and World Markets*, Ithaca, N.Y., Cornell University Press.

Keegan, W. (1984), *Mrs Thatcher's Economic Experiment*, Harmondsworth, Penguin.

Keegan, W. (1985), *Britain Without Oil*, Harmondsworth, Penguin.

Kilpatrick, A. and Lawson, T. (1980), 'On the Nature of Industrial Decline in the UK', *Cambridge Journal of Economics*, vol. 4, no. 1.

Kilroy, B. (1979), 'Housing Finance: Why So Privileged?', *Lloyds Bank Review*, July.

Kingman, J. (1986), 'Science and the Public Purse', *Government and Opposition*, vol. 21, no. 1.

Kinsey, R., Lea, J. and Young, J. (1986), *Losing the Fight Against Crime*, Oxford, Basil Blackwell.

Klein, R. (1983), *The Politics of the National Health Service*, London, Longman.

Korpi, W. (1980), 'Social Policy and Distributional Conflict in the Capitalist Democracies', *West European Politics*, vol. 3, no. 3.

Krieger, J. (1986), *Reagan, Thatcher and the Politics of Decline*, Cambridge, Polity Press.

Laing, W. (1985), *Private Health Care*, London, Office of Health Economics.

Land, H. (1978), 'Who Cares for the Family?', *Journal of Social Policy*, vol. 7, part 3.

Laslett, P. and Wall, R. (1974), *Household and Family in Past Time*, Cambridge, Cambridge University Press.

Lee, R. M. (1985), 'Redundancy, Labour Markets and Informal Relations', *Sociological Review*, vol. 33, no. 3.

Lees, S. (1986), *Losing Out: Sexuality and Adolescent Girls*, London, Hutchinson.

Lewis, R. (1986), 'The Role of the Law in Employment Relations', in Lewis, R. (ed.), *Labour Law in Britain*, Oxford, Basil Blackwell.

Lipset, S. M. (1983), 'Radicalism or Reformism: The Sources of Working Class Politics', *American Political Science Review*, vol. 77, no. 1.

Lloyd, J. (1986), 'The Sparks are Flying', *Marxism Today*, March.

Long, R. (1986), 'Ten Years on from Bullock', *Personnel Management*, March.

Lynes, T. (1984), 'William Beveridge', in P. Barker (ed.), *Founders of the Welfare State*, London, Heinemann.

McCarthy, W. E. J. (ed.) (1985), *Trade Unions*, 2nd edition, Harmondsworth, Penguin.

McKee, L. and Bell, C. (1984), 'His Unemployment: Her Problem, The Domestic and Marital Consequences of Male Unemployment', Paper presented to the Annual Conference of the British Sociological Association, Bradford, 1984.

McKeown, T. (1979), *The Role of Medicine*, Oxford, Basil Blackwell.

McKibbin, R. (1974), *The Evolution of the Labour Party, 1910–24*, Oxford, Oxford University Press.

McKibbin, R. (1984), 'Why Was There No Marxism in Great Britain?', *English Historical Review*, vol. 99, no. 341.

McLoughlin, I., Smith, J. H. and Dawson, P. (1983), *The Introduction of a Computerised Freight Information System in British Rail: TOPS*, University of Southampton, New Technology Research Group.

McRae, H. and Cairncross, F. (1985), *Capital City*, revised edition, London, Methuen.

Maier, C. (1981), 'The Two Post-war Eras and the Conditions for Stability in Twentieth-Century Western Europe', *American Historical Review*, vol. 86, no. 2.

Malpass, P. (1986), 'Councils That Check Their Tenants', *Roof*, vol. 11, no. 3.

Mann, M. (1987), 'Citizenship and Ruling Class Strategies', *Sociology*, vol. 21, no. 2.

Mark, R. (1978), *In the Office of Constable*, London, Collins.

Marshall, G., Rose, D., Vogler, C. and Newby, H. (1985), 'Class, Citizenship and Distributional Conflict in Modern Britain', *British Journal of Sociology*, vol. 36, no. 2.

Marshall, T. H. (1963), *Society at the Crossroads*, London, Heinemann.

Martin, J. and Roberts, C. (1984), *Women and Employment: a Lifetime Perspective*, London, HMSO.

Martin, J. P. and Wilson, G. (1969) *The Police: A Study in Manpower*, London, Heinemann.

Martin, W. E. (ed.) (1981), *The Economic of the Profits Crisis* London, HMSO.

Massey, D. (1984), *Spatial Divisions of Labour*, London and Basingstoke, Macmillan.

Massey, D. and Meegan, R. (1982), *The Anatomy of Job Loss*, London and New York, Methuen.

Matthews, R. (1985), *Managing for Success*, London, Confederation of British Industry.

Merrett, S. with Gray, F. (1982), *Owner-Occupation in Britain*, London, Routledge and Kegan Paul.

Metcalf, D. and Nickell, S. (1985), 'Jobs and Pay', *Midland Bank Review*, Spring.

Middlemas, K. (1979), *Politics in Industrial Society*, London, André Deutsch.

Milward, A. S. (1984), *The Reconstruction of Western Europe, 1948–51*, London, Methuen.

Minns, R. (1980), *Pension Funds and British Capitalism*, London, Heinemann.

Moon, J. and Richardson, J. J. (1985), *Unemployment in the UK*, Aldershot, Gower.

Moore, R. and Levie, H. (1985), 'New Technology and the Unions', in T. Forrester (ed.), *The Information Technology Revolution*, Oxford, Basil Blackwell.

Moos, M. (1985), 'From Education to Training or Whatever Happened to the DES?', in K. Jones and M. Brenton (eds.), *Yearbook of Social Policy*, London, Routledge and Kegan Paul.

Moran, M. (1986), 'Industrial Relations', in H. Drucker, P. Dunleavy, A. Gamble and G. Peele, (eds.), *Developments in British Politics 2* London, Macmillan.

Morgan, K. (1986), 'The Spectre of "Two Nations" in Contemporary Britain', *Catalyst*, vol. 2, no. 2.

Morris, L. (1985), 'Renegotiation of the Domestic Division of Labour in the Context of Male Redundancy', in H. Newby, J. Bujra, P. Littlewood, G. Rees and T. Rees (eds.), *Restructuring Capital*, London, Macmillan.

Nairn, T. (1977), *The Break-Up of Britain*, London, New Left Review.

National Advisory Commission on Civil Disorders (1968), *Report*, Washington, D.C., US Government Printing Office.

National Communications Union (1984), *The Broad Strategy: A New Concept*, London, NCU.

National Economic Development Council (1984), *Education, Training and Industrial Performance*, London, HMSO.

New Society (1986), 'GCSE: A Guide to the New Exam', March 1986.

Newby, H. (1985), 'Introduction: Recession and Re-organisation in Industrial Society', in H. Newby, J. Bujra, P. Littlewood, G. Rees and T. L. Rees (eds.), *Restructuring Capital*, Basingstoke, Macmillan.

Newman, O. (1972), *Defensible Space*, New York, Macmillan.

Nissel, M. and Bonnerjea, L. (1982), *Family Care of the Handicapped Elderly: Who Pays?*, London, Policy Studies Institute.

Noble, T. (1981), *Structure and Change in Modern Britain*, London, Batsford.

Northcott, J. (1986), *Microelectronics in Industry: Promise and Performance*, London, Policy Studies Institute.

Northcott, J. and Rogers, P. (1984), *Microelectronics in British Industry: The Pattern of Change*, London, Policy Studies Institute.

Northcott, J. and Rogers, P. (1985), *Microelectronics in Industry: an International Comparison*, London, Policy Studies Institute.

Oakley, A. (1974), *The Sociology of Housework*, London, Martin Robertson.

O'Connor, J. (1973), *The Fiscal Crisis of the State*, New York, St Martin's Press.

Office of Population Censuses and Surveys (1977), *Monitor No. 1.*

O'Higgins, M. (1983), 'Rolling Back The Welfare State: The Rhetoric and Reality of Public Expenditure and Social Policy under the Conservative Government', in C. Jones and J. Stevenson (eds.), *The Yearbook of Social Policy in Britain 1982*, London, Routledge and Kegan Paul.

O'Higgins, M. (1985), 'Inequality, Redistribution and Recession: The British Experience 1976–1982', *Journal of Social Policy*, vol. 14, part 3.

O'Higgins, M. (1986), 'Public–Private Interaction in Social Policy: A Comparative Study of Pensions Provisions in Sweden, West Germany and the United Kingdom', in M. Rein and L. Rainwater (eds.), *The Public–Private Interplay in Social Protection: A Comparative Study*, New York, M. E. Sharpe.

Olson, M. (1984), *The Rise and Decline of Nations*, New Haven, Yale University Press.

Open University (1985), *Caring for Health: dilemmas and prospects*, Milton Keynes, Open University Press.

Pahl, R. E. (1984), *Divisions of Labour*, Oxford, Basil Blackwell.

Panitch, L. (1980), 'Recent Theorizations of Corporatism: Reflections on a Growth Industry', *British Journal of Sociology*, vol. 31, no. 2.

Parker, G. (1985), *With Due Care and Attention: A Review of Research on Informal Care*, London, Family Policy Studies Centre.

Parker, R. (1981), 'Tending and Social Policy', in E. M. Goldberg and S. Hatch (eds.), *A New Look at the Personal Social Services*, London, Policy Studies Institute.

Pavitt, K. and Soete, L. (1980), 'Innovative Activities and Export Shares: Some Comparisons Between Industries and Countries', in K. Pavitt (ed.), *Technical Innovation and British Economic Performance*, London, Macmillan.

Pawley, M. (1986), 'Sell Up and Play the Stock Market', *Roof*, vol. 11, no. 3.

Pearson, G. (1983), *Hooligan: A History of Respectable Fears*, London, Macmillan.

Penn, R. and Scattergood, H. (1985), 'Deskilling or Enskilling?: An Empirical Investigation of Recent Theories of the Labour Process', *British Journal of Sociology*, vol. 36, no. 4.

Phelps Brown, E. H. (1959), *The Growth of British Industrial Relations*, London, Macmillan.

Pinchbeck, I. and Hewitt, M. (1973), *Children in English Society*, vol. 2, London, Routledge and Kegan Paul.

Plender, J. (1982), *That's the Way the Money Goes*, London, André Deutsch.

Policy Studies Institute (1983) *Police and People in London*, London, PSI. (Page references are to the paperback edition, Aldershot, Gower 1985.)

Pollard, S. (1982), *The Wasting of the British Economy*, London, Croom Helm.

Porter, M. (1983), *Home, Work and Class Consciousness*, Manchester, Manchester University Press.

Prais, S. J. (1981), 'Vocational Qualifications of the Labour Force in Britain and Germany', *National Institute Economic Review*, November.

Radical Statistics Health Group (1985), 'Unsafe in Their Hands', *Medicine in Society*, vol. 11, no. 2.

Rapoport, R. N., Fogarty M. P. and Rapoport, R. (eds.) (1982), *Families in Britain*, London, Routledge and Kegan Paul.

Reddin, M. (1982), 'Occupation, Welfare and Social Policy', in C. Jones and J. Stevenson (eds.), *The Yearbook of Social Policy in Britain 1980–1*, London, Routledge and Kegan Paul.

Reiner, R. (1978), *The Blue-Coated Worker*, Cambridge, Cambridge University Press.

Reiner, R. (1985), *The Politics of the Police*, Brighton, Wheatsheaf Books.

Reiss, A. J. and Bordua, D. J. (1967), 'Environment and Organisation: A Perspective on the Police', in D. J. Bordua, (ed.), *The Police: Six Sociological Essays*, New York, Wiley.

Richards, M. (1982), 'Do Broken Marriages Affect Children', *Health Visitor*, vol. 55, no. 4.

Robinson, R. (1986), 'Restructuring the Welfare State: An Analysis of Public Expenditure 1979/80 – 1984/5', *Journal of Social Policy*, vol. 15, part 1.

Rossiter, C. and Wicks, M. (1982), *Crisis or Challenge? Family Care, Elderly People and Social Policy*, London, Study Commission on the Family.

Rothwell, R. and Zegveld, W. (1985), *Re-industrialization and Technology*, Harlow, Longman.

Rowthorn, B. (1986), 'Unemployment—The Resistable Force', *Marxism Today*, vol. 30, no. 9.

Royal Commission on Trade Unions and Employers' Associations (1968), *Report*, Cmnd. 3623, London, HMSO.

Royal Society (1983), *Demographic Trends and Future University Candidates*, London, Royal Society.

Rubinstein, W. D. (1981), *Men of Wealth*, London, Croom Helm.

Saifullah-Khan, V. (ed.) (1979), *Minority Families in Britain*, London, Macmillan.

Sarlvik, B. and Crewe, I. (1983), *Decade of Dealignment: The Conservative Victory of 1979 and Electoral Trends in the 1970s*, Cambridge, Cambridge University Press.

Saunders, P. (1980), *Urban Politics*, Harmondsworth, Penguin Books.

Saunders, P. (1984), 'Beyond Housing Classes: The Sociological Significance of Private Property Rights in Means of Consumption', *International Journal of Urban and Regional Research*, vol. 8, no. 2.

Scarman, Lord (1981), *The Brixton Disorders, 10–12 April 1981*, Cmnd. 8427, London, HMSO.

Scase, R. and Goffee, R. (1980), *The Real World of the Small Business Owner*, London, Croom Helm.

Seabrook, J. (1978), *What Went Wrong? Working People and the Ideals of the Labour Movement*, London, Gollancz.

Searle, G. R. (1971), *The Quest for National Efficiency*, Oxford, Oxford University Press.

Semmel, B. (1960), *Imperialism and Social Reform*, London, Routledge and Kegan Paul.

Sen, G. (1984), *The Military Origins of Industrialisation and International Trade Rivalry*, London, Frances Pinter.

Shonfield, A. (1965), *Modern Capitalism*, London, Oxford University Press.

Silburn, R. (ed.) (1985), *The Future of Social Security*, London, Fabian Society.

Simon, B. and Taylor, W. (eds.) (1981), *Education in the Eighties*, London, Batsford.

Sinfield, A. (1968), *The Long-Term Unemployed*, Paris, Organisation for Economic Cooperation and Development.

Sinfield, A. (1978), 'Analyses in the Social Division of Welfare', *Journal of Social Policy*, vol. 7, part 2.

Sinfield, A. (1981), *What Unemployment Means*, London, Martin Robertson.

Sinfield, A. (1984), 'The Wider Impact of Unemployment', in OECD, *High Unemployment: A Challenge for Income Support Policies*, Paris, Organisation for Economic Cooperation and Development.

Sinfield, A. and Showler, B. (1981), 'Unemployment and the Unemployed in 1980', in B. Showler and A. Sinfield (eds.), *The Workless State*, Oxford, Martin Robertson.

Smith, D. J. (1974), *The Extent of Racial Discrimination*, London, Political and Economic Planning, Report No. 547.

Smith, K. (1984), *The British Economic Crisis*, Harmondsworth, Penguin Books.

Spencer, K., Taylor, A., Smith, B., Mawson, J., Flynn, N. and Batley, R. (1986), *Crisis in the Industrial Heartland: A Study of the West Midlands*, Oxford, Clarendon Press.

Stopford, J. M. and Turner, L. (1985), *Britain and the Multinationals*, Chichester and New York, John Wiley and Sons.

Stout, D. K. (1977), *International Price Competitiveness, Non-Price Factors and Export Performance*, London, National Economic Development Office.

Strang, J. (1984), 'Changing the Image of the Drug Taker', *Health and Social Service Journal*, 11 October 1984.

Strange, S. (1971), *Sterling in Decline*, London, Oxford University Press.

Tawney, R. H. (1937), *The Acquisitive Society*, London, Bell.

Taylor, A. J. P. (1977), 'Accident Prone, or What Happened Next', *Journal of Modern History*, vol. 49, no. 1.

Taylor-Gooby, P. (1985), *Public Opinion, Ideology and State Welfare*, London, Routledge and Kegan Paul.

Taylor-Gooby, P. (1985), 'The Politics of Welfare: Public Attitudes and Behaviour', in R. Klein and M. O'Higgins (eds.), *The Future of Welfare*, Oxford, Basil Blackwell.

Therborn, G. (1986), *Why Some Peoples are More Unemployed than Others*, London, Verso.

Titmuss, R. (1963), *Essays on the Welfare State*, London, Unwin University Books.

Tocqueville, A. de (1958), *The Old Regime and the French Revolution*, New York, Anchor Books (first published 1858).

Townsend, A. (1986), 'Spatial Aspects of the Growth of Part-time Employment in Britain', *Regional Studies*, vol. 20, no. 4.

Townsend, A. R. (1983), *The Impact of Recession*, London, Croom Helm.

Townsend, P. (1979), *Poverty in the United Kingdom*, London, Allen Lane and Penguin Books.

Townsend, P. and Davidson, N. (1982), *Inequalities in Health*, Harmondsworth, Penguin Books.

Trades Union Congress (1974), 'Industrial Democracy', Annex B to *TUC Report 1974*, London, TUC.

Tuck, M. and Southgate, P. (1981), *Ethnic Minorities and Policing*, (Home Office Research Study No. 70), London, HMSO.

Wainwright, H. (1984), 'Women and the Division of Labour', in P. Abrams and R. Brown (eds.), *UK Society: Work, Urbanism and Inequality*, London, Weidenfeld and Nicolson.

Walker, A. (ed.) (1982), *Community Care*, Oxford, Basil Blackwell.

Walker, R., Lawson, R. and Townsend, P. (1984), *Responses to Poverty: Lessons from Europe*, London, Heinemann/Gower.

Warr, P. (1983), 'Work, Jobs and Unemployment', *Bulletin of the British Psychological Society*, vol. 36.

Wedderburn, Lord (1986), *The Worker and the Law*, 3rd edition, Harmondsworth, Penguin.

Weiss, L. (1984), *Small Capital and the State: the Italian case, 1945-75*, Unpublished PhD Thesis, University of London.

Whiteley, P. and Winyard, S. (1983), 'Influencing Social Policy: The Effectiveness of the Poverty Lobby in Britain', *Journal of Social Policy*, vol. 12, no. 1.

Wiener, M. (1981), *English Culture and the Decline of the Industrial Spirit*, Cambridge, Cambridge University Press.

Wilkin, D. (1979), *Caring for the Mentally Handicapped Child*, London, Croom Helm.

Wilks, S. (1983), 'Liberal State and Party Competition: Britain', in K. Dyson and S. Wilks (eds.), *Industrial Crisis*, Oxford, Basil Blackwell.

Williams, K., Williams, J. and Thomas, D. (1983), *Why Are the British Bad at Manufacturing?*, London, Routledge and Kegan Paul.

Williams, R. (1975), *The Country and the City*, St Albans, Paladin.

Wilson, H. (1971), *The Labour Government 1964-70*, London, Weidenfeld and Nicolson and Michael Joseph.

Winchester, D. (1983), 'Industrial Relations in the Public Sector', in G. S. Bain (ed.), *Industrial Relations in Britain*, Oxford, Basil Blackwell.

Winckler, V. (1985), 'Tertiarization and Feminization at the Periphery: The Case of Wales', in H. Newby, J. Bujra, P. Littlewood, G. Rees and T. L. Rees (eds.), *Restructuring Capital: Recession and Re-organisation in Industrial Society*.

Winter, J. M. (1983), 'Unemployment, Nutrition and Infant Mortality in Britain 1920-1950', in J. M. Winter (ed.), *The Working Class in Modern British History*, Cambridge, Cambridge University Press.

Winyard, S. (1985), 'Towards Two Nations', *Poverty*, no. 61.

Wragg, T. (1985), 'Rollercoaster Teachers', *New Society*, February 1985.

Young, M. (1984), 'Police Wives: A Reflection of Police Concepts of Order and Control', in H. Callan and S. Ardener (eds.), *The Incorporated Wife*, London, Croom Helm.

Author Index

Abrams, P. and Brown, R. xi
Alderson, J. 176–7
Allan, G. 133
Alleway, L. 151
Alt, J. 14
Anderson, F. 150
Anderson, M. 122
Arthur, P. 19
Audit Commission 111

Bain, G.S. and Price, R. 60, 62
Ball, M. 101
Banton, M. 168
Barnett, A. 34
Batstone, E. 27
Beechey, V. 8
Blank, S. 218
Bleasdale, A. 138
Boddy, M., Lovering, J. and
    Bassett, K. 11
Booth, A. 12
Bosanquet, N. 156
Braverman, H. 10–11
Brittan, S. 2, 204
Brown, C.J.F. and Sheriff, T.D.
    22
Brown, J.C. 92, 94, 95
Buchanan, D. and Huczynski,
    A. 45
Buck, N., Gordon, I., Young,

K., with Ermisch, J. and Mills,
    L. 6
Burgoyne, J. and Clark, D. 132

Cain, M. 168, 170
Cameron, D.R. 11–12, 21, 28
Campbell, B. 139
Carrington, J.C. and Edwards,
    G.T. 24
Causer, G.A. 217
Central Statistical Office 20
Chatterton, M. 168
Clark, J. 10, 11
Clark, J., Jacobs, A., King, R.
    and Rose, H. 72
Clark, J., King, R., McLoughlin,
    I. and Rose, H. 74
Clark, J. and Lord Wedderburn
    64
Clarke, M. 30
Clarke, R.V. and Hough, M.
    167, 174
Coakley, J. and Harris, L. 25,
    30, 86
Coates, D. and Hillard, J. 20
Coleman, A. 109
Commissioner of Police for the
    Metropolis 164, 174, 177
Confederation of British
    Industry 43, 47, 50

Connor, H. and Pearson, R. 11
Cooke, P. 6–7
Coombes, D. 29
Critchley, T.A. 173, 181
Crouch, C. 29, 204, 208

Dale, R. 195
Daniel, W.W. 18
Daniel, W.W. and Millward, N., 61
Darby, J. 19
Davies, N. 164
Deacon, A. 79, 94
Deacon, A. and Bradshaw, J. 80, 91
Department of Education and Science 186, 189–90, 192, 194–5, 196, 198–9
Dilnot, A.W., Kay, J.A. and Morris, C.N. 112
Donnison, D. 96, 97
Duclaud-Williams, R.H. 102
Dunleavy, P. 13
Dunleavy, P. and Husbands, C.T. 15
Dunleavy, P. and Rhodes, R.A.W. 13
Dyson, K. 28, 29

Edgell, S. 125
Edmonds, J. 62–3, 67–8
Eekelaar, J. and Clive, E. 131
Esping-Andersen, G. and Korpi, W. 91
European Communities 92, 93

Fagin, L. and Little, M. 136, 152
Field, F. 18, 84
Finch, J. and Groves, D. 133
Fine, B. and Harris, L. 27
Flanders, A. 73, 74
Foot, M. 82
Forrester, P.G. 41

Fothergill, S. and Gudgin, G. 7
Fox, A. 14, 66
Fox, I. 188
Franklin, M. 13
Fryer, B., Manson, A. and Fairclough, A. 72

Gamble, A. 20, 23, 28
Gamble, A. and Walkland, S.A. 28, 32, 35
Garnsey, E., Rubery, J. and Wilkinson, F. 9
Geary, D. 208
Gelb, A. and Bradley, K. 215
George, V. and Lawson, R. 83
George, V. and Wilding, P. 143–4, 155
Glendinning, C. 134
Glyn, A. and Sutcliffe, R. 215
Godley, W. 36
Golding, P. and Middleton, S. 81
Goldthorpe, J.H. 46–7, 84, 96, 206
Goldthorpe, J.H. and Payne C. 18
Gough, I. 2, 143

Habermas, J. 204
Hall, J.A. 12, 19, 203–5, 207
Hare, P. 24, 35
Harris, J. 79–80
Harrison, A. and Gretton, J. 145, 146, 148, 150, 151, 154–5
Harrop, M. 16–17
Hawkins, C. 25
Heath, A., Jowell, R. and Curtice, J. 15–16, 19
Holdaway, S. 168, 176
Huhne, C. 18
Hunt, P. 125, 126
Husbands, C.T. 13, 14
Hutton, S. and Lawrence, P. 42

Independent Schools Information Service 188
Ingham, G. 25, 29, 30, 215
Institute of Manpower Studies 49
Institute of Marketing 50

Jenkins, R. 19
Jenkins, R., Bryman, A., Ford, J., Keil, T. and Beardsworth, A. 10
Johnson, P. 4
Jones, B. 11

Kahn, P., Lewis, N., Livock, R. and Wiles, P. 179
Katzenstein, P. 206
Keegan, W. 22, 23, 33
Kilpatrick, A. and Lawson, T. 27
Kilroy, B. 105
Kingman, J. 212
Kinsey, R., Lea, J. and Young, J. 2
Klein, R. 141–2, 155, 160–1
Korpi, W. 94
Krieger, J. 1

Laing, W. 157
Land, H. 137
Laslett, P. and Wall, R. 122
Lawson, R. 2
Lee, R.M. 10
Lees, S. 125
Lewis, R. 64
Lipset, S.M. 204, 208
Lloyd, J. 68, 71
Long, R. 75–6
Lynes, T. 80

McCarthy, W.E.J. 73
McKee, L. and Bell, C. 138
McKeown, T. 153
McKibbin, R. 204, 208

McLoughlin, I., Smith, J.H. and Dawson, P. 54
McRae, H. and Cairncross, F. 30
Maier, C. 210
Malpass, P. 102
Mann, M. 205, 208
Mark, R. 174
Marshall, G., Rose, D., Vogler, C. and Newby, H. 14
Marshall, T. 77, 80, 82
Martin, J. and Roberts, C. 8, 123, 138
Martin, J.P. and Wilson, G. 164, 165
Martin, W.E. 25
Massey, D. 7, 19
Massey, D. and Meegan, R. 7
Matthews, R. 50
Merrett, S., with Gray, F. 101, 116
Metcalf, D. and Nickell, S. 17
Middlemas, K. 12
Milward, A.S. 217
Minns, R. 86
Moon, J. and Richardson, J.J. 21
Moore, R. and Levie, H. 69
Moos, M. 194
Moran, M. 10
Morgan, K. 6
Morris, L. 137

Nairn, T. 2, 219
National Advisory Commission on Civil Disorders, *Report* 178
National Economic Development Council 194
Newby, H. 3
Newman, O. 109
Nissel, M. and Bonnerjea, L. 134
Noble, T. xi, 214
Northcott, J. 5
Northcott, J. and Rogers, P. 5, 54

Oakley, A. 122
O'Connor, J. 143
Office of Population Censuses and Surveys 188
O'Higgins, M. 17, 88, 89, 147
Olson, M. 206

Pahl, R.E. 9, 15, 123–4, 137
Panitch, L. 12
Parker, G. 133
Parker, R. 134
Pavitt, K. and Soete, L. 27
Pawley, M. 105
Pearson, G. 128
Penn, R. and Scattergood, H. 11
Phelps Brown, E.H. 64
Pinchbeck, I. and Hewitt, M. 128
Plender, J. 86, 88
Policy Studies Institute 167, 168, 170, 171, 173
Pollard, S. 20, 28
Porter, M. 125
Prais, S.J. 193

Radical Statistics Health Group 148
Rapoport, R.N., Fogarty, M. and Rapoport, R. 122
Reddin, M. 84
Rees, A.M. 18
Reiner, R. 166, 168, 170, 171, 173
Reiss, A.J. and Bordua, D. 166
Richards, M. 131
Robinson, R. 98, 99–100, 145, 147–9
Rossiter, C. and Wicks, M. 133
Rothwell, R. and Zegveld, W. 26–7
Rowthorn, B. 12
Royal Commission on Trade Unions and Employers' Associations, *Report* 66
Royal Society 198

Rubinstein, W.D. 209

Saifullah-Kahn, V. 122
Sarlvik, B. and Crewe, I. 2
Saunders, P. 13, 106
Scarman, Lord 176, 177–8, 179
Scase, R. and Goffee, R. 46
Seabrook, J. 15
Semmel, B. 209, 215
Sen, G. 209
Shonfield, A. 82–3
Silburn, R. 88, 89
Sinfield, A. 78, 92, 96, 136
Smith, D.J. 18
Smith, K. 4, 20, 21, 33, 35
Spencer, K., Taylor, A., Smith, B., Mawson, J., Flynn, N. and Batley, R. 6
Stopford, J.M. and Turner, L. 31, 43
Stout, D.K. 33
Strang, J. 151
Strange, S. 22, 217

Tawney, R.H. 38
Taylor, A.J.P. 203, 217
Taylor-Gooby, P. 97, 143
Therborn, G. 11–12, 84, 96
Titmuss, R. 85
Tocqueville, A. de 207
Townsend, A.R. 7, 8
Townsend, P. and Davidson, N. 152–3
Trades Union Congress 65
Tuck, M. and Southgate, P. 172

Wainwright, H. 18, 123, 125
Walker, A. 133
Walker, R., Lawson, R. and Townsend, P. 83, 87
Warr, P. 136
Wedderburn, Lord 65
Weiss, L. 217

Whiteley, P. and Winyard, S. 93
Wiener, M. 214
Wilkin, D. 134
Wilks, S. 34
Williams, K., Williams, J. and
    Thomas, D. 24, 25, 26, 27, 34
Williams, R. 120

Wilson, H. 88
Winchester, D. 65
Winckler, V. 8
Winter, J.M. 137
Winyard, S. 95

Young, M. 169

Subject Index

Acquired Immune Deficiency
    Syndrome (AIDS) 151–2
adversary politics 28
alcohol consumption 150–1
Amalgamated Engineering
    Union (AEU) 69
ancillary employment structure
    10
anti-industrial culture thesis
    46–7, 213–15
Aston, University of 199
Attlee, Clement 211–12
Austria 12

Baker, Kenneth 202
Bank of England 215
banks
    clearing 24
    merchant 24–5, 86, 215
Benn, Tony 220–1
Beveridge Report 77–81, 85
Bevin, Ernest 211–12
Biffen, John 221
Bradford, University of 199
British Institute of Management
    49
British Rail 53
British Telecom 54, 71–2
Brixton 177–8
building societies 24, 105

business schools 39, 48

Callaghan, James 184, 191
capital, character of British 12,
    24–6, 29–30, 90, 208–9
Certficate of Secondary
    Education (CSE) 186–7
chief constables 165, 181
child abuse 128
childhood, attitudes to 127
children 126–9, 139, 145–6,
    149
Churchill, Sir Winston 211
City of London 29–30, 85–6,
    118, 209, 215, 216, 218
civil liberties 171, 219
civil service 28–9, 46, 56, 214
class
    and state 203–5
    conflict 14
    middle 16, 18, 78, 80, 81, 88,
        207–8
    structure 17–19, 21, 123–4
    working 15–16, 18, 207–8,
        218–19
    upper 18, 207
Clydeside 6
collective bargaining 65–6
community care 133–5
community policing 176–7

company welfare state 84–5
computerisation
   and management 44–5, 51,
     54–5
   of police work 166–7
Confederation of British
   Industry 49–51
Conservative Government 12,
   15–16, 32–3, 35, 40, 64, 81,
   83, 84, 88, 89, 94, 96, 99,
   101–2, 103–4, 113, 114, 147,
   155–6, 159–60, 184, 186–7,
   191, 195, 212
Conservative Party 1, 12, 17, 79,
   88, 103
corporatism 12, 29, 90, 205,
   215–16
crime
   clear-up rates 173–4
   prevention, as function of
     police 173
   rates 2
Crossman, Richard 141–2
Croydon 106

Day, Graham 57
decolonisation 211
deindustrialisation 22–3
demographic change 145–7
Department of Education and
   Science 183, 192, 194–5
deskilling 10–11
divorce 121, 129–31
drug abuse 151

East Anglia 6
economic planning 34–5
economic policy 32–5
economic restructuring 3–11
economy
   balance of payments 21–2,
     35–6
   growth rate 1, 20–1, 82–4, 219

   imports and exports 21–2, 43,
     47
   international competitiveness
     27, 33, 42–4, 50–1, 220
   internationalisation of 30–2
   share in world trade 21–2, 43
Edmonds, John 62–3, 67–8
Education Act, 1986 188
education
   demand for 182–3, 197–8
   employer attitudes to 192–3
   provision of 182–5
educational achievement 182–3
educational decision-making
   184–5
educational standards 186–8
Edwardes, Michael 56
Eisenhower, Dwight D. 213
elderly
   and health services 145–6, 148
   care of 127, 133–5, 145, 158–9
   numbers 145
Electrical, Electronic,
   Telecommunication and
   Plumbing Union (EETPU)
   11, 68–9
employment
   female 5, 8–9, 23, 122–3, 125
   location of 6–8
   male 8–9, 61–2
   manufacturing 4, 22–3, 37,
     60–1
   part-time 5, 8–9, 23, 126
   public sector 60, 65
   service sector 5, 23, 24, 37, 61
engineers, in Britain and West
   Germany 42
ethnic minorities
   and education 188, 201–2
   and unemployment 21
   family structure 122
   police attitudes to 171–2
European Economic

Community (EEC) 213, 217, 221
European Monetary System (EMS) 36, 215

family cycle 121
family structure, diversity of 121–2
France 28, 87, 93
full employment 35, 83, 84

gender socialislation 125
General Certificate of Education (GCE) 183, 186–7
General Certificate of Secondary Education (GCSE) 187
General, Municipal, Boilermakers and Allied Trade Union (GMBATU) 11, 62, 67–8
Gormley, Joe 66
Griffiths Report 154, 157–8
Griffiths, Roy 154, 157
Gross Domestic Product (GDP) 20

Hammond, Eric 68
health
    inequalities in 152–4
    needs 145–7, 149–52
health services
    private 157
    use of 145–7
    see also National Health Service
Henderson, Arthur 208
high technology firms 31, 69
higher education 196–200
hippies, police attitude to 171
Holland 206
homelessness 93, 109, 123

Hong Kong 220
House Purchase and Housing Act 1959 102
households
    composition 121–2
    expenditure 111–12, 154
    income 9, 63, 89, 91
    work strategies 123
Housing and Town Planning Act 1919 101
housing
    and industrial investment 24, 105
    benefit 100
    conditions 113–15
    costs 111–12
    expenditure 99–100, 147
    management 110–11
    provision 101, 104
    public 98–104, 109–10, 116, 123
    subsidies 102, 107, 111–13
    tenure 13–14, 98–9, 106

Imperial Chemical Industries (ICI) 47
income distribution 17
incomes policy 33–4, 63–4
industrial disputes
    as cause of economic problems 33–4, 216
    policing of 179–80
Industrial Reorganisation Corporation (IRC) 34
inequalities
    in education 183, 201
    in health 152–4
    in earnings 17–19
    in wealth distribution 18
inflation 13, 14, 21, 183
inner cities 2, 7, 19, 185, 201, 219
Institute of Personnel Management (IPM) 49

insurance companies 25, 81–6
investment
    in U.K. 24
    international comparisons 24,
        105
Italy 93, 206, 217

Japan 28, 35, 47, 105, 191, 200,
        206
Johnson, Lyndon B. 178
Joseph, Sir Keith 187, 198

Kautsky, Karl 208
Kennedy, John F. 66, 213
Kerner Report 178
Kinnock, Neil 121

labour force
    polarisation of 11, 95–6, 117
    sectoral distribution 4–5, 13,
        60–1
labour law 33–4, 64–5
labour markets 9–11, 84, 95–6
Labour Government 15, 32,
        34–5, 40, 79, 82, 84, 88–9,
        90, 94, 99, 114, 183–4, 212
Labour party 1, 64, 88, 103, 214
Lenin, V.I. 208
liberal imperialism 209
Liberal Party 2, 16
Liberal/S.D.P. Alliance 2, 16,
        64, 97, 221
London 6, 164

McGregor, Ian 56–7
Macmillan, Harold 21, 101
management
    and professionalism 55–6
    and technological change
        52–5
    education 39, 48–9
    origins and status 46–7
    qualifications 41

quality 39–41
Mann, Thomas 214
Manpower Services
    Commission (MSC) 193–6
Mark, Sir Robert 168, 170, 174
marriage 124–6, 130, 137–8, 139
Marshall Plan 212
mergers and takeovers 25, 45,
        51–2, 61
Methodism 208
Metropolitan Police 164–5,
        169–70, 173
monetarism 32–3, 201
mortgages
    access to 113
    tax relief on interest 103
multinational companies 31–2,
        43, 61

National Advisory Board
    (NAB) 197
National Communications
    Union (NCU) 71–2
National Health Service
    demands on 141–2, 145–6
    expenditure 147
    public attitudes to 156
    resources 142, 147–9
    see also health services
national insurance 82, 85
National Plan 34
National Union of Public
    Employees (NUPE) 72
natonalism
    Scottish 2, 14
    Welsh 2
new technology 4–5, 10–11, 37,
        44–5, 52–5, 69
New Technology Research
    Group 53
Newman, Sir Kenneth 170
News International 10, 70
North Atlantic Treaty

Organisation (NATO) 205
North Sea oil 15, 21–2, 35, 219
Northern Ireland 20, 219
Norway 12
Notting Hill 3
Nottingham 3

O'Brien, Sir Richard 193
occupational welfare 78, 81,
    84–7, 88
one-parent families 93, 101, 121,
    131, 146
Open University 49, 200
Owen, Dr David 221
owner-occupation 14–15, 98,
    102–3, 112–13, 116–17

panda cars 165–6
parents 127–8, 132, 139, 182,
    187–8
Pension Act 1975 88–9
pension funds 25, 85–6, 93
Post Office Engineering Union
    (POEU) 71
Police Acts 1964 181
Police Complaints Authority
    173
police
    and public order 19, 177–80
    corruption 174
    manpower 163–5
    organisation of 162–5
    subculture 167–73
policing, technology of 19,
    165–7, 178, 181
political elite 28–9, 216–17, 220
polytechnics 48, 185, 197
Portugal 206
poverty 17, 80, 92–6
Powell, Enoch 141–2
profitability of British industry
    25
protectionism 36, 209

public expenditure
    attitudes toward 14, 78, 96–7
    distribution of 37, 144, 148,
        201
    level of 13, 83, 147–8
Public Health Act 1875 108

Rate Support Grant (RSG) 184
Reagan, Ronald 143, 213
research and development (r. &
    d.) 26–7, 37, 42, 43, 212
riots 2, 3, 19, 177–80, 201
Robbins Report 196–7
Roosevelt, Franklin D. 211

Salford, University of 199
Scarman, Lord 177–9
schools
    comprehensive 183
    private 188
Scotland 5, 6, 7
Second International 205
shop stewards 66, 75
small firms 43, 45–6
Smith, Adam 207
smoking 150, 153
Social Democratic Party (SDP)
    16
    see also Liberal/S.D.P.
        Alliance
social integration 2, 120
social mobility 18
social security 9, 78, 80–1, 87–9,
    91–4, 100, 147, 158–60
South East Asia 206
South Wales 6, 7
Spain 206, 222
Stalin, J. 210
state benefits 9, 78, 83, 113, 123
state, character of British 28, 90,
    207–13
state theory 203–5
step-families 121, 132

sterling 28, 29–30, 218
Stock Exchange 30
stock market 25, 86
strikes (see industrial disputes)
subcontracting 10, 45, 62
supplementary benefits 91, 95,
    101, 131
Sweden 28, 84, 87, 216, 220

Taiwan 220
teachers
    pay 190–1
    quality 189
    training 189–91
Tebbit, Norman 137
Technical and Vocational
    Education Initiative
    (TVEI) 195–6
technological innovation 26–7
Television South (TVS) 53
terrorism 174–5
Thatcher, Margaret 1, 12, 16,
    40, 63, 98, 143, 195, 221
Thatcherism 12–14, 16–17, 220
third world 4
Trade Union Act 76
trade unions
    and job security 71–2
    challenges to 59–67
    membership 58, 60–3
    strategies in 1980s 67–71
Trade Union Congress 73
Transport and General
    Workers' Union (TGWU)
    60
Treasury 215
Trident missiles 212–13
Trotsky, Leon 205

United States of America,
    relations with Britain
    210–13
unemployment

and health 136–7, 152
and occupational welfare 89
and the family 136–8
and trade unions 59–60
distribution 5–8, 20–1, 97,
    135–6
female 138–9
international variations 11–12
youth 139–40
unit beat policing 165–6, 171,
    175–6
universities 48, 184, 196–200
University Grants Committee
    (UGC) 196–8

voting behaviour
    class and 15–16
    housing and 15, 106
    trends in 2, 15–17

wealth distribution 18
welfare backlash 94, 143
welfare consensus 2–3, 79–80,
    159
welfare, public and private
    systems 78, 81–2, 87–90
welfare state, crisis of 1, 81,
    143–4
West Germany 42, 47, 83–4, 93,
    191, 193–4, 200, 216, 220
West Midlands 6
Westland 213
Wilson, Harold 40, 88, 218
women
    and domestic care 134–5
    and occupational pensions 88
    and state benefits 90
    earnings 125–6
    employment 5, 8–9, 18, 62,
        122–3, 125
    in police force 165, 166
    trade union membership
        61–2, 72

working practices 27, 53
World War Two 79, 210

Youth Opportunities

Programme (YOP) 194
Youth Training Scheme (YTS)
136, 194–5